Spiritual Gurus Ancient

Edited by
P. K. Das
M. K. Singh

MP
MAHAVEER PUBLISHERS

Published by
MAHAVEER PUBLISHERS
4764/2A, 23-Ansari Road, Daryaganj
New Delhi – 110002
Ph. : 011 – 66629669–79–89
e-mail : mahaveerpublishers@gmail.com

This book is purely a Collection taken from the different sources like magazines, religious books, internet etc. and represented in simple and easily readable form.

First Edition: July 2012

Spiritual Gurus: Ancient
ISBN(10) : 8183520359
ISBN(13) : 9788183520355

Distributed in India by
VAIBHAV BOOK SERVICE
e-mail : vaibhavbookservice@gmail.com

Distributed in Nepal by
BAJRANGBALI BOOK ENTERPRISES PVT. LTD.
Jyatha, Mushyabahal, Ward No. 27, Kathmandu, Nepal
e-mail : bajrangbalibooks@gmail.com

Printed & Bound in India

Preface

The Book, "Spiritual Gurus," provides an exposition of the lives and teachings of some great masters, spiritual gurus and yogis who were born during the ancient time. Their greatest gift to humanity is to bring the depth of wisdom of ancients sages to the modern seekers.

It forms a part of the series of 'Spiritual Gurus' which is intended to bring to focus the lives and teaching of eminent spiritual gurus, saints and yogis of the ancient time. They encourage self-awareness through practice of yoga, meditation and contemplation with an attitude of self-reliance.

In all major and minor religions in the world, Spiritual Masters have sprung up from time to time to teach and preach values to be inculcated in life according to their faith and belief.

Religions are to unite human race and not to divide or destroy whatever may be the reasons whether material or non-material. Spiritual Masters all over the globe for centuries irrespective of their religious championed eloquently about the goal of existence to ensure useful, purposeful and pleasant life on the earth ending in peaceful death and non-violent ever. Spiritual enlightenment is necessary to keep such instincts in full control to attain various levels of mental fulfilment and satisfaction. Spirituality is above all religions, secularions, morals and ethics. It speaks of universally accepted value system, endorsed by all religions of the world all times, for the human race to live in peace while achieving progress and prosperity leading to both physical, mental and metaphysical happiness during the life span.

World Spiritual leaders spring up time and again in mankind to purify the society preaching universal spiritual and sacred values to get rid of the reigning evils enabling human race to ascend the ladder from demonality to divinity.

Contents

1

Adi Shankara

Adi Shankara (788 CE-820 CE), also known as Shankara Bhagavatpadacharya and Adi Shankaracharya was an Indian philosopher from Kalady of present day Kerala who consolidated the doctrine of advaita vedanta. His teachings are based on the unity of the atman and brahman— non-dual brahman, in which brahman is viewed as nirguna brahman, brahman without attributes.

Shankara travelled across India and other parts of South Asia to propagate his philosophy through discourses and debates with other thinkers. He is reputed to have founded four mathas ("monasteries"), which helped in the historical development, revival and spread of 'Advaita Vedanta.' Adi Shankara is believed to be the organizer of the Dashanami monastic order and the founder of the Shanmata tradition of worship.

His works in Sanskrit concern themselves with establishing the doctrine of advaita (nondualism). He also established the importance of monastic life as sanctioned in the Upanishads and Brahma Sutra, in a time when the Mimamsa school established strict ritualism and ridiculed monasticism. Shankara represented his works as elaborating on ideas found in the Upanishads, and he wrote copious commentaries on the Vedic canon (Brahma Sutra, principal upanishads and Bhagavad Gita) in support of his thesis. The main opponent in his work is the Mimamsa school of thought, though he also offers arguments against the views of some other schools like Samkhya and certain schools of Buddhism.

Life

Traditional accounts of Adi Shankara's life can be found in the Shankara Vijayams, which are poetic works that contain a mix of biographical and legendary material, written in the epic style. The most important among these biographies are the Madhaviya Shankara Vijayam (of Madhava, c. 14th century), the Cidvilasiya Shankara Vijayam (of Cidvilasa, c. between 15th century and 17th century), and the Keraïiya Shankara Vijayam (of the Kerala region, extant from c. 17th century).

Birth and Childhood

Shankara was born in the Brahmin community to Sri Sivaguru and Aryamba in or near Kaladi in central (present day) Kerala. According to lore, it was after his parents, who had been childless for many years, prayed at the Vadakkunnathan temple, Thrissur that Sankara was born under the star Thiruvathira.

His father died while Shankara was very young. Shankara's upanayanam, the initiation into student-life, had to be delayed due to the death of his father, and was then performed by his mother. As a child, Shankara showed remarkable scholarship, mastering the four Vedas by the age of eight.

Sannyasa

From a young age, Shankara was inclined towards sannyasa, but it was only after much persuasion that his mother finally gave her consent. He only received her consent when bathing in a pond one day. A crocodile caught hold of his leg. Shankara appealed to his mother, who had arrived at the pond, asking for permission to become a sanyasi. His mother finally gave consent, only to have the crocodile let go of young Shankara. Shankara then left Kerala and travelled towards North India in search of a guru. On the banks of the Narmada River, he met Govinda Bhagavatpada, the disciple of Gaudapada. When Govinda Bhagavatpada asked Shankara's identity, he replied with an extempore verse that brought out the Advaita Vedanta philosophy. Govinda Bhagavatapada was impressed and took Shankara as his disciple.

The guru instructed Shankara to write a commentary on the Brahma Sutras and propagate the Advaita philosophy. Shankara travelled to Kashi, where a young man named Sanandana, hailing from Chola territory in South India, became his first disciple. According to legend, while on his way to the Vishwanath Temple, Sankara came upon an untouchable accompanied by four dogs. When asked to move aside by Shankara's disciples, the untouchable replied: "Do you wish that I move my ever lasting Atman ("the Self"), or this body made of flesh?" Realizing that the untouchable was none other than god Shiva himself, and his dogs the four Vedas, Shankara prostrated himself before him, composing five shlokas known as Manisha Panchakam.

At Badari he wrote his famous Bhashyas ("commentaries") and Prakarana granthas ("philosophical treatises").

Meeting with Mandana Mishra

One of the most famous debates of Adi Shankara was with the ritualist Mandana Mishra. Mandana Mishra held the view that the life of a householder was far superior to that of a monk. This view was widely shared and respected throughout India at that time. Thus it would have been important for Adi Shankara to debate with him. Madana Mishra's guru was the famous Mimamsa philosopher, Kumarila Bhamma. Shankara sought a debate with Kumarila Bhamma and met him in Prayag where he had buried himself in a slow burning pyre to repent for sins committed against his guru: Kumarila Bhamma had learned Buddhist philosophy from his Buddhist guru under false pretenses, in order to be able to refute it. Learning anything without the knowledge of one's guru while still under his authority constitutes a sin according to the Vedas. Kumarila Bhamma thus asked Adi Shankara to proceed to Mahicmati (known today as [[Mahishi], District Saharsa in Bihar) to meet Mandana Mishra and debate with him instead.

After debating for over fifteen days, with Mandana Mishra's wife Ubhaya Bharati acting as referee, Mandana Mishra accepted defeat. Ubhaya Bharati then challenged Adi Shankara to have a debate with her in order to 'complete' the victory. She asked him questions related to sexual congress between man and woman a subject in which Shankaracharya had no knowledge, since he was a true celibate and sanyasi. Sri Shankracharya asked for a "recess" of 15 days. As per legend, he used the art of "para-kaya pravesha" (the spirit leaving its own body and entering another's) and exited his own body, which he asked his disciples to look after, and psychically entered the dead body of a king. The story goes that from the King's two wives, he acquired all knowledge of "art of love." The queens, thrilled at the keen intellect and robust love-making of the "revived" King, deduced that he was not their husband, as of old. The story continues that they sent their factotums to "look for the lifeless body of a young sadhu and to cremate it immediately" so that their "king" (Shankracharya in the king's body) would continue to live with them. Just as the retainers piled Shankracharaya's lifeless corpse upon a pyre and were about to set fire to it, Shankara entered his own body and regained consciousness. Finally, he answered all questions put to him by Ubhaya Bharati; and she allowed Mandana Mishra to accept sannyasa with the monastic name Suresvaracharya, as per the agreed-upon rules of the debate.

Philosophical Tour

Adi Shankara then travelled with his disciples to Maharashtra and Srisailam. In Srisailam, he composed Shivanandalahari, a devotional hymn in praise of Shiva. The Madhaviya Shankaravijayam says that when Shankara was about to be sacrificed by a Kapalika, the god Narasimha appeared to save Shankara in response to Padmapadacharya's prayer to him. As a result, Adi Shankara composed the Laksmi-Narasimha stotra.

He then travelled to Gokarma, the temple of Hari-Shankara and the Mukambika temple at Kollur. At Kollur, he accepted as his disciple a boy believed to be dumb by his parents. He gave him the name, Hastamalakacharya ("one with the amalaka fruit on his palm," i.e., one who has clearly realised the Self). Next, he visited sringeri to establish the Sharada Pimham and made Tomakacharya his disciple.

After this, Adi Shankara began a Dig-vijaya "tour of conquest" for the propagation of the Advaita philosophy by controverting all philosophies opposed to it. He travelled throughout India, from South India to Kashmir and Nepal, preaching to the local populace and debating philosophy with Hindu, Buddhist and other scholars and monks along the way.

With the Malayali King Sudhanva as companion, Shankara passed through Tamil Nadu, Andhra Pradesh and Vidarbha. He then started towards Karnataka where he encountered a band of armed Kapalikas. King Sudhanva, with his Nairs, resisted and defeated the Kapalikas. They safely reached Gokarna where Shankara defeated in debate the Shaiva scholar, Neelakanta.

Proceeding to Saurashtra (the ancient Kambhoja) and having visited the shrines of Girnar, Somnath and Prabhasa and explaining the superiority of Vedanta in all these places, he arrived at Dwarka. Bhamma Bhaskara of Ujjayini, the proponent of Bhedabeda philosophy, was humbled. All the scholars of Ujjayini (also known as Avanti) accepted Adi Shankara's philosophy.

He then defeated the Jainas in philosophical debates at a place called Bahlika. Thereafter, the Acharya established his victory over several philosophers and ascetics in Kamboja (region of North Kashmir), Darada and many regions situated in the desert and crossing mighty peaks, entered Kashmir. Later, he had an encounter with a tantrik, Navagupta at Kamarupa.

Accession to Sarvajnapitha

Adi Shankara visited Sarvajnapimha (Sharada Peeth) in Kashmir (now in Pakistan-occupied Kashmir). The Madhaviya Shankaravijayam states this temple had four doors for scholars from the four cardinal directions. The southern door (representing South India) had never been opened, indicating that no scholar from South India had entered the Sarvajna Pitha. Adi Shankara opened the southern door by defeating in debate all the scholars there in all the various scholastic disciplines such as Mimamsa, Vedanta and other branches of Hindu philosophy; he ascended the throne of Transcendent wisdom of that temple.

Towards the end of his life, Adi Shankara travelled to the Himalayan area of Kedarnath-Badrinath and attained videha mukti ("freedom from embodiment"). There is a samadhi mandir dedicated to Adi Shankara behind the Kedarnath temple. However, there are variant traditions on the location of his last days. One tradition, expounded by Keraliya Shankaravijaya, places his place of death as Vadakkunnathan temple in Thrissur, Kerala. The followers of the Kanchi kamakoti pitha claim that he ascended the Sarvajnapimha and attained videha mukti in Kanchipuram (Tamil Nadu).

Dates

Several dates have been proposed for Shankara:

788–820 CE: This is the mainstream scholarly opinion, placing Shankara in mid to late 8th century CE. These dates are based on records at the Shegeri Sharada Pimha, which is the only matha to have maintained a relatively unbroken record of its Acharyas; starting with the third Acharya, one can with reasonable confidence date the others from the 8th century to the present. The Sringeri records state that Shankara was born in the 14th year of the reign of "Vikram Aditya," but it is unclear as to which king this name refers. Though some researchers identify the name with Chandragupta II (4th. c. CE), modern scholarship accepts the Vikram Aditya as being from the Chalukya dynasty of Badami, most likely Vikram Aditya II (733–746 CE), which would place him in the middle of the 8th c. Max Muller, Macdonnel, Pathok, Deussen and Radhakrishnan all accept the dates 788-820 CE. The date 788–820 is also among those considered acceptable by Swami Tapasyananda, though he raises a number of questions.

509–477 BCE: This dating, more than a millennium ahead of all others, is based on records of the heads of the Shankara Mamhas at Dwaraka Pitha and Govardhana matha and the fifth Peetham at Kanchi. However, such an early date is not consistent with the fact that Shankara quotes the Buddhist logician Dharmakirti, who finds mention in Xuanzang (7th c.). Also, his near-contemporary Kumarila Bhamma is usually dated ca. 8th c. CE. Most scholars feel that due to invasions and other discontinuities, the records of the Dwaraka and Govardhana mathas are not as reliable as those of Sringeri. Thus, while considerable debate exists, the pre-Christian Era dates are usually discounted, and the most likely period for Shankara is during the 8th c. CE.

44-12 BCE: Anandagiri believed that he was born at Chidambaram in 44 BCE and died in 12 BCE.

6th Century CE: Telang placed him in this century. Sir R G Bandarkar believed that he was born in 680 CE.

805-897 CE: A D Venkiteswara not only places Adishankara later than most, but also had the opinion that it would not have been possible for him to have achieved all the works apportioned to him, and has him live ninety two years.

Mathas

Adi Shankara founded four Mamhas to guide the Hindu religion. These are at Sringeri in Karnataka in the south, Dwaraka in Gujarat in the west, Puri in Orissa in the east, and Jyotirmath (Joshimath) in Uttarakhand in the north. Hindu tradition states that he put in charge of these mathas his four main disciples: Sureshvara, Hastamalakacharya, Padmapada, and Totakacharya respectively. The heads of the mathas trace their authority back to these figures. Each of the heads of these four mathas takes the title of Shankaracharya ("the learned Shankara") after the first Shankaracharya.

Philosophy and Religious Thought

Advaita ("non-dualism") is often called a monistic system of thought. The word "Advaita" essentially refers to the identity of the Self (Atman) and the Whole (Brahman). Advaita Vedanta says the one unchanging entity (Brahman) alone exists, and that changing entities do not have absolute existence, much as the ocean's waves have no existence in separation from the ocean. The key source texts for all schools of Vedanta are the Prasthanat rayi–the canonical texts consisting of the Upanishads, the Bhagavad Gita and the Brahma Sutras.

Adi Shankara was the first in the tradition to consolidate the siddhanta ("doctrine") of Advaita Vedanta. He wrote commentaries on the Prasthana Trayi. A famous quote from Vivekacsamani, one of his prakarana granthas that succinctly summarises, his philosophy is:

Brahma satyam jagat mithya, jivo brahmaiva naparah

Brahman is the only truth, the spatio-temporal world is an illusion, and there is ultimately no difference between Brahman and individual self.

Advaita Vedanta is based on shastra ("scriptures"), yukti ("reason") and anubhava ("experience"), and aided by karmas ("spiritual practices"). This philosophy provides a clear-cut way of life to be followed. Starting from childhood, when learning has to start, the philosophy has to be realised in practice throughout one's life, even up to death. This is the reason why this philosophy is called an experiential philosophy-the underlying tenet being "That thou art," meaning that ultimately there is no difference between the experiencer and the experienced (the world) as well as the universal spirit (Brahman). Among the followers of Advaita, as well those of other doctrines, they are believed to have appeared Jivanmuktas, ones liberated while alive. These individuals (commonly called Mahatmas, great souls, among Hindus) are those who realised the oneness of their self and the universal spirit called Brahman.

Adi Shankara's Bhashyas (commentaries) on the Upanishads, the Bhagavad Gita and the Brahma Sutras are his principal works. Although he mostly adhered to traditional means of commenting on the Brahma Sutra, there are a number of original ideas and arguments to establish that the essence of Upanishads is Advaita. He taught that it was only through direct knowledge that one could realize Brahman. "A perception of the fact that the object seen is a rope, will remove the fear and sorrow which result from the illusory idea that it is a serpent." Cited from Shankara's "Vivekachuudaamani"/verse #12/translated by Mohini M Chatterji. This metaphor was borrowed from Yogacara Buddhist thinkers, who used it in a different context.

Adi Shankara's opponents accused him of teaching Buddhism in the garb of Hinduism, because his non-dualistic ideals seemed rather radical to contemporary Hindu philosophy. However, although Advaita proposes the theory of Maya, explaining the universe as a "trick of a magician," Adi Shankara and his followers see this as a consequence of their basic premise that Brahman alone is real. Their idea of Maya emerges from their belief in the reality of Brahman, as opposed to Buddhist doctrines of emptiness, which emerge from the empirical Buddhist approach of observing the nature of reality.

Historical and Cultural Impact

Because of his unification of two seemingly disparate philosophical doctrines, Atman and Brahman, Westerners who know about him perceive him as the "St. Thomas Aquinas of Indian thought" and "the most brilliant personality in the history of Indian thought."

At the time of Adi Shankara's life, Hinduism was increasing influence in India at the expense of Buddhism and Jainism.

Hinduism was divided into innumerable sects, each quarrelling with the others. The followers of Mimamsa and Sankhya philosophy were atheists, insomuch that they did not believe in God as a unified being. Besides these atheists there were numerous theistic sects. There were also those who rejected the Vedas, like the Charvakas.

Adi Shankara held discourses and debates with the leading scholars of all these sects and schools of philosophy to controvert their doctrines. He unified the theistic sects into a common framework of Shanmata system. In his works, Adi Shankara stressed the importance of the Vedas, and his efforts helped Hinduism regain strength and popularity. Many trace the present worldwide prominence of Vedanta to his works. He travelled on foot to various parts of India to restore the study of the Vedas.

Even though he lived for only thirty-two years, his impact on India and on Hinduism was striking. He reintroduced a purer form of Vedic thought. His teachings and tradition form the basis of Smartism and have influenced Sant Mat lineages. He is the main figure in the tradition of Advaita Vedanta. He was the founder of the Dashanami Sampradaya of Hindu monasticism and banmata of Smarta tradition. He introduced the Pancayatana form of worship.

Adi Shankara, along with Madhva and Ramanuja, was instrumental in the revival of Hinduism. These three teachers formed the doctrines that are followed by their respective sects even today. They have been the most important figures in the recent history of Hindu philosophy. In their writings and debates, they provided polemics against the non-Vedantic schools of Sankhya, Vaisheshika etc. Thus they paved the way for Vedanta to be the dominant and most widely followed tradition among the schools of Hindu philosophy. The Vedanta school stresses most on the Upanishads (which are themselves called Vedanta, End or culmination of the Vedas), unlike the other schools that gave importance to the ritualistic Brahmanas, or to texts authored by their founders. The Vedanta schools hold that the Vedas (which include the Upanishads) are unauthored, forming a continuous tradition of wisdom transmitted orally. Thus the concept of apaurusheyatva ("being unauthored") came to be the guiding force behind the Vedanta schools. However, along with stressing the importance of Vedic tradition, Adi Shankara gave equal importance to the personal experience of the student. Logic, grammar, Mimamsa and allied subjects form main areas of study in all the Vedanta schools.

Regarding meditation, Shankara refuted the system of Yoga and its disciplines as a direct means to attain moksha, rebutting the argument that it can be obtained through concentration of the mind. His position is that the mental states discovered through the practices of Yoga can be indirect aids to the gain of knowledge, but cannot themselves give rise to it. According to his philosophy, knowledge of brahman springs from inquiry into the words of the Upanishads, and the knowledge of brahman that shruti provides cannot be obtained in any other way. It has to be noted that it is generally considered that for Shankara the Absolute Reality is attributeless and impersonal, while for Madhava and Ramanuja, the Absolute Truth is Vishnu. This has been a subject of debate, interpretation, and controversy since Shankara himself is attributed to composing the popular 8th century Hindu devotional composition Bhaja Govindam (literal meaning, "Worship Govinda"). This work of Adi Shankara is considered as a good summary of Advaita Vedanta and underscores the view that devotion to God, Govinda, is not only an important part of general spirituality, but the concluding verse drives through the message of Shankara: "Worship Govinda, worship Govinda, worship Govinda, Oh fool! Other than chanting the Lord's names, there is no other way to cross the life's ocean." Bhaja Govindam invokes the almighty in the aspect of Vishnu; it is therefore very popular not only with Sri Adi Shankaracharya's immediate followers, the Smarthas, but also with Vaishnavas and others.

A well known verse, recited in the Smarta tradition, in praise of Adi Shankara is:

Shruti smriti purananashalayam karunalayam|

Namami Bhagavatpadashamkaram lokacœamkaram||

I salute the compassionate abode of the Vedas, Smritis and Puranas known as Shankara Bhagavatpada, who makes the world auspicious.

Adi Shankara begins his Gurustotram or Verses to the Guru with the following Sanskrit Sloka, that has become a widely sung Bhajan:

Guru Brahma, Guru Vishnu, Guru Deva Maheshwara. Guru Sakshath Parambrahma, Tasmai Shri Gurave Namaha. (tr: Guru is the creator Brahma, Guru is the preserver Vishnu, Guru is the destroyer Shiva. Guru is directly the supreme spirit — I offer my salutations to this Guru.)

Works

Adi Shankara's works deal with logically establishing the doctrine of Advaita Vedanta as he saw it in the Upanishads. He formulates the doctrine of Advaita Vedanta by validating his arguments on the basis of quotations from the Vedas and other Hindu scriptures. He gives a high priority to svanubhava ("personal experience") of the student. His works are largely polemical in nature. He directs his polemics mostly against the Sankhya, Buddha, Jaina, Vaisheshika and other non-vedantic Hindu philosophies.

Traditionally, his works are classified under Bhacya ("commentary"), Prakarana grantha ("philosophical treatise") and Stotra ("devotional hymn"). The commentaries serve to provide a consistent interpretation of the scriptural texts from the perspective of Advaita Vedanta. The philosophical treatises provide various methodologies to the student to understand the doctrine. The devotional hymns are rich in poetry and piety, serving to highlight the relationship between the devotee and the deity.

Adi Shankara wrote Bhashyas on the ten major Upanishads, the Brahma Sutras and the Bhagavad Gita. In his works, he quotes from Shveshvatara, Kaushitakai, Mahanarayana and Jabala Upanishads, among others. Bhashyas on Kaushitaki, Nrisimhatapani and Shveshvatara Upanishads are extant but the authenticity is doubtful. Adi Shankara's is the earliest extant commentary on the Brahma Sutras. However, he mentions older commentaries like those of Dravida, Bhartrprapancha and others.

In his Brahma Sutra Bhashya, Adi Shankara cites the examples of Dharmavyadha, Vidura and others, who were born with the knowledge of Brahman acquired in previous births. He mentions that the effects cannot be prevented from working on account of their present birth. He states that the knowledge that arises out of the study of the Vedas could be had through the Puranas and the Itihasas. In the Taittiriya Upanishad Bhashya 2.2, he says:

Sarvesham cadhikaro vidyayam ca shreyah: kevalaya vidyaya veti siddham

It has been established that everyone has the right to the knowledge (of Brahman) and that the supreme goal is attained by that knowledge alone.

Some western academics consider only Upadeúasahasri among independent philosophical works as authentic. Many other such texts exist, among which there is a difference of opinion among scholars on the authorship of Viveka Chudamani. The former pontiff of Sringeri Math, Shri Shri Chandrashekhara Bharati III has written a voluminous commentary on the Viveka Chudamani.

Adi Shankara also wrote commentaries on other scriptural works, such as the Vishnu Sahastranam and the Sanatsujatiya. Like the Bhagavad Gita, both of these are contained in the Mahabharata.

Film

In 1983 a film directed by G. V. Iyer named Adi Shankaracharya was premiered, the first film ever made entirely in Sanskrit language in which all of Adi Shankaracharya's works were compiled. The movie received the National Film Awards for Best Film, Best Screenplay, Best Cinematography and Audiography and has been known as a master piece.

2

Brahmarshi Prem Nirmal

Brahmarshi Prem Nirmal more fondly known as "Guruji" is a living enlightened master and founder of the TASC, Tao Anand Spiritual Center, which aims at holistic development of individuals as well as society. He is a Holistic Counsellor, Corporate Trainer, Kriya Yogi, Scientific Mystic, Enlightenment Educationist, scholar of Kashmir Shaivism,an exponent in 32 Vidyas, 10 Maha Vidyas and the various scriptures.

He has done extensive research in the areas of stress management, intuition development, aura reading and meditation therapy. He is also founder of SVT (Shiv Vyapti Trust) which is involved in various humanitarian activities.

Life

Brahmarshi Prem Nirmal was born to Smt. Bhagirathi and Sri Devji Nirmal who stayed at Bayath, a small village in Mandvi taluka of Kutch district, Gujarat, India. He was named "Premji." His early schooling was completed in Kutch, Gujarat, before moving to Mumbai (former 'Bombay'). He completed his matriculation from Elphinston Technical High School, Mumbai and Higher secondary education from Amulakh Amichand Bhimji Vividhlakshi Vidhyalay. He, thereafter, pursued his Electrical and Power Electronics Engineering from V.J.T.I., Mumbai University and did his Post Graduate studies in Cybernetics through the Baroda Productivity Council.

After working for about 2 years with Applied Electronic Limited (Aplab) company in Thane, Maharashtra, and one more year in Hybrid Electronics, Mumbai, he started his own business of manufacturing SMPS and invertors, Nirmal Power Systems. After successfully running the business for 22 years, he closed his business at the age of 47. Since then, he is completely involved in spreading Kriya yoga. He is founder director of TASC, TAO Anand Spiritual Center at Thane and has been conducting workshops on various topics like "Art and Science of Holistic Living," Power of Super Conscious Mind, Enlightened Billionaire, secrets of enlightenment, Scientific Spirituality, Swar Yoga, Shree Vidya, Astral Travel, Aura reading with naked eyes and Chakra workshop, Ascension and Akashik records etc. He has wide experience in Personal Counseling, Consultancy and Training and has deep insights in human behavior and body-mind healing.

In the year 1996 Nirmal Kriya i.e process of enlightenment was revealed unto him by Sri Mahavatar Babaji while he was at his residence. Guruji thereafter is teaching Nirmal Kriya to all the aspiring seekers. He shares the secrets of enlightenment through nature camps and programs at TAO Center.

He was the visiting faculty for Stress Management at various reputed organizations such as Welingkar Institute of Management and IIT-Mumbai. He is empanelled with the Life Positive Holistic Practitioners board. Prem Nirmal was conferred with the title of Brahmarshi on 23 June 2009 by Brahmarshi Subhash Patri at TAO, Thane. Guruji has also travelled to countries like Singapore, Kenya, U.A.E. and Oman to spread his message.

Teachings

Prem Nirmal, along with his wife Bharati Nirmal, promote Householder's Spirituality. Prem Nirmal's wife Bharati says, that being a householder is the fastest way to transcend desires, grow in all dimensions and move towards a fulfilling life. Perm Nirmal encourages honest enquiry and has perfect methodology through which he guides his friends and disciples on the spiritual path. He has a scientific approach towards spirituality.

Various third eye experiences/Astral body experiences/Cosmic body experiences (Body expansions etc.), even though indicative of some progress on the path, are just the passing phase of meditation. Meditation needs to be supplemented with intense 'Swadhyaya' the 'self-study' to develop the intense and clear "UNDERSTANDING" of how the mind functions and governs the behaviorural patterns. He also advocates the concept of 'Enlightened Billionaire', i.e a "Jivan Mukta" who is living this material world as a householder yet detached from inside, thus balancing material and spiritual sides of life to grow in wisdom and lead a balanced life in holistic way. 'Nirmal Kriya' which was revealed unto him, is a practical way of accomplishing this.

Nirmal Kriya

Nirmal Kriya i.e process of enlightenment is a process through which all the five bodies, i.e Physical, etheric, emotional, mental and causal are cleansed. Nirmal Kriya automatically leads to a stateless state i.e no-mind state or meditation. Nirmal Kriya helps reduce mental stress, relieve depression and anxiety, improves immunity and cures various diseases and disorders. However, Prem Nirmal says that Nirmal Kriya's purpose is much beyond these physical improvements. It is a process of enlightenment. Once you practice Kriya which prepares the background, it naturally throws you in a space of non-thinking, called meditation. It creates the high levels of Prana in your body-brain system that makes it easier for you to be aware of your breath and your thoughts simultaneously. You can easily get the knack of meditation when you do Kriya. Simply remain silent after doing Kriya, and keep your attention on your natural breathing process. Simultaneously keep witnessing your thoughts. You will experience very low levels of thought traffic, as in high Prana state thoughts cannot linger for long. Even if the No-thought state remains just for few seconds, you will experience the surge of energy and vitality, bringing back the positive qualities of Zest, love and joy!

3

Dnyaneshwar

Dnyaneshwar (or Jñaneshwar) (1275–1296), also known as Jñanadeva, was born into a Deshastha Brahmin Kulkarni family.

He was a 13th century Maharashtrian Hindu saint (Sant-a title by which he is often referred), poet, philosopher and yogi of the Nath tradition whose works Bhavartha Deepika Teeka (a commentary on Bhagavad Gita, popularly known as "Dnyaneshwari"), and Amrutanubhav are considered to be milestones in Marathi literature.

Traditional History

According to Nath tradition Sant Dnyaneshwar was the second of the four children of Vitthal Govind Kulkarni and Rukmini, a pious couple from Apegaon near Paithan on the banks of the river Godavari. Vitthal had studied Vedas and set out on pilgrimages at a young age. In Alandi, about 30 km from Pune,

Sidhopant, a local Yajurveda brahmin, was very much impressed with him and Vitthal married his daughter Rukmini.

After some time, getting permission from Rukmini, Vitthal went to Kashi(Varanasi in Uttar Pradesh, India), where he met Ramananda Swami and requested to be initiated into sannyas, lying about his marriage. But Ramananda Swami later went to Alandi and, convinced that his student Vitthal was the husband of Rukmini, he returned to Kashi and ordered Vitthal to return home to his family. The couple was excommunicated from the brahmin caste as Vitthal had broken with sannyas, the last of the four ashrams. Four children were born to them; Nivrutti in 1273, Dnyandev (Dnyaneshwar) in 1275, Sopan in 1277 and daughter Mukta in 1279. According to some scholars their birth years are 1268, 1271, 1274, 1277 respectively. It is believed that later Vitthal and Rukmini ended their lives by jumping into the waters at Prayag where the river Ganges meets Yamuna hoping that their children would be accepted into the society after their death.

The couple set out on a pilgrimage with their children to Tryambakeshwar, near Nashik, where their elder son Nivrutti (at the age of 10) was initiated in to the Nath tradition by Gahininath. The paternal great grandfather of Dnyaneshwar had been initiated into the Nath cult by Goraksha Nath (Gorakh Nath). The orphaned children grew up on alms. They approached the brahmin community of Paithan to accept them but the brahmins refused. According to the disputed "Shuddhi Patra" the children were purified by the brahmins on condition of observing celibacy. Their argument with the brahmins earned the children fame and respect due to their righteousness, virtue, intelligence, knowledge and politeness. Dnyaneshwar became the student of Nivruttinath along with his younger siblings Sopan and Mukta at the age of 8. He learnt and mastered the philosophy and various techniques of kundalini yoga.

Writings

Jnanadeva, from the Ravi Varma Press, 1910's.

The child moved to Nevasa, a village in Ahmednagar district, where Dnyaneshwar began his literary work when Nivruttinath instructed him to write a commentary on Bhagavad Gita. The Dnyaneshwari or Bhavartha Deepika Teeka was written down by Sacchidananandbaba from discourses by Dnyaneshwar. By the time the commentary was complete Dnyaneshwar was only 15 years old.TIKITIKI

Considered a masterpieces of Marathi literature, the Dnyaneshwari's 18 chapters are composed in a metre called "ovi." Dnyaneshwar liberated the "divine knowledge" locked in the Sanskrit language to bring that knowledge into Prakrit (Marathi) and made it available to the common man. He was confident that he would write in marathi in as good or better manner than Sanskrit.

Amrutanubhav, written some time after, is difficult and finds fewer readers. Containing 10 chapters and 806 ovi, the basis of this book is non dualism (advaita siddhanta). The seventh and biggest chapter (295 ovi) is the most important. Apart from Dnyaneshwari and Amrutanubhav works like Changdev Paasashti (a collection of 65 ovi addressed to an allegedly 1400 years old yogi named Changdev Maharaj),

Haripath and around 1000 “abhanga” (authorship of many is disputed due to differences in writing style) are attributed to Dnyaneshwar.

Siblings

The siblings Muktabai, Sopan, Dnyaneshwar and Nivruttinath seated on the flying wall greet Changdev seated on a tiger. In the centre, Changdev bows to Dnyaneshwar.

Nivruttinath was the elder brother of Dnyaneshwar. Nivrutti was an authority on philosophy of the Nath sect. Gahininath, one of the nine Nath gurus, accepted Nivrutti as his disciple and initiated him into the Nath sect, instructing him to propagate devotion to Krishna. Dnyaneshwar accepted his elder brother as his own guru. After the early Samadhi of Dnyaneshwar, Nivrutti travelled with his sister Mukta on a pilgrimage along the Tapi river where they were caught in a thunderstorm and Mukta was swept away. Nivrutti took to salvation (Samadhi) at Tryambakeshwar. Around 375 abhangas are attributed to him but, the authorship of many of them is disputed due to difference in writing style and philosophy.

Sopandev was a younger brother who attained 'samadhi' at Saswad near Pune. He wrote a book “Sopandevi” based on the Bhagvadgita's Marathi interpretation along with 50 or so abhangas. Muktabai was the youngest of the siblings, Muktai or Muktabai was known for her simple and straightforward expression of thoughts. She could be considered as one of the first poetesses in Marathi along with Mahadamba. There are around 40 abhangas attributed to her. She accepted Yogi Changdev as her disciple.

Varkari Movement

Dnyaneshwar's palkhi (palanquin), holding the footwear of the saint, is carried with honour in a silver bullock cart from Alandi to Pandharpur.

Dnyaneshwar was probably introduced into the Vaishnava Sampradaya (or Vitthala Sampradaya) of Pandharpur (founder of the Varkari movement), influenced by the piety of contemporary members of the movement such as Namdev, Gora Kumbhar, Savta Mali, Janabai, Narhari Sonar, Chokha Mahar and Sena Nhavi, after his writing of Dnyaneshwari since there is no mention of it in that work. The Varkaris soon considered him their teacher and spiritual leader, who initiated his contemporaries associated with the Dvaita (dualism) school of the bhakti movement into Advaita (non-dualism). He strongly advocated jnana yukta bhakti (devotion guided by knowledge) and believed that one can not be liberated unless one attains the true and divine knowledge of Brahman.

For year 2011-12 the Palakhi is scheduled on June 23 from Alandi.

Entering into a State of Samadhi

After having composed Amritanubhava, Dnyaneshwar made a pilgrimage to northern India with Namdev and other saints. After completing this pilgrimage he expressed his intention to enter into a state of Samadhi because he felt that the mission of his life was complete. At the age of 21 on 13th day of the second half of Kartik in Shaka 1218, Dnyaneshwar entered into a permanent state of Sanjeevan Samadhi at Alandi in Maharashtra, India.

An account of this incident is described by the contemporary Saint Namdev in a set of Abhangas named as Samadheeche Abhanga (translation: The Abhangas of Samadhi).

Miracles

Stories recounted in many holy books of the Bhagawata Sampradaya sect about Dnyaneshwar's life are full of miracles, such as the baking of bread (mande, or roti in Hindi) on his heated back, and his making a wall move.

Pasayadan

Dnyaneshwar wrote the Pasayadan which is a prayer for the general well being of the people. Pasayadan is included at the end of the Dynaneshwari.

4

Guru Ravidas

Ravidas (also Raidas, Rohidas and Ruhidas in eastern India) was a North Indian Sant mystic of the bhakti movement who was active in the 15th century CE. Venerated in the region of Uttar Pradesh as well as the Indian state of Maharashtra, his devotional songs and verses made a lasting impact upon the bhakti movement. He is often given the honorific "Bhagat" or "Sant."

A shoemaker of the Chamar caste, all of his devotional songs were preserved and included in the Sikh holy book, the Adi Granth, by the fifth Sikh Guru, Guru Arjan Dev. There is also a larger body of hymns passed on independently that is claimed and attributed by some to Ravidas ji. Ravidas was subversive in that his devotionalism implied a levelling of the social divisions of caste and gender, yet ecumenical in that it tended to promote crossing of sectarian divides in the name of a higher spiritual unity. He taught that one is distinguished not by one's caste (jati) but by one's actions (karma) and that every person has the right to worship God and read holy texts.

In the mid 20th centuries there emerged a distinct sect, the Ravidasis, for whom he is the chief Guru. Ravidasis are mainly Punjabi Chamar caste and their faith, the Ravidassia Religion, is a socio-religious identity. A temple was built at his birthplace in 1978. Ravidas Jayanti is celebrated with a procession, bearing the portrait of the great ascetic in the main streets and bazaars of the city with music.

Background

The details of Guru Ravidas' life are controversial. According to some, he was born in 1376/7 or else 1399 CE but many scholars offer later dates. Schaller estimates his lifespan as 1450-1520 while the Encyclopaedia Britannica contents itself with a floreat of 15th-16th century CE. Partly this is due to traditions that make him, on one hand, like his contemporary Kabir, the disciple of Ramananda (he is mentioned as such c.1600 CE in Nabhadas' Bhaktamal) but also, on the other, the guru of Meera (according to a song attributed to her: "guru miliyaa raidasjee"). However, as Schaller points out, the importance of such claims lies in their establishing the authority of a lineage of gurus (parampara). One may count oneself a disciple of a master without having actually met him.

His origin and parents are also given differently. According to one account he was born in a village named Seer Govardhanpur, near Varanasi in Uttar Pradesh, India: his father Baba Santokh Das was a leather merchant (chamar) and Mata

Kalsa Devi was his mother. His father got him married to Mata Lona Devi at early age and according to the Ravidas Purana he had a son named Vijaydas. A region between Ahmednagar and Benares is named after him.

The queen of Chittorgarh is said to have been a disciple (this may be connected with Meera, who was married to the ruler of Chittorgarh). It is said that the conservative Brahmins of Kashi could not stand the popularity of this "untouchable saint." A complaint was made to the king that he was working against age-old norms of social order (varnashrama dharma)-a cobbler was not supposed to talk of God or do work of advising or teaching. The ruler arranged for an assembly of learned men. Ravidas was also invited and was felicitated publicly. A procession was arranged (shobha yatra) and the king himself participated.

Today he is respected, as when Bangaru Laxman (Organiser, 6-8-1995) accused Congress leader Sitaram Kesri of showing "disrespect to Dalit saints like Ravidas, Satyakam Jabali, Sadhna Kasai, Banka Mahar, Dhanna Chamar and others who protected Hindus against foreign onslaughts."

Songs and teachings

How to escape? I recite the name Ram.

Lord, if you are sandalwood, I am water;

With the fragrance in all parts of my body.

Lord, if you are a cloud, I am a peacock;

Looking for you like a chakora for the moon.

Lord, if you are a lamp, I am the wick;

With a light burning day and night.

Lord, if you are a pearl, I am the thread;

Together like gold and bracelet.

Lord, you are the master and I servant;

thus is the devotion of Raidas.

This song demonstrates several key facets of Ravidas' sant bhakti'. His similes for the divine-water, cloud, light, gold-suggest the one god (Ik Onkar) and state that he himself is inseparable from that formless(Waheguru) yet that he is the one who gives it form.

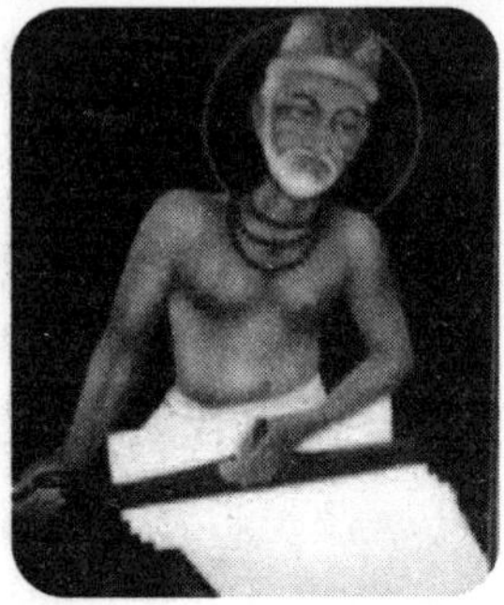

5

Kabir

Kabir (also Kabira) (1440–1518) was a mystic poet and saint of India, whose writings have greatly influenced the Bhakti movement. The name Kabir comes from Arabic al-Kabir which means 'The Great'-the 37th name of God in Islam.

Apart from having an important influence on Sikhism, Kabir's legacy is today carried forward by the Kabir Panth ("Path of Kabir"), a religious community that recognizes him as its founder and is one of the Sant Mat sects. Its members, known as Kabir panthis, are estimated to be around 9,600,000. They are spread over north and central India, as well as dispersed with the Indian diaspora across the world, up from 843,171 in the 1901 census. His writings include Bijak, Sakhi Granth, Kabir Granthawali and Anurag Sagar.

Early Life and Background

Not much is known of Kabir's birth parents, but it is known that he was brought up in a family of Muslim weavers. He was found by a Muslim weaver named Niru and his wife, Nima, in Lehartara, situated in Varanasi. They adopted the boy and taught him the weaver's trade.

The story is told that on one particular day of the year, anyone can become a disciple by having a master speak the name of God over him. It is common for those who live near the Ganges to take their morning bath there in the sacred waters. The bhakti saint Ramananda was in the habit of arising before dawn to take his bath. On this special day too, he awoke before dawn and found his way down to the steps of the Ganges. As he was walking down the steps to the waters, a little hand reached out and grabbed the saint's big toe. Ramananda was taken by surprise, and he involuntarily called out the name of God. Looking down, he saw in the early morning light the hand of the young Kabir. After his bath, he noticed that on the back of the little one's hand was written in Arabic the name Kabir. He adopted him as son and disciple and brought him back to his ashram, much to the consternation of his Hindu students, some of whom left in protest.

Not much is known about what sort of spiritual training Kabir may have received. He did not become a sadhu, nor did he ever abandon worldly life. Kabir chose instead to live the balanced life of a householder and mystic, a tradesman and contemplative.

Kabir's family is believed to have lived in the locality of Kabir Chaura in Varanasi. Kabir mamha, a mamha located in the back alleys of Kabir Chaura, celebrates his life and times. Accompanying the property is a house named Nirumila which houses Niru and Nima's graves. The house also accommodates students and scholars who live there and study Kabir's work.

Philosophies

Kabir was influenced by the prevailing religious mood of his times, such as old Brahmanic Hinduism, Hindu and Buddhist Tantrism, the teachings of Nath yogis and the personal devotionalism of South India mixed with the imageless God of Islam. The influence of these various doctrines is clearly evident in Kabir's verses. Eminent historians like R.C. Majumdar, P.N. Chopra, B.N. Puri and M.N. Das have held that Kabir is the first Indian saint to have harmonised Hinduism and Islam by preaching a universal path which both Hindus and Muslims could tread together. But there are a few critics who contest such claims.

The basic religious principles he espoused are simple. According to Kabir, all life is an interplay of two spiritual principles. One is the personal soul (Jivatma) and the other is God (Paramatma). It is Kabir's view that salvation is the process of bringing these two divine principles into union. The incorporation of much of his verse in Sikh scripture, and the fact that Kabir was a predecessor of Guru Nanak, have led some western scholars to mistakenly describe him as a forerunner of Sikhism.

His greatest work is the Bijak (the "Seedling"), an idea of the fundamental one. This collection of poems elucidates Kabir's universal view of spirituality. Though his vocabulary is replete with Hindu spiritual concepts, such as Brahman, karma and reincarnation, he vehemently opposed dogmas, both in

Hinduism and in Islam. His Hindi was a vernacular, straightforward kind, much like his philosophies. He often advocated leaving aside the Qur'an and Vedas and simply following Sahaja path, or the Simple/Natural Way to oneness in God. He believed in the Vedantic concept of atman, but unlike earlier orthodox Vedantins, he spurned the Hindu societal caste system and murti-poojan (idol worship), showing clear belief in both bhakti and Sufi ideas. The major part of Kabir's work as a bhagat was collected by the fifth Sikh guru, Guru Arjan Dev, and forms a part of the Sikh scripture Guru Granth Sahib.

Poetry

Kabir composed in a pithy and earthy style, replete with surprise and inventive imagery. His poems resonate with praise for the true guru who reveals the divine through direct experience, and denounce more usual ways of attempting god-union such as chanting, austerities, etc. Kabir, being illiterate, expressed his poems orally in vernacular Hindi, borrowing from various dialects including Avadhi, Braj, and Bhojpuri. His verses often began with some strongly worded insult to get the attention of passers-by. Kabir has enjoyed a revival of popularity over the past half century as arguably the most accessible and understandable of the Indian saints, with a special influence over spiritual traditions such as those of Sant Mat, Garib Das and Radha Soami.

Legacy

A considerable body of poetical work has been attributed to Kabir. And while two of his disciples, Bhagodas and Dharmadas, did write much of it down, "...there is also much that must have passed, with expected changes and distortions, from mouth to mouth, as part of a well-established oral tradition."

Poems and songs ascribed to Kabir are available today in several dialects, with varying wordings and spellings as befits an oral tradition. Opinions vary on establishing any given poem's authenticity. Despite this, or perhaps because of it, the spirit of this mystic comes alive through a "unique forcefulness... vigor of thought and rugged terseness of style."

Kabir and his followers named his poetic output as 'baòis,' utterances. These include songs, as above, and couplets, called variously dohe, Shloka (Sanskrit Shloka), or sakhi. The latter term, meaning 'witness,' best indicates the use that Kabir and his followers envisioned for these poems: "As direct evidence of the Truth, a sakhi is... meant to be memorized... A sakhi is... meant to evoke the highest Truth." As such, memorizing, reciting, and thus pondering over these utterances constitutes, for Kabir and his followers, a path to spiritual awakening.

Kabir's Poetry Today

There are several allusions to Kabir's poetry in mainstream Indian film music. The title song of the Sufi fusion band Indian Ocean's album Jhini is an energetic rendering of Kabir's famous poem "The intricately woven blanket," with influences from Indian folk, Sufi traditions and progressive rock.

Documentary filmmaker Shabnam Virmani, from the Kabir Project, has produced a series of documentaries and books tracing Kabir's philosophy, music and poetry in present day India and Pakistan. The documentaries feature Indian folk singers such as Prahlad Tipanya, Mukhtiyar Ali and the Pakistani Qawwal Fareed Ayaz.

Kabir's poetry has appeared prominently in filmmaker Anand Gandhi's films Right Here Right Now and Continuum.

6

Lahiri Mahasaya

Shyama Charan Lahiri (September 30, 1828 – September 26, 1895), best known as Lahiri Mahasaya, was an Indian yogi and a disciple of Mahavatar Babaji. He was also popularly known as Yogiraj and Kashi Baba. He revived the yogic science of Kriya Yoga when he learned it from Mahavatar Babaji in 1861. Lahiri Mahasaya was also the guru of Sri Yukteswar Giri. Mahasaya is a Sanskrit, spiritual title translated as 'large-minded."

He was unusual among Indian holy men in that he was a householder — marrying, raising a family, and working as an accountant for the Military Engineering Department of the British Indian government. Lahiri lived with his family in Varanasi rather than in a temple or monastery. He achieved a substantial reputation among 19th century Hindu religionists.

He became well known in the west through Paramhansa Yogananda, a disciple of Sri Yukteswar Giri, and through

Yogananda's Autobiography of a Yogi. Yogananda wrote that Lahiri was chosen by Mahavatar Babaji to reintroduce the lost practice of Kriya Yoga to the world. Lahiri's disciples included both of Yogananda's parents as well as Yogananda's own guru. Lahiri Mahasaya prophesied that the infant Yogananda would become a yogi, and "As a spiritual engine, he will carry many souls to God's kingdom."

Biography

Early Life

Lahiri was born into a Brahmin family in the Ghurni village (presently a neighbourhood of Krishnanagar town) in Nadia district of Bengal Province. He was the youngest son of Muktakashi, wife of Gaur Mohan Lahiri. His mother died when he was a child — there is very little known about her, except that she was a devotee of Lord Shiva. At the age of three or four, he was often seen sitting in meditation, with his body buried in the sand up to his neck. When Lahiri was five, the family's ancestral home was lost in a flood, so the family moved to Varanasi, where he spent most of his life.

As a child, he studied Urdu and Hindi, gradually moving on to Bengali, Sanskrit, Persian, French and English at the Government Sanskrit College, along with study of the Vedas. Reciting the Vedas, bathing in the Ganges, and worship were part of his daily routine.

In 1846, he was married to Srimati Kashi Moni. They had two sons, Tincouri and Ducouri, and two daughters. His work as an accountant in the Military Engineering Department of the English government took him all over India. After the death of his father, he took on the role of supporting the entire family in Varanasi.

Teacher of Kriya Yoga

In 1861, Lahiri was transferred to Ranikhet, in the foothills of the Himalayas. One day, while walking in the hills, he heard a voice calling to him. After climbing further, he met his Guru Mahavatar Babaji, who initiated him into the techniques of Kriya Yoga. Babaji told Lahiri that the rest of his life was to be given to spreading the Kriya message.

Soon after, Lahiri Mahasaya returned to Varanasi, where he began initiating sincere seekers into the path of Kriya Yoga. Over time, more and more people flocked to receive the teachings of Kriya from Lahiri. He organized many study groups and gave regular discourses on the Bhagavad Gita at his "Gita Assemblies." He freely gave Kriya initiation to those of every faith, including Hindus, Muslims, and Christians, at a time when caste bigotry was very strong. He encouraged his students to adhere to the tenets of their own faith, adding the Kriya techniques to what they already were practicing.

He continued his dual role of accountant and supporter to his family, and a teacher of Kriya Yoga, until 1886, when he was able to retire on a pension. More and more visitors came to see him at this time. He seldom left his sitting room, available to all who sought his darshan. He often exhibited the breathless state of superconscious samadhi.

Over the years he gave initiation to gardeners, postmen, kings, maharajas, sannyasis, householders, people considered to be lower caste, Christians, and Muslims. At that time, it was unusual for a strict Brahmin to associate so closely with people from all castes.

Some of his notable disciples included Sri Panchanon Bhattacharya, Swami Sri Yukteswar Giri, Swami Pranabananda, Swami Keshabananda, Sri Bhupendranath Sanyal, and the parents of Paramhansa Yogananda. Others who received initiation into Kriya Yoga from Lahiri included Swami Bhaskarananda Saraswati of Benares, Balananda Brahmachari of Deogarh, Maharaja Iswari Narayan Sinha Bahadur of Benares and his son. One biographer even speculates that Lahiri initiated Sai Baba of Shirdi into Kriya Yoga, based on a passage in Lahiri's secret diary.

He gave permission to one disciple, Panchanon Bhattacharya, to start an institution in Kolkata to spread the teachings of Kriya Yoga. The Arya Mission Institution published commentaries by Lahiri on the Bhagavad Gita, along with other spiritual books, including a Bengali translation of the Gita. Lahiri himself had printed thousands of small books with excerpted passages from the Gita, in Bengali and Hindi, and distributed them for free, an unusual idea at that time.

In 1895 he began gathering his disciples, letting some of them know that he would soon be leaving the body. Moments before his passing, he said simply, "I am going home. Be comforted; I shall rise again." He then turned his body around three times, faced north, and consciously left his body, entering mahasamadhi. Lahiri Mahasaya died on September 26, 1895.

Teachings

Kriya Yoga

The central spiritual practice which he taught to his disciples was Kriya Yoga, a series of inner pranayama practices that quickly hasten the spiritual growth of the practitioner. He taught this technique to all sincere seekers, regardless of their religious background. In response to many types of problems that disciples would bring him, his advice would be the same — to practice more Kriya Yoga. Regarding Kriya Yoga, he said:

Always remember that you belong to no one, and no one belongs to you. Reflect that some day you will suddenly have to leave everything in this world–so make the acquaintanceship of God now. Prepare yourself for the coming astral journey of death by daily riding in the balloon of God-perception. Through delusion you are perceiving yourself as a bundle of flesh and bones, which at best is a nest of troubles. Meditate unceasingly, that you may quickly behold yourself as the Infinite Essence, free from every form of misery. Cease being a prisoner of the body; using the secret key of Kriya, learn to escape into Spirit.

He taught that Kriya practice would give the yogi direct experience of truth, unlike mere theoretical discussion of the scriptures, and to:

Solve all your problems through meditation. Exchange unprofitable religious speculations for actual God-contact. Clear your mind of dogmatic theological debris; let in the fresh, healing waters of direct perception. Attune yourself to the active inner Guidance; the Divine Voice has the answer to every dilemma of life. Though man's ingenuity for getting himself into trouble appears to be endless, the Infinite Succor is no less resourceful.

The Guru-Disciple Relationship

Lahiri often spoke of the Guru-Disciple relationship in the context of Kriya Yoga. He always gave the Kriya technique as an initiation, and taught that the technique was only properly learned as part of the Guru-Disciple relationship. Frequently he referred to the realization that comes through practicing Kriya as taught by the Guru, and the grace that comes through the 'transmission' of the Guru. He also taught that the grace of the Guru comes automatically if his instructions are followed. He suggested contacting the Guru during meditation, counselling that it wasn't always necessary to see his physical form.

Regarding the necessity of the help of a Guru to deep yoga practice, he said:

It is absolutely necessary for all devotees to totally surrender to their Guru. The more one can surrender to the Guru, the more he can ascertain the subtlest of the subtle techniques of yoga from his Guru. Without surrender, nothing can be derived from the Guru.

The relationship Lahiri Mahasaya had with his own disciples was very individual. He even taught the Kriya Yoga practice slightly differently to each, depending on the spiritual needs of the individual disciple.

Other Teachings

Lahiri taught that if one is earning an honest living and practicing honesty, then there was no need to alter one's external life in any significant way in order to become aware of God's presence. If a student neglected his worldy duties, he would correct him. It was extremely rare for him to advise sannyas, or complete worldly renunciation by becoming a swami. Instead, he advised marriage for most of his disciples along with Kriya Yoga practice.

He generally eschewed organized religion. However, this wasn't a strict dogma for him, as he allowed at least one of his advanced disciples, Panchanon Bhattacharya, to open the "Arya Mission Institution" in Kolkata to spread the Kriya teachings. Other disciples of Lahiri also started organizations to spread the Kriya Yoga message, including Swami Sri Yukteswar Giri with his Satsanga Sabha. Generally, he preferred Kriya to spread naturally.

Lahiri frequently taught the wisdom of the Bhagavad Gita. His regular Gita assemblies, called Gita Sabha, attracted many disciples. He asked several of his close disciples to write interpretations of the Gita by tuning in to his own realization. Lahiri taught that the battle of Kurukshetra was really an inner psychological battle, and that the different characters in the battle were actually psychological traits within the struggling yogi. This understanding would later become the foundation of Paramhansa Yogananda's commentaries on the Bhagavad Gita. He also taught that the epic story of the Mahabharata showed the soul's descent into matter, and its challenges in retracing its way back to spirit.

7

Mahavatar Babaji

Mahavatar Babaji is the name given to an Indian saint by Lahiri Mahasaya and several of his disciples who met Mahavatar Babaji between 1861 and 1935. Some of these meetings were described by Paramhansa Yogananda in his book Autobiography of a Yogi (1946), including a first hand telling of Yogananda's own meeting with Mahavatar Babaji. Another first hand account was given by Sri Yukteswar Giri in his book The Holy Science. All of these accounts, along with additional meetings with Mahavatar Babaji, are described in various biographies of those mentioned by Yogananda.

Mahavatar Babaji's given name and date of birth are not known, so those who met him during that period all called him by the title first given to him by Lahiri Mahasaya. "Mahavatar" means "great avatar," and "Babaji" simply means "revered father." Some of the encounters included two or more witnesses—discussions between those who met Mahavatar Babaji indicate that they all met the same person.

Meetings with Mahavatar Babaji, 1861-1966

Lahiri Mahasaya

The first reported encounter with Mahavatar Babaji was in 1861, when Lahiri Mahasaya was posted to Ranikhet in his work as an accountant for the British government. One day while walking in the hills of Dunagiri above Ranikhet, he heard a voice calling his name. Following the voice up the mountain, he met a "tall, divinely radiant sadhu." He was amazed to find that the sadhu knew his name. This sadhu was Mahavatar Babaji.

Mahavatar Babaji told Lahiri Mahasaya that he was his guru from the past, then initiated him into Kriya Yoga and instructed Lahiri to initiate others. Lahiri wanted to remain with Mahavatar Babaji, who told him instead that he must return to the world to teach Kriya Yoga and that "Kriya Yoga sadhana would spread through the people of the world through his (Lahiri's) presence in the world."

Lahiri Mahasaya reported that Mahavatar Babaji did not give his name or background, so Lahiri gave him the title "Mahavatar Babaji." Many sadhus in India are called Babaji, and sometimes even "Babaji Maharaj," which has caused confusion between Mahavatar Babaji and other sadhus with similar names.

Lahiri Mahasaya had many meetings with Mahavatar Babaji, recounted in several books, including Paramhansa Yogananda's Autobiography of a Yogi, Yogiraj Shyama Charan

Lahiri Mahasaya, and Purana Purusha: Yogiraj Sri Shama Churn Lahiri, among others.

Disciples of Lahiri Mahasaya

Several disciples of Lahiri Mahasaya also said they met Babaji. Through discussion with each other, and the fact that some of these encounters included two or more witnesses, they confirmed that the person they saw was the same sadhu that Lahiri called Mahavatar Babaji.

In 1894, at the Kumbha Mela in Allahabad, Sri Yukteswar Giri, a disciple of Lahiri Mahasaya, met Mahavatar Babaji. He was surprised by the striking resemblance between Lahiri Mahasaya and Mahavatar Babaji. Others who met Babaji also commented on the resemblance. It was at this meeting that Mahavatar Babaji instructed Sri Yukteswar to write the book that was to become Kaivalya Darshanam, or The Holy Science. Sri Yukteswar had two more meetings with Mahavatar Babaji, including one in the presence of Lahiri Mahasaya.

Swami Pranabananda Giri, another disciple of Lahiri Mahasaya, also met Mahavatar Babaji in the presence of Lahiri Mahasaya, at Lahiri's home. Pranabananda asked Mahavatar Babaji his age. Mahavatar Babaji responded that he was about 500 years old at that time.

Swami Keshabananda, a disciple of Lahiri Mahasaya, tells of meeting Mahavatar Babaji in the mountains near Badrinath around 1935, after he became lost wandering in the mountains. At that meeting, Pranabananda reported that Babaji gave him a message for Yogananda, that "I won't see him this time, as he is eagerly hoping; but I shall see him on some other occasion."

Other disciples of Lahiri Mahasaya who reported meetings with Mahavatar Babaji include Swami Kebalananda Giri and Ram Gopal Muzumdar, who recounted meeting Mahavatar Babaji and his sister, whom he called Mataji. In addition, a woman disciple of Trailanga Swami, Shankari Mata (also called Shankari Mai Jiew) met Mahavatar Babaji while visiting Lahiri Mahasaya.

Traditional Legends about Mahavatar Babaji

Legendary powers and age have been attributed to Mahavatar Babaji by the disciples of Lahiri Mahasaya. These stories have led many to believe that Mahavatar Babaji is a legendary person, rather than a real sadhu that was seen by numerous witnesses from 1861 to 1935.

Paramhansa Yogananda, in his Autobiography, described Mahavatar Babaji's role on earth:

The Mahavatar is in constant communion with Christ; together they send out vibrations of redemption, and have planned the spiritual technique of salvation for this age. The work of these two fully-illumined masters–one with the body, and one without it–is to inspire the nations to forsake suicidal wars, race hatreds, religious sectarianism, and the boomerang-evils of materialism. Babaji is well aware of the trend of modern times, especially of the influence and complexities of Western civilization, and realizes the necessity of spreading the self-liberations of yoga equally in the West and in the East.

In addition, Babaji is reputed to be ageless, according to some accounts, and about 500 years old around the late 1800's, according to Swami Pranabananda. Yogananda reports that, according to the disciples of Lahiri Mahasaya, nobody knows Babaji's age, family, place of birth, true name, or other details "dear to the annalist's heart."

According to Yogananda's Autobiography, he has a sister called Mataji (meaning "Holy Mother") who also has lived throughout the centuries. Her level of spiritual attainment is comparable to her brother's, and she lives in a state of spiritual ecstasy in an underground cave. Although only three pages in the book are dedicated to her, she is described by Ram Gopal as "young and surpassingly lovely" as well as a "glorious woman."

Mahavatar Babaji as Krishna

Lahiri Mahasaya wrote in his diary that Mahavatar Babaji was Lord Krishna. Two disciples of Paramhansa Yogananda report that he also stated Mahavatar Babaji was Krishna in a former lifetime. Yogananda also frequently prayed out loud to "Babaji-Krishna."

Modern Claims and Popular References

Babaji and the 18 Siddha Kriya Yoga Tradition by M. Govindan, claims to build upon the story of Mahavatar Babaji by giving details of his life. According to Govindan, Babaji was named Nagaraj (king of serpents) by his parents. He was born on the 30th day of November 203 A.D., in a small coastal village now known as Parangipettai, in Tamil Nadu, India. This information was given by Babaji Nagaraj in 1953 to two disciples, yogi S.A.A. Ramaiah and V.T. Neelakantan.

Between 1861 and 1924, Hariakhan Baba, a Hindu Saint who taught throughout northern India near the Himalayas, was identified as Mahavatar Babaji by Mahendra Baba.

An overview of the Babaji phenomenon was presented by journalist Carter Phipps in WIE Magazine.

In Book 3 of Conversations with God, by Neale Donald Walsch, it is suggested that Babaji may at one time have resurrected himself from the dead.

The 2002 Tamil film Baba written by Rajinikanth was based on Babaji. Paramhansa Swami Maheshwarananda writes in his book The hidden power in humans, that the Guru of the legendary Babaji is Sri Alakh Puriji.

8

Mandana Mishra & Ubhaya Bharti

Mandana Mishra was a Hindu philosopher of Mimamsa and Advaita Vedanta. Mandana Mishra, also known as Sureshvaracharya, was a follower of the Karma Mimamsa, School of philosophy and a staunch defender of the holistic Sphota doctrine of language. His wife Ubhaya Bharati, who was considered to be an incarnation of the Goddess Saraswati is also a younger sister of Kumarila Bhatta.

Mandana Mishra lived in the ancient village Mahishmati (Mahishi) of Mithila now in Bihar in 8th century. He was a renowned philosopher of India in those days. Even Adi Shankaracharya had to come to Mahishi for most famous religious debate of his life.

Mandana Mishra is best known as the author of the Brahmasiddhi, his other major works are Vidhiviveka, Sphota-vada, Mimansaanukramanikaa.

When Adi Sankaracharya was proceeding on his Jaitra Yatra (victory march), the great scholar Mandana Mishra in Mahishmati presently Mahishi, Sankaracharya entered into a scholarly debate with him. Ubhaya Bharati, the wife of Mandana Mishra, was also a great scholar. She was well-versed in the principles of Ritham, Sathyam, Mahattattwam, etc. It was decided that Mandana Mishra would take to Sannyasa if he were to be defeated in the debate. Sankaracharya chose Ubhaya Bharati to be the adjudicator of the contest. As the debate was in progress, she listened to the arguments and counter arguments with utmost concentration. She was impartial in her judgement and declared Sankaracharya to be the winner. Being one of wisdom, she did not feel dejected that her husband was defeated in the debate. Mandana Mishra took to Sannyasa in accordance with the terms and conditions of the debate. Ubhaya Bharathi, being his Ardhangi (better half), followed suit. Both husband and wife renounced the world and propagated the path of wisdom. Human life has no value if one does not acquire wisdom. "To have the vision of the effulgent light of Atma, you have to remove the soot of ego covering your mind". This was the teaching of Ubhaya Bharati. She was living in a hermitage on the banks of the river Ganga, imparting spiritual teachings to women. Many women had become her disciples. Every day in the morning, they used to go the Ganges to have a bath. On the way, there lived a Sannyasi whom people called Brahma Jnani. Truly, he was a renunciant and one of wisdom. However, he was very much attached to a small earthen pot in which he used to preserve water. One day, he was lying down using the pot as a pillow, lest somebody might steal it. Ubhaya Bharati who was on her way to Ganges with her disciples observed this and remarked, "Though he is one of wisdom, there is a small defect in him. He has renounced the world, but is attached to his earthen pot which he is using as his pillow." The Sanyasi overheard their conversation and became angry. When Ubhaya Bharati and her disciples were coming back from Ganges, he threw away the pot on the road, just to show that he was not attached to it. Seeing this, Ubhaya Bharati said, "I thought there was only one defect in him -Abhimana (attachment). Now I realise that he has another defect also – Ahamkara (ego). How can one with Ahamkara and Abhimana be a Jnani (one of wisdom)?" It was an eye-opener for the Sanyas. Ubhaya Bharati toured the length and breadth of the country preaching and propagating the path of wisdom.

9

Nigamananda

Swami Nigamananda Paramahansa (18 August 1880 — 29 November 1935) was born into a Brahmin family, in the hamlet of Kutabpur in Nadia district (at present Meherpur district in Bangladesh). His followers idealized him as their worshiped and beloved thakura.

Nigamananda was a sannyasi of the Shankar's cult. After his ordination as a sannyasi, he came to be known as Paribrajakacharya Paramahansa Srimat Swami Nigamananda Saraswati Deva.

Nigamananda also was a sadguru and a sadhu from India. He was a yogi and a hindu spiritual leader, well known in Eastern India. He was also an Indian hindu guru, a hindu philosopher, associated with the shakti cult, and was viewed as a perfect spiritual master for tantra, gyan, yoga and prema or bhakti

In 1930 Indian spiritual writer, social reformer Durga Charan Mohanty met Swami Nigamananda at Nilachala Kutir Puri and recognized him as sadguru. He wrote a lot of books for Nilachala Saraswata Sangha Puri, founded by Swami Nigamananda in 1934, and translated Swamiji's writings from Bengali to Oriya language. Under Mohanty's encouragement, more than hundred Nigamananda ashrams have been opened at difference places of Orissa, which are running now. He continued to spread the message of Swami Nigamananda till his worldly departure on 7 Dec 1985 at Biratunga.

Swami Nigamananda's followers believe that he achieved siddhi (perfection) in four different sadhanas (spiritual disciplines): tantra, gyan, yoga and prema. Based on these experiences, he wrote five books in the Bengali language: Brahamcharya Sadhana. (These books are now widely available in Oriya, written by Durga Charan Mohanty).

Nigamananda reportedly experienced the state of Nirvikalpa Samadhi.

Life

Childhood, studies and Service Life (1880 — 1901)

At his birth, Nigamananda was named Nalinikanta, per the wishes of his father, Bhuban Mohan Bhattacharya, and the advice of his father's guru, Swami Bhaskarananda Saraswati. At the age of thirteen (1893) he lost his mother "Manikya Sundari Devi," who died of cholera, causing him to fall into depression. In 1894-95 he passed the student scholarship examination and studied at Meherpur High School. In 1895 he took admission at Dhaka Asanulla Engineering College for studying survey. In

1897 his father married him to a thirteen year old girl named "Sudhansubala Devi" of Halisahar. He completed his study in 1899 and joined a service in the District Board of Dinajpur, the estate of Rani Rashmoni to earn his sustenance. As noted, at the end of Vadra, 1901 (approximately five years after marriage) when he was serving as the supervisor of the Narayanpur Estate (Zamindari), in one night suddenly Nalinikanta saw the shadowy image of "Sudhansubala Devi"(his wife) standing at the table glowering and silent while she was supposed to be away at Kutabpur(Nalinikanta's village) at that time. He went to Kutabpur to inquire and came to know that "Sudhansubala Devi" had died just an hour before he saw her image at Narayanpur(Nalinikanta's work place), again an emotional blow to Nalinikanta. He attempted to reach his wife through occult science, but in vain.

Turning Point

This incident further drew him inwards. Earlier, he had the impression that death is the ultimate end of an individual but after this incident, Nalinikanta started believing that there must be life after death. Nalinikanta became desperate to know all about the elusive phenomenona of life and death. These began to worry him all the time. This inquiry took him in Chennai to the Theosophical Society at Adyar. He ascertained all the hypotheses and exercises that theosophy could offer and through a medium, was able to talk to Sudhansubala Devi(his wife) but Nalinikanta could not see her physically. With the experience, he was not satisfied at all. He came to know by a discussion with the members of the Society that the knowledge about the phenomena of "life and death" was the perquisite of the Hindu yogis. With such realization he began to search a true yogi who would fulfill his desire to meet his dead wife and teach him more about "life after death."

Spiritual Experience (1902 — 1905)

As noted, one night in his dreams Nalinikanta saw a sadhu with a brilliant aura around him. He woke up to find the sadhu actually standing beside his bed. The sadhu handed him a leaf with a mantra written on it and then vanished. Nalinikanta asked many to understand the meaning of the mantra. Finally he met Bamakshepa, a famous tantrik, of Tara Pitha, Birbhum district. Nalinikanta took initiation from him and was directed to chant said mantra for 21 days. Under Bamakhepa's guidance he had physical darshan of Maa Tara Devi in the form of "Sudhansubala Devi." This darshan led him to another mystery. He saw Tara Devi coming out of his body and again mingling with him. To solve this mystery, Bamakshepa advised him to attain the knowledge of Advaita from a vedantic guru. In 1902 Nigamananda travelled again to search a Gyani guru, and met "Satchidananda Saraswati," who was a guru from vedantic order, at the holy place of Pushkar in the state of Rajasthan(India). He instantaneously realized that "Satchidananda Saraswati" was the sadhu who had given him the tara mantra in his dream. Nalinikanta became his disciple, and learned all the theories of Brahma (god as the formless one), Brahma Sutras and Vedanta, was initiated by the Satchidananda into renunciation and according to the principle changed his name to Nigamananda.

Satchidananda directed Nigamananda to undertake pilgrimages to the four institutions (Char Dham) of religious seats and realize for himself the significance of each, as the Hindus held these places of worship as very dear to them for their sacredness. After pilgrimages, he arrived back to the ashram.

On his arrival at the ashram, Sachidanand reviewed Nigamananda's Pilgrimages and said: My boy! You have travelled widely and seen the religious places and acquired knowledge and experience. All that I had to teach you has been accomplished but it is for you now to put my teachings in to practice. You have to experience for yourself the truth of your being and this can only be done through concerted efforts as well as the practice and observance of your Yogic principles. Thus you now have to seek out a guru who will provide you the proper guidance in this line.

I had rambled like a mad chap caring little for bodily comforts for God and Guru. God never descended for a moment to assist me. The day I traced my Guru and received His blessings, things turned in my favour. Prior to that although I had undertaken various practices they did not yield any result. As soon as I come under the guidance of my Gurudev whatever practices I followed, I got success in each of them. It is therefore very important that a blessing of guru is very essential for success in spiritual sadhana-Swami Nigamananda

Again Nigamananda went out to seek a guru. In 1903 he met a "yogi guru" (yoga master)-whom he called "Sumeru Das Ji" (otherwise known as Koot Hoomi Lal Singh or Kuthumi).

Under Sumeru Das Ji's guidance he learned the secrets of yoga. After hard practice Nigamananda was able to master savikalpa samadhi (the trance in which the Yogi loses his body consciousness and acquires a transcendental consciousness while his individual identity is still retained) in the month of Poush,1904. Soon after Nigamananda desired to experience the state of Nirvikalpa-the most advanced of Yogic Samadhis. Nigamananda's followers believe that he did enter by way of this Samadhi and returned into his body with the residual consciousness of "I am the Master or Guru" at Kamakshya, in Guwahati Assam (Nilachal Hill). and in yoga he had visualized and practically understood in his own body the Vedic knowledge he had learned from his guru, Satchidananda.

As noted, in 1904, it was Kashi (now known as Varanasi, in U.P., India), one night Goddess Annapurna appeared in his dream and said, his knowledge is limited to formless God and not gone beyond that, hence he was still unfulfilled or incomplete. Nigamananda was awakened from his slumber and soon he became alive to the facts of the case as indicated to him by Goddess Annapurna. So he went to Gouri Devi, (a siddhayogini). She accepted him as a disciple and taught him bhakti or prem (eternal nature of divine love to realize this physical world as the transformation of god in bhava sadhana.

As Swami Nigamananda through a long and continued search discovered his Guru, same principle was followed by many of his disciples to find him out. A few such stories are narrated by his disciples.

Recognition as Paramahaonsa (1904)

Nigamananda went to Allahabad to see Kumbha Mela in 1904 and learned that his master Satchidandand was in the area, staying with Sankaracharya of Sringeri Matha and become anxious to see his guru. Nigamananda went to Sankaracharya's camp, where he found the mahant (superior) sitting on an elevated throne surrounded by 125 sadhus, including his guru "Satchidananda." Seeing him, Nigamananda went to first pay his respects to his guru, and only afterwards to the higher-ranking mahant. The sadhus were upset by this perceived disrespect in not honoring the "mahant" first, but in response Nigamananda quoted the scripture: Manathaha Shri Jagannatha Madguru Shri Jagadguru Madatma Sarvabhutatma Tasmai Shri Gurave Namaha and said My guru is highest in the whole world. Nigamananda further explained to the "sadhu" assemblies that on the basis of the Vedanta philosophy there was no difference between his "Guru" (Shri Satchidanand Saraswati) and "Jagadguru" (Shri Shankarcharya).

Jagadguru Sankaracharya endorsed this response and recognized Nigamananda as one who had achieved spiritual enlightenment. According to instruction of Jagadguru, Nigamananda was conferred with the title paramahansa, then came to be known as "Paribrajakacharay a Paramahansa Shree Mad Swami Nigamananda Saraswati Deva."

Death (1935)

Swami Nigamananda spent the last fourteen years of his life in Puri, Orissa. He died in Calcutta on 29 November 1935.

Swami Nigamananda's followers have continued to honor his memory, and gather together on, annual congregation (sammilan), ceremonial occasions. In 1997, a fire broke out at a gathering of 12,000 who had come together to commemorate Swami Nigamananda at Madhuban grounds, on the outskirts of Baripada in Orissa. The fire and ensuing stampede killed 177 devotees. His ashram at Halisahar, and Sundarbans are places of pilgrimage.

Mission

Swami Nigamananda's mission was:

1. To propagate Sanatana Dharma, i.e. spiritual foundation of the Hindu religion,
2. To spread the right kind of education among people (and publish spiritual literature with emphasis on character building), and
3. To provide service to all created beings, in general, with the attitude of serving the indwelling God.

In order to realize these objectives he enjoined upon his devotees to:

1. Lead an ideal family life (Adarsha Grihastha Jeevan Gathan)
2. Combine the power of spiritual associations (Sangha Shakti Pratishta)
3. Sharing or exchanging of spiritual feelings (Bhava Binimaya)

In order to achieve the above objectives he initiated several thousand interested men and women of all walks of life and taught them his unique spiritual practices devoid of any sectarian bias in the form of a complete package of worship, prayer and meditation. He encouraged his disciples to meet periodically in groups (Sangha) of three or more for offering prayer and worship to the Guru, exchanging spiritual experiences, chanting of "jayaguru" (a non-sectarian word meaning "Glory due to the Master," which he invented), reading spiritual books and dwelling on the ideas therein, devising ways and means for the management of the Math and the Ashrams and pledging to lead the life of a spiritually inspired ideal householder. He had advised his disciples that, the glory of God or Guru is experienced through the medium of these syllable, "Jayaguru" one can reach at God through this name since God is the Guru or Master of the Universe. People belonging to any sect or creed can accept this name without any detriment to their progress in the religious life.

Philosophy and Teachings

Nigamananda was a Sanyasi of the Shankar's cult. The Vedanta philosophy due to the Shankaracharya had been studied by Nigamananda after he was initiated as a Sanyasi of that Order.

Swami Nigamananda's core teachings were, guru and istha are one and identical and to follow the ideals of Lord Shankar and the path of Lord Gaurang. Though he also indicated the philosophical treaties propounded by Lord Shankar which is hard to be practiced by the people of this age but easier to tread the path of devotion shown by Lord Gaurang. His view was Shankar and Gaurang which is a sweet combination of Gyan and Bhakti can lead the world in the right way.

According to Swami Chetanananda Saraswati, Nigamananda's philosophy and teachings as described below:

Avatar and Sadguru

According to view of "Chetanananda Saraswati," Swami Nigamananda never admitted that he was God-incarnate or an Avatar although many of his disciples fancied to identify him as one. He stated that an incarnation is an exclusive descent of God on earth to uphold spiritual order in a region, country or even the whole world. Although he could, the Avatar ordinarily does not enlighten or guide individuals, per se. Through his agency, righteousness is established and demoniac forces are destroyed at large. Swami Nigamananda wanted that he should be treated as a Sadguru (a perfect spiritual Master, also one form of God) who, on account of his long quest over succession of births and deaths, attained to the knowledge of his Swaroop (true or potential nature, i.e., supreme universal consciousness). There is scriptural evidence to show that Gautam himself had to pass through many births before acquiring the qualities to realise the truth and become the great Buddha! Swami Nigamananda further pointed out that an "Avatar" does not always remain in the state of super-human consciousness so as to be able to take part in Leela i.e. divine play! Sadguru, Jagadguru and God.

According to Swami Nigamananda, the disciple should take his Guru (a Sadguru, of course) to be the Jagadguru (or the World Master, the Purushottama) and not an ordinary human being, in tune with Lord Krishna's statement in the Bhagavadgeeta:

He who truely knows My birth and activities to be divine is not born again but attains to Me-Bhagavadgeeta (4.9).

Also like in Patanjali's aphorism: "By contemplating on the form of one who has no attachments, concentration of mind is attained," Swami Nigamananda advised his disciples to meditate on his physical form such that all the admirable qualities and attributes in him would get automatically transferred into their beings and fashion their souls. Further he assured that because he had, by triple modes of spiritual practice, simultaneously experienced the nature of Brahman, Paramatma (supreme universal self) and Bhagawan (Personal and universal Godhead) as the ultimate spiritual goals of the seekers, his true disciples also would simultaneously have such experience. That, he said, "was his only expectation from his disciples and he would love to wait for the day to see that fulfilled" the Order of Spiritual Attainments.

According to Swami Nigamananda, the theory of self realization requires expanding the individual self to the status of the supreme universal self and it can be directly practiced only by the most competent among the aspirant Sanyasis by means of precise intellectual inquiry, analysis and deep meditation, although the service to the Master holds the key to success in such pursuits as well. However, Nigamananda pointed out that true transcendental divine love and ecstasy could be properly experienced by the most fortunate ones only after they had attained monistic realisation of the supreme as declared by Lord Krishna himself in the Bhagavadgita:

Having realized the state of oneness with the supreme self or Parabrahma and attaining tranquility in spirit, the aspirant neither grieves nor desires and regarding all beings as alike he attains supreme devotion to Me-Bhagavadgita (18.54).

Reconciliation of Monistic and Dualistic Pursuits

Unlike some other saints who recognized and preached a diversity of equally valid doctrines for self/God realisation and as many valid paths to attain to those, Swami Nigamananda suggested the realisation of oneness of self and the supreme universal self as the true and the highest goal of human life.

And the path leading to it, in the case of most aspirants, is one of true devotion for the perfect spiritual Master (Sadguru) who initiates them. Rendering personal Service to the Master and invoking his grace through prayers, chanting and simple meditation are the chief modes of spiritual practice for them. They will thus, not only acquire non-dualistic realization knowing, for sure, that their Master is a realised soul and trying to live up to his teachings, but also experience bliss due to intense love for him in course of time, when they are enabled to participate in his Leela for helping others to achieve self/God realisation.

Swami Nigamananda pointed out that the path shown by Gouranga Mahaprabhu who practiced and preached unconditional devotion and love for God was rather narrow, in as much as it was directed to Sri Krishna as the only God. In order to broad-base that path, Swami Nigamananda suggested to take the Master as an embodiment of Sri Krishna (or any other deity whom the aspirant loved), in which case the guide himself becomes his goal. In this way Swami Nigamananda convincingly formulated a reconciliation of the two apparently contradictory creeds, one due to the great Shankaracharya, the founder of the monistic school of Vedanta philosophy and the other due to Gauranga Mahaprabhu who advocated the principle and practice of apparent duality between the devotee and God. After all, Swami Nigamananda pointed out that in the path of devotion and love the aspirant has to subdue or tame his ego adequately and hence he attains to the same stage as that of the monistic aspirant whose ego loses its identity on attaining to his goal. In the former case, the individuality of the devotee is reduced to a trifling, overpowered by personal god-consciousness, whereas in the latter the aspirant loses his self-consciousness in the ocean of impersonal universal consciousness.

Gyanchakra

Nigamananda pointed out that although the doctrine of monistic vedanta philosophy treats the supreme reality in terms of oneness of individual and universal consciousness, it does not systematically explain the structure of the material creation which, on the other hand, is done by Sankhya philosophy.

But this latter does not treat the supreme reality as well. Similarly, whereas Christianity emphasises on service and surrender as means to god realization, the Indian philosophy of Poorva Mimamsa prescribes various ritualistic actions for the attainment of personal and collective happiness despite cycles of birth and death.

By means of a Gyanachakra chart (the spheres of spiritual cosmology) which he visualized and presented in a pictorial form, Swami Nigamananda identified different layers of human consciousness inter-woven in the microcosm (body) and the macrocosm (the universe) and pointed out the levels which the aspirants of different spiritual orders and sects may ultimately reach. In this chart he placed Sri Krishna and Sri Radha in the transition between the non qualified (Nirguna) Brahman and qualified (Saguna) Brahman, which he called as the Nitya or the Bhavaloka. (Yogamaya is a form of divine power, which incessantly attracts the earth-bound souls and helps them realise their true blissful nature and participate in the divine play).

Other Key Teachings

- To be able to get spiritually liberated one needs the help of a liberated person (a Master Sadguru or simply Guru). In the Hindu scriptures that person is known as the Guru. Without his grace or favor none can make any progress in the path leading to liberation. Also he who has attained the ultimate reality (Paramatman or Brahman) as one and the same as himself (the Atman) is the Guru.
- The Guru who helps in getting one liberated cannot be equated in importance to formal learning, pilgrimage or divinity. If we do not offer our deep devotion and love to Him, who else then is fit for getting our utmost respect?
- The Guru indeed is the embodiment of the essence of what the Vedanta teaches – the individual self (the Atman) is one and the same as the cosmic self (Paramatman or Brahman).

- A Sadguru never curses anyone. Even if He appears to be angry, that too is going to do good to the disciple. The advantage of depending on a Sadguru is unique. One doesn't have the same advantage depending even on God because God never materializes to give instructions. The Guru in practice provides the required guidance leading the disciple to the ultimate goal.
- The Guru and the disciple are inseparable in a way. The Guru cannot exist without being a part of a true disciple's personality or character.
- There are two pathways to attain spiritual liberation: one is by initiation into and observing the austerities of sanyas yoga and the other – by service rendered to a Sadguru who has had realization of Brahma. The former is an extremely arduous path – the disciple must die in a sense even while he remains in his body. In other words, he has to loose his body consciousness. But if one unconditionally loves the Guru by way of rendering service to him sincerely, spiritual liberation may be obtained relatively easily.
- Nothing substantial can be achieved without Guru's grace. I have been wandering far and wide like a bird as if with its voice box mutilated but have not had God coming and helping me. But the day I was able to have the grace or the benefit of the Guru (Who is God in human form), I started making real progress.
- The Guru, 'the mantra' that he gives during initiation and the disciple's choicest divinity (or Ista) are one and

the same. Unless the Guru becomes the choicest divinity, the mantra received from Him looses its power.

- Acquisition of disciples through initiation is not Guru's profession; it is the inspiration of His heart. The Guru's inifiation takes care and guides the disciple hoping that one day the disciple will get spiritually enlightened.
- The Guru is the embodiment of both the monistic (or non-dual) ideology due to the Great Shankaracharya and love divine as preached by Sri Sri Gouranga Mahaprahbu. If the disciple submits himself to the Guru, his latent characteristic attitude is bound to unfold. Spiritual life based on such a universal (non-sectarian) and sweet relationship between the Guru and the disciple can help harmonize the diverse faiths in the world.

Yoga, Theories and Techniques

Few Nigamananda's teachings as noted by Durga Charan Mohanty are furnished here:

Theory of Jibanamukta Upasana

One of Nigamananda's major concepts was the theory of Jibanamukta Upasana, which he believed could lead the sadhaka to quick self-realisation.

Karmic Theory

According to Swami Nigamananda, Karma is of three kinds viz. Kriyaman, Sanchita and Prarbdha. When the results of one's labour is enjoyed during his life time is called Kriyaman; if he dies before enjoying the fruits of his labour, it is called Sanchita

Karma or accumulated labour. As he takes rebirth to enjoy the balance of accumulated Karma of the past life this is called Prarbdha. By virtue of one's Sadhana, the effects of Kriyaman and Sanchita can be wiped out during one's own life but it is not possible to erase out the effects of Prarbdha Karma. So long as a person is possessed with worldly ambitions, he is sure to take the endless journey of birth and death. Jivtma leaves the gross body to travel sometime in the astral world which is called the spirit world or Pret Lok. After undergoing some of its Karmic effects, it returns to the gross world with a gross body for the fulfillment of his further desires that he had during his last incarnation. How it moves from one world to another being ignorant of the same is a matter of great mystery. Yogies can perceive the mystery clearly and tell the past Sanskar of Jiva.

Theory of Process of Thinking on Death

Swami Nigamananda's insight into the mysteries of death would remain as a guideline for them to tread the path of virtue and justice and face the dragon of death without the least fear.

You are not to live here for ever. Someday you will have to depart from this world. If you prepare yourself to face death you have to realise what death is, what exists after death and what happens to the soul when it makes its exit from this body. Man need not fear death since it is a process of promotion to a better life-Swami Nigamananda

Swami Nigamananda said, one should remember all the time that he has to die one day. We do not know at what moment death will visit us. Before working on good or evil deeds, one should also remember that he has to die one day and that day is not very far off. Death will drive out from one's mind the anxiety for sense pleasure and evil thoughts. Man would refrain from committing any act of injustice on poor if he thinks of this. Attachment to wealth and relations will then fail to dominate the feelings of man. All the earthly matters to which man is tied so much will continue to remain as they are even after his departure from this world. Only the spiritual wealth that has been earned during one's life time remains as an asset to the individuals. Those who have acquired wealth and learning by virtue of their intellect and have puffed with pride on account of this will submit to the God of death meekly when that particular hour comes. Being drunk with pride, some persons ill-treat their fellow brethren who have been ill placed in their life without giving the least thought that they will be paid back in the same coins at an appropriate time with compound interest. A day is awaiting for them when they will be left in the deserted crematory ground with the beasts and birds around who will joyously wait to feast upon his flesh and worn-out tissues. Their inert bodies will lie there in silent submission to these beings. If one thinks of this all the evil thoughts will disappear from his mind. Those who are blind to the truth of life and have plunged themselves in the temporary pleasures of the world will be able to change their course of life if the foregoing lines get into their mind. Those of you have become wise enough and quite alert to the truth will not be afraid of death and they will accept it as a passage to the superior world.

Yoga

Swami Nigamananda had written a great deal on Yoga, the theories and techniques can be found in his book "Yogi Guru." Out of them few produced here:

Hatha yoga and Laya yoga: According to Swami Nigamananda, the practice of Hatha Yoga can be carried out when the body is made fit for the purpose; the body should be cleansed first of the impurities through Sat Sadhna i.e. the six elementary practices of Yoga. Hatha Yoga is completely different from Laya Yoga. The practices of Hatha Yoga can make the body strong which can enable it to survive for a period of about four hundred years or more, whereas Laya Yoga helps the aspirant to attain union with the supreme. If the body is not kept purified both externally and internally through the practices of Hatha Yoga, the succeeding steps of Laya Yoga would yield no result.

Dharana and dhyan: Swami Nigamananda taught that, since the breathing system is closely connected with the intricate workings of the mind, practice of Pranayama leads to regulate the breath and thereby maintains tranquility of mind. Mind is subjected to forces of disturbed thoughts owing to the irregularity in the process of breathing. He said I had applied myself to the higher practices of Yoga, thereafter, i.e. Dharana and Dhyan (meditation). The Sadhaka is likely to peril his life if he does not take assistance of another during these advance practices. During the practices of Dharana, the Sadhaka experiences his own progress and when the estimated height in Sadhana is achieved, he enters into the successive step of progress. While being absorbed in the practice of Dhyan, the Sadhaka may cross over to the state of Samadhi and it is not predictable when he is to stumble across this state of consciousness. Till the experience of Samadhi, the Sadhaka goes on groping in the darkness where Guru comes to his aid to steer him through the difficult passages of Yoga.

Sampragyant samadhi: Nigamananda pointed out that if earlier practices are perfected, the succeeding steps yield good and a biding results. These practices are under one's own control. At that state the Sadhaka would enter in to Samadhi is a matter of his own experience and could experience the awakening of Kundalini. The upward and downward motion of Kundalini is called Sampragyant Samadhi.

Works

Garohill Yoga Ashram

Nigamananda founded his first Yoga Ashram in 1905 (1312 BS) at Kodaldhoa in Garo Hills, which is called now "Garohill-Yogashrama." His famous yoga book "Yogi Guru," was written and composed here in 14 days of time as noted.

Saraswata Matha

Nigamananda founded "Shanti Ashram" in 1912 at Jorhat to fulfill his three missons i.e. To propagate Sanatana Dharma (spreading eternal religion), spreading true education and serve everybody as god incarnate,

He took a plot of land of Jorhat in Sibsagar district and founded this ashram there on Akshaya Tritiya, in the month of Baishakh (in 1319 BS according to Bengal calendar). This was called "Shanti Ashram" or Saraswata Matha,which went by the name of Assam-Bengal Saraswata Matha in the later years.

Rishi Vidyalaya was an important school founded under this Matha for Yoga training to students.

Retirement

Swami Nigamananda initiated ten of his devout disciples into Samnyas in the tradition of the "Saraswati" by order due to the great Sankaracharya, the juniormost among whom were "Swami Nirvanananda Saraswati" (an erudite scholar, philosopher and writer who became famous as Anirvan later on) and "Swami Prajnananda Saraswati." Swearing in Swami Prajnanandaji as the Mahant and Trustee of the "Saraswat Matha and Ashrama Establishments." Swami Nigamananda retired and resided in Nilachala Kutir in Puri for several years, till 1935 CE.

100 Years of Saraswata Matha (1912–2011)

This Institution(Shanti Ashram) or "Saraswata Matha" founded by Swami Nigamananda in 1912(1319 BS) now steped into hundred years of its life on Akshaya Tritiya Baishakh, 2011 (1418 BS), i.e. 6 May 2011.

He expressed his views stating that this Matha is very dear to my heart, I can sacrifice my life hundred times for the sake of this Matha.

Nilachala Saraswata Sangha

Swami Nigamananda retired form his work and resided in Nilachala Kutir, Puri, Orissa. Puri is a holy city of the Hindus as a part of the Char Dham pilgrimages also known as city of Lord Jagannath. Nigamananda believed Lord Jagannath as "symbol of truth" and liked very much to the culture of Lord Jagannath of Puri, as it embodies in itself the culture of truth, unity and integrity. He spent his rest 12 years of his life in Puri.

The day 24 August 1934(Friday), fullmoon day (Sravan Purnima) Friday, Nilachala Saraswata Sangha was established by Swami Nigamananda himself at Nilachala Kutir, Puri. The

Oriya devotees gathered there to celebrate his birthday. He advised these people to form a religious circle among them. As per his wishes some devotees started an association for religious talk and thus "Nilachala Saraswata Sangha" (the Sangha) came into existence by the gradual growth of the group discussion and prayer, to fulfill the triple objectives as, (1)leading an Ideal family life, (2)establishment of combined power and (3)sharing of feelings.

Guru Braham Ashrams

Swami Nigamananda established Guru Brahama Ashrams where people from any faith can come here and pray to god in his own way.

He instituted five Ashrams in five divisions of undivided Bengal, they are Purba Bangala Saraswat Ashram at Moinamati, Comilla (Bangaladesh), now at Tripura, Madhya Bangala Saraswat Ashram at Kalni, Dacca, now Purbasthali Bardhaman district, Uttar Bangala Saraswat Ashram at Bogra, Paschima Bangala Saraswat Ashram at Kharkusama, Midnapore, Dakhina Bangala Saraswat Ashram at Halisahar, 24 Paraganas.

Swami Nigamananda installed Jagat Gurus Ashan, in the year 1915 at Kokilamukh, Jorhat, Assam. and established many Ashrams and made thousands of disciples in the Guru-shishya tradition.

Other foundations

Followers of Nigamananda run numerous schools and educational institutions in India.

Publications

Arya Darpan

Nigamananda also published Arya Darpan, a monthly magazine on sanatana dharma and believed to be intended for disseminating non-sectarian spiritual knowledge among the masses who are apt to be misguided by narrow religious faith lacking in a rational basis. Many essays on important topics relating to religious and scriptural matters have been included in this magazine.

Thakurer Chithi

Advising to his desciples, Nigamananda had written numerous letters, out of them hundred letters are collected and stored in a book called "Thakurer Chithi." This information is being published in a Calcutta based magazine Modern Review, founded by Ramananda Chatterjee, on 26 December 1938.

Other few Nigamananda collection of spiritual books are 'Maayer Kripa,' "Vedanta Vivek" and "Tattvamala."

Bhakta Sammelan

He categorized the "Bhakta Sammelan" into two parts one is Sarbabhouma i.e. Country wide and other is Pradeshika i.e. State wide. The first Sarbabhouma Bhakta Sammelan was established by Swami Nigamananda at Kokilamukh, Jorhat, Assam in 1915, and first "Pradeshika Bhakta Sanarpn" was held in the year 1947 by "Nilachala Saraswata Sangha, Puri" at Ankoli in the district of Ganjam, Orissa during full moon day of Maagha.

Swami Sammelan Nigamananda had instructed to each of his disciples and devotees to assemble in the Sammilani every year to enjoy the divine pleasures from the eternal fount of bliss that overflows from the assembly of devotees. He had also introduced for the women disciples a different prayer day in the Annual "Sammelan" where they alone could participate and exchange their views."

He said in one of "Sammelan" as noted that my devotees are fully aware that I am pleased to see them congregated in this Sammelan, once in a year during the X-mas. Such gathering would bring fame to the Maths and it would also do good to the world at large

10

Ramakrishna

Ramakrishna (18 February 1836 – 16 August 1886), born Gadadhar Chattopadhyay, was a famous mystic of 19th-century India. His religious school of thought led to the formation of the Ramakrishna Mission by his chief disciple Swami Vivekananda – both were influential figures in the Bengali Renaissance as well as the Hindu renaissance during the 19th and 20th centuries. Many of his disciples and devotees believe he was an Avatar or incarnation of God. He is also referred as "Paramahamsa" by his devotees, as such he is popularly known as Ramkrishna Paramhamsa.

Ramakrishna was born in a poor Brahmin Vaishnava family in rural Bengal. He became a priest of the Dakshineswar Kali Temple, dedicated to the goddess Kali, which had the influence of the main strands of Bengali bhakti tradition. His first spiritual teacher was an ascetic woman skilled in Tantra and Vaishnava bhakti. Later an Advaita Vedantin ascetic taught him non-dual meditation, and according to Ramakrishna, he experienced nirvikalpa samadhi under his guidance. Ramakrishna also experimented with other religions, notably Islam and Christianity, and said that they all lead to the same God. Though conventionally uneducated, he attracted the attention of the middle class, upper middle class and numerous Bengali intellectuals.

Biography

Birth and Childhood

Ramakrishna was born on 18 February 1836, in the village of Kamarpukur, in the Hooghly district of West Bengal, into a very poor but pious, orthodox brahmin family. Located far from the railroad, Kamarpukur was untouched by the glamour of the city and contained rice fields, tall palms, royal banyans, a few lakes, and two cremation grounds. His parents were Khudiram Chattopadhyaya and Chandramani Devi. According to his followers, Ramakrishna's parents experienced supernatural incidents, visions before his birth. His father Khudiram had a dream in Gaya in which Lord Gadadhara (a form of Vishnu), said that he would be born as his son. Chandramani Devi is said to have had a vision of light entering her womb from Shiva's temple.

Ramakrishna attended a village school with some regularity for 12 years, he later rejected the traditional schooling saying that he was not interested in a "bread-winning education." Kamarpukur, being a transit-point in well-established pilgrimage routes to Puri, brought him into contact with renunciates and holy men. He became well-versed in the Puranas, the Ramayana, the Mahabharata, and the Bhagavata Purana, hearing them from wandering monks and the Kathaks—a class of men in ancient India who preached and sang the PuraGas. He could read and write in Bengali. While the official biographies write that the name Ramakrishna was given by Mathura Bisv'as—chief patron at Dakshineswar Kali Temple, it has also been suggested that this name was given by his own parents.

Ramakrishna describes his first spiritual ecstasy at the age of six: while walking along the paddy fields, a flock of white cranes flying against a backdrop of dark thunder clouds caught his vision. He reportedly became so absorbed by this scene that he lost outward consciousness and experienced indescribable joy in that state. Ramakrishna reportedly had experiences of similar nature a few other times in his childhood—while worshipping the goddess Vishalakshi, and portraying god Shiva in a drama during Shivaratri festival. From his tenth or eleventh year on, the trances became common, and by the final years of his life, Ramakrishna's samadhi periods occurred almost daily.

Ramakrishna's father died in 1843, after that time, family responsibilities fell on his elder brother Ramkumar. This loss drew him closer to his mother, and he spent his time in household activities and daily worship of the household deities and became more involved in contemplative activities such as reading the sacred epics. When Ramakrishna was in his teens, the family's financial position worsened. Ramkumar started a Sanskrit school in Calcutta and also served as a priest.

Ramakrishna moved to Calcutta in 1852 with Ramkumar to assist in the priestly work.

Priest at Dakshineswar Kali Temple

In 1855 Ramkumar was appointed as the priest of Dakshineswar Kali Temple, built by Rani Rashmoni—a rich woman of Calcutta who belonged to the kaivarta community. Ramakrishna, along with his nephew Hriday, became assistants to Ramkumar, with Ramakrishna given the task of decorating the deity. When Ramkumar died in 1856, Ramakrishna took his place as the priest of the Kali temple.

After Ramkumar's death Ramakrishna became more contemplative. He began to look upon the image of the goddess Kali as his mother and the mother of the universe. Ramakrishna reportedly had a vision of goddess Kali as the universal Mother, which he described as "... houses, doors, temples and everything else vanished altogether; as if there was nothing anywhere! And what I saw was an infinite shoreless sea of light; a sea that was consciousness. However far and in whatever direction I looked, I saw shining waves, one after another, coming towards me."

Marriage

Rumors spread to Kamarpukur that Ramakrishna had become unstable as a result of his spiritual exercises at Dakshineswar. Ramakrishna's mother and his elder brother Rameswar decided to get Ramakrishna married, thinking that marriage would be a good steadying influence upon him—by forcing him to accept responsibility and to keep his attention on normal affairs rather than his spiritual practices and visions. Ramakrishna reportedly mentioned that they could find the bride at the house of

Ramchandra Mukherjee in Jayrambati, three miles to the north-west of Kamarpukur. The five-year-old bride, Saradamani Mukhopadhyaya (later known as Sarada Devi) was found and the marriage was duly solemnised in 1859. Ramakrishna was 23 at this point, but the age difference was typical for 19th century rural Bengal. They later spent three months together in Kamarpukur. Sarada Devi was fourteen while Ramakrishna was thirty-two. Ramakrishna became a very influential figure in Sarada's life, and she became a strong follower of his teachings. After the marriage, Sarada stayed at Jayrambati and joined Ramakrishna in Dakshineswar at the age of 18.

By the time his bride joined him, Ramakrishna had already embraced the monastic life of a sannyasi; as a result, the marriage was never consummated. As a priest Ramakrishna performed the ritual ceremony—the Shodashi Puja–where Sarada Devi was made to sit in the seat of goddess Kali, and worshiped as the Divine mother. Ramakrishna regarded Sarada as the Divine Mother in person, addressing her as the Holy Mother, and it was by this name that she was known to Ramakrishna's disciples. Sarada Devi outlived Ramakrishna by 34 years and played an important role in the nascent religious movement.

Religious Practices and Teachers

After his marriage Ramakrishna returned to Calcutta and resumed the charges of the temple again, and continued his sadhana. According to his official biographers, he continued his sadhana under teachers of Tantra, Vedanta and Vaishnava

Bhairavi Brahmani and Tantra

In 1861, Ramakrishna accepted Bhairavi Brahmani, an orange-robed, middle-aged female ascetic, as a teacher. She carried with her the Raghuvir Shila, a stone icon representing Ram and all Vaishnava deities. She was thoroughly conversant with the texts of Gaudiya Vaishnavism and practiced Tantra. According to the Bhairavi, Ramakrishna was experiencing phenomena that accompany mahabhava—the supreme attitude of loving devotion towards the divine –and quoting from the bhakti shastras, she said that other religious figures like Radha and Chaitanya had similar experiences.

The Bhairavi initiated Ramakrishna into Tantra. Tantrism focuses on the worship of shakti and the object of Tantric training is to transcend the barriers between the holy and unholy as a means of achieving liberation and to see all aspects of the natural world as manifestations of the divine shakti. Under her guidance, Ramakrishna went through sixty four major tantric sadhanas which were completed in 1863. He began with mantra rituals such as japa and purascarana and many other rituals designed to purify the mind and establish self-control. He later proceeded towards tantric sadhanas, which generally include a set of heterodox practices called vamachara (left-hand path), which utilize as a means of liberation, activities like eating of parched grain, fish and meat along with drinking of wine and sexual intercourse. According to Ramakrishna and his biographers, Ramakrishna did not directly participate in the last two of those activities, all that he needed was a suggestion of them to produce the desired result. Ramakrishna acknowledged the left-hand tantric path, though it had "undesirable features," as one of the "valid roads to God-realization," he consistently cautioned his devotees and disciples against associating with it. The Bhairavi also taught Ramakrishna the kumari-puja, a form of ritual in which the Virgin Goddess is worshiped symbolically in the form of a young girl. Under the tutelage of the Bhairavi, Ramakrishna also learnt Kundalini Yoga. The Bhairavi, with the yogic techniques and the tantra played an important part in the initial spiritual development of Ramakrishna.

Vaishnava Bhakti

The Vaishnava Bhakti traditions speak of five different moods, referred to as bhavas—different attitudes that a devotee can take up to express his love for God. They are: Shanta, the "peaceful attitude"; dasya, the attitude of a servant; sakhya, the attitude of a friend; vatsalya, the attitude of a mother toward her child; and madhura, the attitude of a woman towards her lover.

At some point in the period between his vision of Kali and his marriage, Ramakrishna practiced dasya bhava, during which he worshiped Rama with the attitude of Hanuman, the monkey-god, who is considered to be the ideal devotee and servant of Rama. According to Ramakrishna, towards the end of this sadhana, he had a vision of Sita, the consort of Rama, merging into his body.

In 1864, Ramakrishna practiced vatsalya bhava under a Vaishnava guru Jatadhari. During this period, he worshipped a metal image of Ramlala (Rama as a child) in the attitude of a mother. According to Ramakrishna, he could feel the presence of child Rama as a living God in the metal image.

Ramakrishna later engaged in the practice of madhura bhava— the attitude of the Gopis and Radha towards Krishna. During the practise of this bhava, Ramakrishna dressed himself in women's attire for several days and regarded himself as one of the Gopis of Vrindavan. According to Sri Ramakrishna, madhura bhava is practised to root out the idea of sex, which is seen as an impediment in spiritual life. According to Ramakrishna, towards the end of this sadhana, he attained savikalpa samadhi—vision and union with Krishna.

Ramakrishna visited Nadia, the home of Chaitanya and Nityananda, the 15th-century founders of Bengali Gaudiya Vaishnava bhakti. According to Ramakrishna, he had an intense vision of two young boys merging into his body. Earlier, after his vision of Kali, he is said to have cultivated the Santa bhava—the child attitude — towards Kali.

Totapuri and Vedanta

In 1865, Ramakrishna was initiated into sannyasa by Tota Puri, an itinerant monk who trained Ramakrishna in Advaita Vedanta, the Hindu philosophy which emphasizes non-dualism.

Totapuri first guided Ramakrishna through the rites of sannyasa—renunciation of all ties to the world. Then he instructed him in the teaching of advaita—that "Brahma alone is real, and the world is illusory; I have no separate existence; I am that Brahma alone." Under the guidance of Totapuri, Ramakrishna reportedly experienced nirvikalpa samadhi, which is considered to be the highest state in spiritual realisation.

Totapuri stayed with Ramakrishna for nearly eleven months and instructed him further in the teachings of advaita. Ramakrishna said that this period of nirvikalpa samadhi came to an end when he received a command from the Mother Kali to "remain in Bhavamukha; for the enlightenment of the people."

Bhavamukha being a state of existence intermediate between samadhi and normal consciousness.

Islam and Christianity

In 1866, Govinda Roy, a Hindu guru who practiced Sufism, initiated Ramakrishna into Islam. Ramakrishna said that he "devoutly repeated the name of Allah, wore a cloth like the Arab Moslems, said their prayer five times daily, and felt disinclined even to see images of the Hindu gods and goddesses, much less worship them—for the Hindu way of thinking had disappeared altogether from my mind." According to Ramakrishna, after three days of practice he had a vision of a "radiant personage with grave countenance and white beard resembling the Prophet and merging with his body."

At the end of 1873 he started the practice of Christianity, when his devotee Shambu Charan Mallik read the Bible to him. Ramakrishna said that for several days he was filled with Christian thoughts and no longer thought of going to the Kali temple. Ramakrishna describes of a vision in which the picture of Madonna and Child Jesus became alive and had a vision in which Jesus merged with his body. In his own room amongst other divine pictures was one of Christ, and he burnt incense before it in the morning and evening. There was also a picture showing Jesus Christ saving St. Peter from drowning in the water.

Arrival of followers

In 1875, Ramakrishna met the influential Brahmo Samaj leader Keshab Chandra Sen. Keshab had accepted Christianity, and had separated from the Adi Brahmo Samaj. Formerly, Keshab had rejected idolatry, but under the influence of Ramakrishna he accepted Hindu polytheism and established the "New Dispensation" (Nava Vidhan) religious movement, based on Ramakrishna's principles—"Worship of God as Mother," "All religions as true" and "Assimilation of Hindu polytheism into Brahmoism." Keshab also publicized Ramakrishna's teachings in the journals of New Dispensation over a period of several years, which was instrumental in bringing Ramakrishna to the attention of a wider audience, especially the Bhadralok (English-educated classes of Bengal) and the Europeans residing in India.

Following Keshab, other Brahmos such as Vijaykrishna Goswami started to admire Ramakrishna, propagate his ideals and reorient their socio-religious outlook. Many prominent people of Calcutta—Pratap Chandra Mazumdar, Shivanath Shastri and Trailokyanath Sanyal—began visiting him during this time (1871–1885). Mozoomdar wrote the first English biography of Ramakrishna, entitled The Hindu Saint in the Theistic Quarterly Review (1879), which played a vital role in introducing Ramakrishna to Westerners like the German indologist Max Müller. Newspapers reported that Ramakrishna was spreading "Love" and "Devotion" among the educated classes of Calcutta and that he had succeeded in reforming the character of some youths whose morals had been corrupt.

Ramakrishna also had interactions with Debendranath Tagore, the father of Rabindranath Tagore, and Ishwar Chandra Vidyasagar, a renowned social worker. He had also met Swami Dayananda. Ramakrishna is considered as one of the main contributors to the Bengali Renaissance. However, some Brahmos like Upadhyay Brahmabandhab disapproved of his avatarahood and ascetic renunciation and considered Ramakrishna's samadhi as a nervous malady.

Among the Europeans who were influenced by Ramakrishna was Principal Dr. W.W. Hastie of the Scottish Church College, Calcutta. In the course of explaining the word trance in the poem The Excursion by William Wordsworth, Hastie told his students that if they wanted to know its "real meaning," they should go to "Ramakrishna of Dakshineswar." This prompted some of his students, including Narendranath Dutta (later Swami Vivekananda), to visit Ramakrishna.

Devotees and Disciples

Most of Ramakrishna's prominent disciples came between 1879–1885, and were influenced by his style of preaching and instruction.

His chief disciples consisted of:

Grihastas or The householders—Mahendranath Gupta, Girish Chandra Ghosh, Akshay Kumar Sen and others.

Monastic disciples who renounced their family and became the earliest monks of the Ramakrishna order—Narendranath Dutta (Swami Vivekananda), Rakhal Chandra Ghosh (Swami Brahmananda), Kaliprasad Chandra (Swami Abhedananda), Taraknath Ghoshal (Swami Shivananda), Sashibhushan Chakravarty (Swami Ramakrishnananda), Saratchandra Chakravarty (Swami Saradananda), Tulasi Charan Dutta (Swami Nirmalananda), Gangadhar Ghatak (Swami

Akhandananda), Hari Prasana (Swami Vijnanananda) and others.

A small group of women disciples including Gauri Ma and Yogin Ma. A few of them were initiated into sanyasa through mantra deeksha. Among the women, Ramakrishna emphasized service to other women rather than tapasya (practice of austerities). Gauri Ma founded the Saradesvari Ashrama at Barrackpur, which was dedicated to the education and uplift of women.

As his name spread, an ever-shifting crowd of all classes and castes visited Ramakrishna. According to Kathamrita it included, childless widows, young school-boys, aged pensioners, Hindu scholars and religious figures, men betrayed by lovers, people with suicidal tendencies, small-time businessmen, and people "dreading the grind of Sansaric life." Ramakrishna's primary biographers, describe him as talkative. According to the biographers, for hours Ramakrishna would reminisce about his own eventful spiritual life, tell tales, explain Vedantic doctrines with extremely mundane illustrations, raise questions and answer them himself, crack jokes, sing songs, and mimic the ways of all types of worldly people, keeping the visitors enthralled. In preparation for monastic life, Ramakrishna ordered his monastic disciples to beg their food from door to door without distinction of caste. He gave them the saffron robe, the sign of the Sanyasi, and initiated them with Mantra Deeksha.

Last Days

In the beginning of 1885 Ramakrishna suffered from clergyman's throat, which gradually developed into throat cancer. He was moved to Shyampukur near Calcutta, where some of the best physicians of the time, including Dr. Mahendralal Sarkar, were engaged. When his condition aggravated he was relocated to a large garden house at Cossipore on December 11, 1885.

During his last days, he was looked after by his monastic disciples and Sarada Devi. Ramakrishna was advised by the doctors to keep the strictest silence, but ignoring their advice, he incessantly conversed with visitors. According to traditional accounts, before his death, Ramakrishna transferred his spiritual powers to Vivekananda and reassured Vivekananda of his avataric status. Ramakrishna asked Vivekananda to look after the welfare of the disciples, saying, "keep my boys together" and asked him to "teach them." Ramakrishna also asked other monastic disciples to look upon Vivekananda as their leader. Ramakrishna's condition gradually worsened and he expired in the early morning hours of August 16, 1886 at the Cossipore garden house. According to his disciples, this was mahasamadhi. After the death of their master, the monastic disciples led by Vivekananda formed a fellowship at a half-ruined house at Baranagar near the river Ganges, with the financial assistance of the householder disciples. This became the first Math or monastery of the disciples who constituted the first Ramakrishna Order.

Biographical Sources

The principal source for Ramakrishna's teaching is Mahendranath Gupta's Sri Sri Ramakrishna Kathamrita and is regarded as a Bengali classic. Kripal calls it "the central text of the tradition." The text was published in five volumes from 1902 to 1932. Based on Gupta's diary notes, each of the five volumes purports to document Ramakrishna's life from 1882–1886.

The most popular translation of the Kathamrita is The Gospel of Sri Ramakrishna by Swami Nikhilananda. Nikhilananda's translation rearranged the scenes in the five volumes of the Kathamrita into a linear sequence. Malcolm Mclean and Jeffrey Kripal argue that the translation is unreliable. Philosopher Lex Hixon writes that the Gospel is "spiritually authentic" and "powerful rendering of the Kathamrita."

Teachings

Ramakrishna's teachings were imparted in rustic Bengali, using stories and parables. These teachings made a powerful impact on Calcutta's intellectuals, despite the fact that his preachings were far removed from issues of modernism or national independence. His spiritual movement indirectly aided nationalism, as it rejected caste distinctions and religious prejudices.

In the Calcutta scene of the mid to late nineteenth century, Ramakrishna was opinionated on the subject of Chakri. Chakri can be described as a type of low-paying servitude done by educated men—typically government or commerce-related clerical positions. On a basic level, Ramakrishna saw this system as a corrupt form of European social organization that forced educated men to be servants not only to their bosses at the office but also to their wives at home. What Ramakrishna saw as the primary detriment of Chakri, however, was that it forced workers into a rigid, impersonal clock-based time structure. He saw the imposition of strict adherence to each second on the watch as a roadblock to spirituality. Despite this, however, Ramakrishna demonstrated that Bhakti could be practiced as an inner retreat to experience solace in the face of Western-style discipline and often discrimination in the workplace.

Ramakrishna emphasised God-realisation as the supreme goal of all living beings. Ramakrishna taught that kamini-kanchana is an obstacle to God-realization. Kamini-kanchan literally translates to "woman and gold." Partha Chatterjee wrote that figure of a woman stands for concepts or entities that have "little do do with women in actuality" and "the figure of woman-and-gold signified the enemy with: that part of one's own self which was susceptible to the temptations of ever-unreliable worldly success." Carl T. Jackson interprets kamini-kanchana to refer to the idea of sex and the idea of money as delusions which prevent people from realizing God. Jeffrey Kripal translates the phrase as "lover-and-gold" and associates it with Ramakrishna's alleged disgust for women as lovers. Kripal's translation is disputed by Swami Tyagananda, who argues this to be a "linguistic misconstruction." Ramakrishna also cautioned his women disciples against purusa-kanchana ("man and gold") and Tyagananda writes that Ramakrishna used Kamini-Kanchana as "cautionary words" instructing his disciples to conquer the "lust inside the mind."

Ramakrishna looked upon the world as Maya and he explained that avidya maya represents dark forces of creation (e.g. sensual desire, evil passions, greed, lust and cruelty), which keep people on lower planes of consciousness. These forces are responsible for human entrapment in the cycle of birth and death, and they must be fought and vanquished. Vidya maya, on the other hand, represents higher forces of creation (e.g. spiritual virtues, enlightening qualities, kindness, purity, love, and devotion), which elevate human beings to the higher planes of consciousness.

Ramakrishna practised several religions, including Islam and Christianity, and taught that in spite of the differences, all religions are valid and true and they lead to the same ultimate goal—God. Ramakrishna's taught that jatra jiv tatra Shiv (wherever there is a living being, there is Shiva). His teaching, "Jive daya noy, Shiv gyane jiv seba" (not kindness to living beings, but serving the living being as Shiva Himself) is considered as the inspiration for the philanthropic work carried out by his chief disciple Vivekananda.

Ramakrishna used rustic colloquial Bengali in his conversations. According to contemporary reports, Ramakrishna's linguistic style was unique, even to those who spoke Bengali. It contained obscure local words and idioms from village Bengali, interspersed with philosophical Sanskrit terms and references to the Vedas, Puranas, Tantras. For that reason, according to philosopher Lex Hixon, his speeches cannot be literally translated into English or any other language. Scholar Amiya P. Sen argued that certain terms that Ramakrishna may have used only in a metaphysical sense are being improperly invested with new contemporaneous meanings.

Ramakrishna was skilled with words and had an extraordinary style of preaching and instructing, which may have helped convey his ideas to even the most skeptical temple visitors. His speeches reportedly revealed a sense of joy and fun, but he was not at a loss when debating with intellectual philosophers. Philosopher Arindam Chakrabarti contrasted Ramakrishna's talkativeness with Buddha's legendary reticence, and compared his teaching style to that of Socrates.

Ramakrishna's explicitly sexual language shocked 19th-century Westerners, even scholars Max Müller who were otherwise his admirers. Müller wrote that his language was at times "abominably filthy." He admitted however that such direct speech was natural to contemporary Hindus, "where certain classes of men walk stark naked," and should not be considered intentional filthiness or obscenity. Citing examples of classical poems like Bhartrihari, the Bible, Homer, and Shakespeare, Müller felt that few of the sayings would have to be bowdlerized..

Reception and Legacy

Several organizations have been established in the name of Ramakrishna. The Ramakrishna Math and Mission is one of the main organizations founded by Swami Vivekananda in 1897. The Mission conducts extensive work in health care, disaster relief, rural management, tribal welfare, elementary and higher education. The movement is considered as one of the revitalization movements of India. Other organizations include the Ramakrishna Vedanta Society founded by Swami Abhedananda in 1923, the Ramakrishna Sarada Math founded by a rebel group in 1929,the Ramakrishna Vivekananda Mission formed by Swami Nityananda in 1976, and the Sri Sarada Math and Ramakrishna Sarada Mission founded in 1959 as a sister organization by the Ramakrishna Math and Mission. Ramakrishna is considered as an important figure in Bengali Renaissance of 19th-20th Century. Max Müller, Mahatma Gandhi, Jawaharlal Nehru, Sri Aurobindo, and Leo Tolstoy have acknowledged Ramakrishna's contribution to humanity. Ramakrishna's influence is also seen in the works of artists such as Franz Dvorak (1862–1927) and Philip Glass.

On Swami Vivekananda's guru, Ramakrishna, Rabindranath Tagore wrote a poem: "To the Ramakrishna Paramahamsa Ramakrishna Deva."

"Diverse courses of worship from varied springs of fulfillment have mingled in your meditation.

The manifold revelation of the joy of the Infinite has given form to a shrine of unity in your life where from far and near arrive salutations to which I join my own."

Tagore was the chief guest on the occasion of birth centenary celebration of Ramakrishna by the Ramakrishna Mission and paid rich tribute to Ramakrishna. During the 1937 Parliament of Religions, which was held at the Ramakrishna Mission in Calcutta, Tagore acknowledged Ramakrishna, whose birth centenary was being celebrated, as a great saint because "the largeness of his spirit could comprehend seemingly antagonistic modes of sadhana, and because the simplicity of his soul shames for all time the pomp and pedantry of pontiffs and pundits."

Religious School of Thought

Several scholars have tried to associate Ramakrishna with a particular religious school of thought—Bhakti, Tantra and Vedanta.

In his influential 1896 essay "A real mahatma: Sri Ramakrishna Paramahansa Dev" and his 1899 book Ramakrishna: His Life and Sayings, the German philologist and Orientalist Max Müller portrayed Ramakrishna as "a wonderful mixture of God and man" and as "...a Bhakta, a worshipper or lover of the deity, much more than a Gyani or a knower."

In London and New York in 1896, Swami Vivekananda delivered his famous address on Ramakrishna entitled "My Master." He said of his master: "this great intellect never learnt even to write his own name, but the most brilliant graduates of our university found in him an intellectual giant." Vivekananda criticized his followers for "brazenly" projecting Ramakrishna as an avatara and miracle-worker. Narasingha Sil has argued that Vivekananda revised and mythologized Ramakrishna's image after Ramakrishna's death. In a 1997 book review of a book by Jeffrey Kripal, Malcolm McLean of Otago University supported Kripal's view and argued that the Movement presents "a particular kind of explanation of Ramakrishna, that he was some kind of neo-Vedantist who taught that all religions are the same." Carl Olson argued that in his presentation of his master, Vivekananda had hid much of Ramakrishna's embarrassing sexual oddities from the public, because he feared that Ramakrishna would be misunderstood. Tyagananda and Vrajaprana argue that Oslon makes his "astonishing claim" based on Kripal's speculations in Kali's Child, which are unsupported by any of the source texts. Amiya Sen writes that that Vivekananda's "social service gospel" stemmed from direct inspiration from Ramakrishna and rests substantially on the "liminal quality" of the Master's message.

Indologist Heinrich Zimmer was the first Western scholar to interpret Ramakrishna's worship of the Divine Mother as containing specifically Tantric elements. Neeval also argued that tantra played a main role in Ramakrishna's spiritual development.

Philosopher Lex Hixon writes Ramakrishna was an Advaita Vedantin. Postcolonial literary theorist Gayatri Chakravorty Spivak wrote that Ramakrishna was a "Bengali bhakta visionary" and that as a bhakta, "he turned chiefly towards Kali." Amiya Prosad Sen writes that "it is really difficult to separate the Tantrik Ramakrishna from the Vedantic," since Vedanta and Tantra "may appear to be different in some respects," but they also "share some important postulates between them."

Psychoanalysis and Sexuality

The dialogue on psychoanalysis and Ramakrishna began in 1927 when Sigmund Freud's friend Romain Rolland wrote to him that he should consider spiritual experiences, or "the oceanic feeling," in his psychological works. Romain Rolland described the mystical states achieved by Ramakrishna and other mystics as an "'oceanic' sentiment," one which Rolland had also experienced. Rolland believed that the universal human religious emotion resembled this "oceanic sense." In his 1929 book La vie de Ramakrishna, Rolland distinguished between the feelings of unity and eternity which Ramakrishna experienced in his mystical states and Ramakrishna's interpretation of those feelings as the goddess Kali.

In 1995, Jeffrey J. Kripal argued in Kali's Child that the Ramakrishna Movement had manipulated Ramakrishna's biographical documents, that the Movement had published them in incomplete and bowdlerized editions (claiming among other things, hiding Ramakrishna's homoerotic tendencies), and that the Movement had suppressed Ram Chandra Datta's Srisriramakrsna Paramahamsadever Jivanavrttanta. These views were disputed by Swami Atmajnanananda, who wrote that Jivanavrttanta had been reprinted nine times in Bengali as of 1995.

Christopher Isherwood who wrote the book Ramakrishna and his Disciples (1965) said in a late interview, "Ramakrishna was completely simple and guileless. He told people whatever came into his mind, like a child. If he had ever been troubled by homosexual desires, if that had ever been a problem he'd have told everybody about them.(...) His thoughts transcended physical love-making. He saw even the mating of two dogs on the street as an expression of the eternal male-female principle in the universe. I think that is always a sign of great spiritual enlightenment." In addition, Isherwood wrote in his autobiographical book, My Guru and his Disciple, "I couldn't honestly claim him as a homosexual, even a sublimated one, much as I would have liked to be able to do so"

In 1998, Kripal wrote that he had "overplayed" the suppression of Jivanavrttanta and "the Ramakrishna Order reprinted Datta's text the very same summer Kali's Child appeared, rendering my original claims of a conscious concealment untenable." The charges of censorship are disputed by Tyagananda.

Goldman, Narasingha Sil, Jeffrey Kripal, and Sudhir Kakar, analyze Ramakrishna's mysticism and religious practices using psychoanalysis, arguing that his mystical visions, refusal to comply with ritual copulation in Tantra, Madhura Bhava, and criticism of Kamini-Kanchana (women and gold) reflect homosexuality. Jeffrey Kripal's controversial Kali's Child: The Mystical and the Erotic in the Life and Teachings of Ramakrishna (1995) argued that Ramakrishna rejected Advaita Vedanta in favor of Shakti Tantra. In this psychoanalytic study of Ramakrishna's life, Kripal argued that Ramakrishna's mystical experiences were symptoms of repressed homoeroticism. Other scholars and psychoanalysts including Romain Rolland, Alan Roland, Kelly Aan Raab, Somnath Bhattacharya, J.S. Hawley and Gayatri Chakravarty Spivak argue that psychoanalysis is unreliable and Ramakrishna's religious practices were in line with Bengali tradition. The application of psychoanalysis has further been disputed by Tyagananda and Vrajaprana as being unreliable in understanding Tantra and interpreting cross-cultural contexts in Interpreting Ramakrishna: Kali's Child Revisited (2010).

In his 1991 book The Analyst and the Mystic, Indian psychoanalyst Sudhir Kakar saw in Ramakrishna's visions a spontaneous capacity for creative experiencing. Kakar also argued that culturally relative concepts of eroticism and gender have contributed to the Western difficulty in comprehending Ramakrishna. Kakar saw Ramakrishna's seemingly bizarre acts as part of a bhakti path to God.

Postcolonial Studies

Postcolonial studies try to locate Ramakrishna in the historical background of Calcutta during the mid-19th Century.

In 1999, postcolonial historian Sumit Sarkar argued that he found in the Kathamrita traces of a binary opposition between unlearned oral wisdom and learned literate knowledge. He argues that all of our information about Ramakrishna, a rustic near-illiterate Brahmin, comes from urban bhadralok devotees, "...whose texts simultaneously illuminate and transform."

Other postcolonial studies have been done by Partha Chatterjee, Amiya P. Sen.

11

Ramanuja

Ramanuja; traditionally 1017–1137, also known as Ramanujacharya, Ethirajar (Yatiraja), Emperumannar, Lakshmana Muni, was a theologian, philosopher, and scriptural exegete. He is seen by Shrivaisnavas as the third and most important teacher (acharya) of their tradition (after Nathamuni and Yamunacharya), and by Hindus in general as the leading expounder of Vishichmadvaita, one of the classical interpretations of the dominant Vedanta school of Hindu philosophy.

Establishing Dates

The traditional biographies of Ramanuja place his life in the period of 1017–1137, yielding a lifespan of 120 years. However, the unusual length and roundness of this lifetime has led scholars to propose that Ramanuja was born 20–60 years later, and died as many as 20 years earlier than the traditional dates.

Any chronology depends crucially on the major historical event mentioned in the traditional biographies: the persecution of Srivaishnavas under the Chola king Kulothunga and Ramanuja's subsequent 12-year exile in Melkote, in Karnataka.

In 1917, T. A. Gopinatha Rao proposed a chronology based on the traditional lifetime of 1017–1137. He identified the Chola king with Kulothunga Chola I (reigned 1070–1120), and dated the exile to Melkote from 1079 to 1126 CE (Rao 1923 cited in Carman 1974:45). However, this would extend the period of exile to 47 years, and in any case, Kulothunga I was not known for being an intolerate Shaivite.

A different chronology was proposed by T. N. Subramanian, an official in the Madras government (Subramanian 1957 cited in Carman 1974:45). This chronology identifies the Chola King with Kulothunga Chola II, who reigned from 1133–50 and was-also arguably-known for his persecution of Vaisnavites. It puts Ramanuja's exile from c. 1137 to 1148. Subramanian's hypothesis is aided by a fragment from the late Tamil biography Ramanujarya Divya Caritai, which states that Ramanuja completed his most important work, the Shribhachya, in 1155–56. Nevertheless, temple inscriptions in Karnataka indicate the presence of Ramanuja and his disciples before 1137. Carman (1974:45) hypothesizes that the traditional biographers conflated two different visits to Mysore into one. This later chronology has been accepted by several scholars, yielding a tentative lifetime of 1077–1157.

Whatever the precise dates of Ramanuja's lifetime, it seems clear that all three of the great Shrivaisnava acharyas lived under the relatively stable and ecumenical climate of the Chola empire, before its decline in the late 12th and 13th centuries (Carman 1974, p. 27).

Historical Background

By the 5th century, the South Indian religious scene was diverse, with popular religion existing alongside Vedic sacrifice and non-Vedic traditions like Buddhism and Jainism. Indeed, the title character of the sixth century Tamil Buddhist epic Manimekalai is advised at one point to study the various Hindu schools of philosophy, such as Sankhya and Vaisheshika as well as Buddhism, Ajivika, Carvaka, and Jainism. It was in this context that fears of a Buddhist or Jain takeover spurred a large Hindu revival that reached its peak in the 7th century and continued nearly into the 2nd millennium.

The popular aspects of this revival took the shape of several mystical and passionate bhakti movements, represented on the Srivaishnavite side by the twelve alvars. The alvars came from a variety of social strata; their ranks include shudras and one woman. The intense devotionalism of their poetry and insistence that caste and sex are no barrier to a relationship with the Divine is uncharacteristic of classical Vedic thought, which laid a strong emphasis on the performance of the social and religious duties proper to one's place in the social structure. Some of these were collected into a definitive canon known as the Nalayira Divya Prabandha ("divine composition of 4000 verses"), by Nathamuni in the 10th century, and came to be seen as a source of revelation equal in authority to the Vedas in the Shrivaisnava community.

On the philosophical side, this period saw the rise of the Vedanta school of philosophy, which focused on the elucidation and exegesis of the speculative and philosophical Vedic commentaries known as the Upanishads. The Advaita, or non-dualist interpretation of Vedanta was developed in this time by Adi Shankara and later by Mandan Mishra. It argued that the Brahman presented in the Upanishads is the static and undifferentiated absolute reality, and that the ultimately false perception of difference is due to avidya, or ignorance.

The goal of proving the Vedantic legitimacy of the popular conception of a personal deity and a genuine personal identity essentially characterizes Ramanuja's project, and the Advaitin school presents a natural object for his polemics. It is this synthesis between the classical Sanskrit writings and the popular Tamil poetry that is the source of one of the names of Ramanuja's system: Ubhaya Vedanta, or "Vedanta of both kinds."

Evaluating Sources

In dealing with the lives of the Vedantic teachers, there is little in the way of actual history, and it is thus necessary to make reference to the many hagiographical works—both in verse and prose—that form a major genre in both Sanskrit and South Indian vernaculars.

The earliest such hagiographies in prose is the Arayirappami Guruparamparaprabhava (the "six thousand" splendour of the succession of teachers) (not to be confused with the well-known commentary on the Divya Prabandha of the same length, also commonly referred to as the "Six Thousand"). This was written by PiIpa;akiya Peruma7 Jiyar in the 13th century in a highly Sanskritized dialect .of Tamil known as MaGipravala. Perhaps earlier was a Sanskrit work of poetry, the Divya Suri Charita or Acts of the Divine Sages, probably written in the 12th century by Garuavahana Panita, a contemporary disciple of Ramanuja's.

In later times, a number of traditional biographies proliferated, such as the 16th or 17th century Sanskrit work Prapannamrta and, following the split of the Shrivaisnava community into the Vamakalais and TeIkalais. The Muvayirappami Guruparamparaprabhava or the "Three Thousand" Splendor of the Succession of Teachers by Brahmatantra Svatantra Jiyar represents the earliest Vamakalai biography, and reflects the Vamakalai view of the succession following Ramanuja. Arayirappami Guruparamparaprabhava, or "Six Thousand" Splendor of the Succession of Teachers referred in the previous paragraph represents the Tenkalai biography.

The various biographies differ in emphasis, facts, and sometimes even entire episodes. In general, the later biographies tend to be more fanciful and elaborate, and the Vamakalai and TeIkalai biographies reflect their sectarian outlook: for instance, the TeIkalai biographies tend to emphasize episodes that reflect more liberal attitudes toward caste on Ramanuja's part, while the Vamakalai biographies generally minimize them. These generalizations are often inaccurate, but the differences in the biographies do at any rate reflect the difficulty of coming up with a single historical narrative. Nonetheless, the traditional biographies agree in most of the facts of Ramanuja's life, and thus an outline of Ramanuja's life and achievements can be sketched.

Formative Years

Ramanuja was born Ilaya Perumal in a Brahmin family in the village of Perumbudur, Tamil Nadu, India in 1017 CE. His father was Asuri Keshava Somayaji Deekshitar and mother was Kanthimathi. To quote from Shyam Ranganathan's article on Ramanuja at the Internet Encyclopedia of Philosophy, "From a young age he is reputed to have displayed a prodigious intellect and liberal attitudes towards caste. At this time he became friendly with a local, saintly Sudra (member of the servile caste) by the name of Kanchipurna, whose occupation was to perform services for the local temple statue of the Hindu deity Vishnu. Ramanuja admired Kanchipurna's piety and devotion to Vishnu and sought Kanchipurna as his guru-much to the horror of Kanchipurna who regarded Ramanuja's humility before him as an affront to caste propriety."

Shortly after being married in his teenage years, and after his father died, Ramanuja and his family moved to the neighbouring city of Kanchipuram. There Ramanuja found his first formal teacher, Yadavaprakasha, who was an accomplished professor of the form of the Vedanta philosophy that was in vogue at the time-a form of Vedanta that has strong affinities to Shankara's Absolute Idealistic Monism (Advaita Vedanta) but was also close to the Difference-and-non-difference view (Bhedabheda Vedanta). ("Vedanta" means the 'end of the Vedas' and refers to the philosophy expressed in the end portion of the Vedas, also known as the Upanishads, and encoded in the cryptic summary by Badharayana called the Vedanta Sutra or Brahma Sutra. The perennial questions of Vedanta are: what is the nature of Brahma, or the Ultimate, and what is the relationship between the multiplicity of individuals to this Ultimate. Vedanta comprises one of the six orthodox schools of Hindu philosophy.)

From a young age, his intelligence and ability to comprehend highly abstract philosophical points were legendary. He took initiation from Yadavaprakasa, a renowned Advaitic scholar. Though his new guru was highly impressed with his analytical ability, he was quite concerned by how much emphasis Ramanuja placed on bhakti. After frequent clashes over interpretation, Yadavaprakasa decided the young Ramanuja was becoming too much of a threat and plotted a way to kill him. However, Ramanuja's cousin Govinda Bhatta (a favourite of Yadavaprakasa) discovered the plot and helped him escape. An alternative version is that one of Yadavaprakasa's students plotted to kill Ramanuja as a means of pleasing their teacher, but Sri Ramanuja escaped in the afore-mentioned manner. Yadavaprakasa was horrified when learnt about the conspiracy. Ramanuja returned to Yadavaprakasa's tutelage but after another disagreement, Yadavaprakasa asked him to leave. Ramanuja's childhood mentor, Kanchipurna, suggested he meet with Kanchipurna's own guru, Yamunacharya. After renouncing the life of a house-holder, Ramanuja travelled to Srirangam to meet an aging Yamunacharya, a philosopher of the remergent Vishishtadvaita school of thought. Yamunacharya had died prior to Ramanuja's arrival. Followers of Ramanuja relate the legend that three fingers of Yamunacharya's corpse were curled. Ramanuja saw this and understood that Yamunacharya was concerned about three tasks. Ramanuja vowed to complete these—

Teach the doctrine of Saranagati (surrender) to God as the means to moksha.

Write a Visishtadvaita Bhashya for the Brahma Sutras of Vyasa which had previously been taught orally to the disciples of the Visishtadvaita philosophy.

That the names of Paraœara, the author of Vishnu Purana, and saint Œaþhakopa should be perpetuated.

Legend goes that on hearing the vow, the three fingers on the corpse straightened. Ramanuja accepted Yamunacharya as his Manasika Acharya and spent 6 months being introduced to Yamunacharya's philosophy by his disciple, Mahapurna although he did not formally join the community for another year. Ramanuja's wife followed very strict brahminical rules of the time and disparaged Mahapurna's wife as being of lower subcaste. Mahapurna and his wife left Srirangam. Ramanuja realized that his life as a householder was interfering with his philosophical pursuit as he and his wife had differing views. He sent her to her parents' house and renounced family and became a sanyasi. Ramanuja started travelling the land, having philosophical debates with the custodians of various Vishnu temples. Many of them, after losing the debates, became his disciples. Ramanuja standardized the liturgy at these temples and increased the standing and the membership of the srivaishnava school of thought. He wrote his books during this time. Ramanuja, who was a Srivaishnavite, might have faced threats from some Shaivite Chola rulers who were religiously intolerant. Ramanuja and a few of his followers moved to the Hoysala kingdom of Jain king Bittideva and queen Shantala Devi in Karnataka. Bittideva converted to Srivaishanavism, in some legends after Ramanuja cured his daughter of evil spirits, and took the name Vishnuvardhana meaning "one who grows the sect of Vishnu." However, the queen and many of the ministers remained Jain and the kingdom was known for its tolerance. Ramanuja re-established the liturgy in the Cheluvanarayana temple in Melukote In Mandya District and Vishnuvardhana re-built it and also built other Vishnu temples like Chennakesava Temple and Hoysaleswara Temple.

Five Acharyas

Swami Ramanuja incorporated teachings from 5 different people who he considered to be his acharyas

Peria Nambigal who performed his samasrayana

Thirukkotiyur Nambigal: who revealed the meaning of Charama slokam to swami on his 18th trip

Periya Thirumalai Nambigal: Ramayana

Tirumalai Aandaan: Bhagavad Vishayam

Azhwar Thiruvaranga Perumal Arayar

Thirukachchi Nambigal : The 6 sentences or Perarulalan, and many others

Two Important Disciples

Koorathazwar

Mudaliyandan

Visishtadvaita Philosophy

Ramanuja's philosophy is referred to as Vishishtadvaita because it combines Advaita (oneness of God) with Vishesha (attributes).

Differences with Shankara

Adi Shankara had argued that all qualities or manifestations that can be perceived are unreal and temporary. Ramanuja believed them to be real and permanent and under the control of the Brahma. God can be one despite the existence of attributes, because they cannot exist alone; they are not independent entities. They are Prakaras or the modes, Sesha or the accessories, and Niyama or the controlled aspects, of the one Brahma.

In Ramanuja's system of philosophy, the Lord (Narayana) has two inseparable Prakaras or modes, namely, the world and the souls. These are related to Him as the body is related to the soul. They have no existence apart from Him. They inhere in Him as attributes in a substance. Matter and souls constitute the body of the Lord. The Lord is their indweller. He is the controlling Reality. Matter and souls are the subordinate elements. They are termed Viseshanas, attributes. God is the Viseshya or that which is qualified.

Ramanuja opines, wrong is the position of the Advaitins that understanding the Upanishads without knowing and practicing dharma can result in Brahma knowledge. The knowledge of Brahma that ends spiritual ignorance is meditational, not testimonial or verbal.

In contrast to Shankara, Ramanuja holds that there is no knowledge source in support of the claim that there is a distinctionless (homogeneous) Brahma. All knowledge sources reveal objects as distinct from other objects. All experience reveals an object known in some way or other beyond mere existence. Testimony depends on the operation of distinct sentence parts (words with distinct meanings). Thus the claim that testimony makes known that reality is distinctionless is contradicted by the very nature of testimony as a knowledge means. Even the simplest perceptual cognition reveals something (Bessie) as qualified by something else (a broken hoof, "Bessie has a broken hoof," as known perceptually). Inference depends on perception and makes the same distinct things known as does perception.

He also holds that the Advaitin argument about prior absences and no prior absence of consciousness is wrong. Similarly the Advaitin understanding of a-vidya (not-Knowledge), which is the absence of spiritual knowledge, is incorrect. "If the distinction between spiritual knowledge and spiritual ignorance is unreal, then spiritual ignorance and the self are one."

The Seven objections to Shankara's Advaita

Ramanuja picks out what he sees as seven fundamental flaws in the Advaita philosophy to revise them. He argues:

I. The nature of Avidya. Avidya must be either real or unreal; there is no other possibility. But neither of these is possible. If Avidya is real, non-dualism collapses into dualism. If it is unreal, we are driven to self-contradiction or infinite regress.

II. The incomprehensibility of Avidya. Advaitins claim that Avidya is neither real nor unreal but incomprehensible, {anirvachaniya.} All cognition is either of the real or the unreal: the Advaitin claim flies in the face of experience, and accepting it would call into question all cognition and render it unsafe.

III. The grounds of knowledge of Avidya. No pramana can establish Avidya in the sense the Advaitin requires. Advaita philosophy presents Avidya not as a mere lack of knowledge, as something purely negative, but as an obscuring layer which covers Brahma and is removed by true Brahma-vidya. Avidya is positive nescience, not mere ignorance. Ramanuja argues that positive nescience is established neither by perception, nor by inference, nor by scriptural testimony. On the contrary, Ramanuja argues, all cognition is of the real.

IV. The locus of Avidya. Where is the Avidya that gives rise to the (false) impression of the reality of the perceived world? There are two possibilities; it could be Brahma's Avidya or the individual soul's {jiva.} Neither is possible. Brahma is knowledge; Avidya cannot co-exist as an attribute with a nature utterly incompatible with it. Nor can the individual soul be the locus of Avidya: the existence of the individual soul is due to Avidya; this would lead to a vicious circle.

V. Avidya's obscuration of the nature of Brahman. Sankara would have us believe that the true nature of Brahma is somehow covered-over or obscured by Avidya. Ramanuja regards this as an absurdity: given that Advaita claims that Brahma is pure self-luminous consciousness, obscuration must mean either preventing the origination of this (impossible since Brahma is eternal) or the destruction of it-equally absurd.

VI. The removal of Avidya by Brahma-vidya. Advaita claims that Avidya has no beginning, but it is terminated and removed by Brahma-vidya, the intuition of the reality of Brahma as pure, undifferentiated consciousness. But Ramanuja denies the existence of undifferentiated {nirguna} Brahma, arguing that whatever exists has attributes: Brahma has infinite auspicious attributes. Liberation is a matter of Divine Grace: no amount of learning or wisdom will deliver us.

VII. The removal of Avidya. For the Advaitin, the bondage in which we dwell before the attainment of Moksa is caused by Maya and Avidya; knowledge of reality (Brahma-vidya) releases us. Ramanuja, however, asserts that bondage is real. No kind of knowledge can remove what is real. On the contrary, knowledge discloses the real; it does not destroy it. And what exactly is the saving knowledge that delivers us from bondage to Maya? If it is real then non-duality collapses into duality; if it is unreal, then we face an utter absurdity.

Bhagavad Ramanuja taught his followers to highly respect all Sri Vaishnavas irrespective of caste.

Cited from Sri Ramanuja, His Life, Religion, and Philosophy, published by Sri Ramakrishna Math, Chennai, India.

Writings

Ramanuja may have written 9 books. They are also referred to as the nine precious gems, the Navarathnas.

His most famous work is known as the Sri Bhasya or Brahma Sutra Bhasya. It is a commentary on the Brahma Sutras, known also as the Vedanta Sutras of Badarayana.

Gadhya Thrayam (three prose hymns). All three are important works in Srivaishnava philosophy:

Vaikuntha Gadyam describing in great detail Vaikuntha, the realm of Vishnu and recommending meditating on it.

Sriranga Gadyam, a prayer of surrender to the feet of Ranganatha

Saranagati Gadyam, an imagined dialogue between Ramanuja and Shri (Lakshmi) and Narayana where he petitions Lakshmi to recommend Narayana to give him grace. Narayana and Lakshmi accept his surrender.

Vedartha Sangraha (a resume of Vedanta). It sets out Ramanuja's philosophy, which is theistic (it affirms a morally perfect, omniscient and omnipotent God) and realistic (it affirms the existence and reality of a plurality of qualities, persons and objects).

Vedanta Saara (essence of Vedanta) an appendix to Sri Bhasya

Vedanta Deepa (the light of Vedanta), another appendix/commentary to Sri Bhasya.

Gita Bhashya (his commentary on the Bhagavad Gita)

Nithya Grantham (About the day to day activities to be performed by all Sri Vaishnavas)

Reverence as an Acharya

Ramanuja's thiruvarasu (sacred burial shrine) is the Ramanuja shrine (sannidhi) located inside the Sri Ranganathaswamy temple (periyakoyil or simply koyil) Srirangam, Tamil Nadu within the temple complex, where he attained his Acharyan

Thiruvadi (the lotus foot of his Acharya). A wax replica of his mortal remains (thirumeni) is placed inside the Sri Ramanuja shrine in "padmasanam" (folded leg posture). It is anointed with chandan (sandalwood paste) and saffron (kungumappoo) twice a year. His shrine is open to the general public for darshan. Acharya Sri Ramanuja is believed to be the titular administrator of the Srirangam temple.

In almost all of Sri Vaishnava temples, Acharya Ramanuja is given the foremost prominence. His blessings are invoked at the beginning of devotional services. Several temples like Sri Venkateswara Temple at Tirumala, Sri Parthasarathy Temple at Chennai, Sri Thirunarayana Swami Temple at Melukote have exclusive shrines dedicated to him. The Sattrumurai, or Appellations made to the Lord, at the end of daily services in a Sri Vaishnava temple always conclude with the words:

Sarva Desa Dasa Kaleshu Avyahata Parakrama |

Ramanuja Arya Divyajna Vardhatam Abhivardhatam ||

Meaning: Let the most Magnificent instruction of Sri Ramanuja increase and pervade through all countries at all times, without any hindrance.

A Living Tradition

Ramanuja's achievements are visible to this day. Iyengar Brahmins in South India follow his philosophical tradition. The Tamil prabhandas are chanted at Vishnu temples on par with the Sanskrit vedas. Persons of all communities, and not just Brahmins, are given roles in rituals at Srirangam and other leading temples. The philosophic discourses have been passed on to subsequent generations by great successors like Pillai Lokacharya, Vedanta Desika and Manavala Mamuni who lived in the 13th and 14th centuries. Several hagiographic accounts suggest that Ramanuja was an incarnation of Sri AdiSesha. Rama Mishra-Famous Swamigal in south India. He was the student of Ramanujacharya. He had followed the thoughts of Bhagvad Ramanujacharya. Title given as Ramamishra Mahadeshiker. The Swaminarayan tradition of Gujarat also traces their acharya-parampara to Ramanuja through Ramananda (who according to legend was administered pancha-sanskaras by Ramanuja).

12

Rama Tirtha

Swami Ram Tirth (October 22, 1873 – 27 October 1906), also known as Swami Ram, was an Indian teacher of the Hindu philosophy of Vedanta. He was among the first notable teachers of Hinduism to lecture in the United States, travelling there in 1902. He was preceded by Swami Vivekananda in 1893, and followed by Paramahansa Yogananda in 1920. During his American tours Swami Rama Tirtha spoke frequently on the concept of 'practical Vedanta' and on education of Indian youth. He proposed bringing young Indians to American universities, and helped establish several scholarships for Indian students.

Biography

Ram Tirth was born to Pandit Hiranand Goswami on the day of Deepawali vikram samvat 1930 (22 October 1873) in the village Muraliwala of Gujranwala District, in Punjab (now in

Pakistan). When he was a few days old, his mother died, and he was raised by his elder brother Gossain Gurudas. After receiving his Masters degree in mathematics from Government College of Lahore, he became Professor of Mathematics at Forman Christian College in Lahore. A chance meeting with Swami Vivekananda in 1897 in Lahore inspired his later decision to take up the life of a sannyasi.

In the late 19th century, he became well known in Punjab for his speeches to Krishna and later through lectures and essays on Advaita Vedanta. He eventually entered the monastic swami order in 1899 on the day of Deepawali, leaving his personal life as a professor as well as his wife, and children. Maharaja Kirti shah Bahadur of Tehri sponsored a trip to Swami Ram Tirth for Japan to teach Hinduism. From Japan he travelled in 1902 to the United States of America, where he spent two years lecturing on the essence of Hinduism and other religions, and a philosophy he called "practical Vedanta."

He frequently spoke about the inequities of the caste system in India and the importance of education for women and the poor, stating that, "Neglecting the education of women and children and the labouring classes is like cutting down the branches that are supporting us, nay, it is like striking a death-blow to the roots of the tree of nationality." Arguing that India needed educated young people—and not missionaries—he began an organization to aid Indian students in American universities. To solve the problem of poverty in India, he suggested bringing young Indians to the U.S. for higher education, and helped to establish a number of scholarships for Indian students during his tour of America.

Upon his return to India in 1904 he was received with great acclaim—large crowds thronged to his lectures. In 1906, weary of the adoration, he completely withdrew from public life and moved to the foothills of the Himalaya. There he prepared to write a book giving a systematic presentation on practical Vedanta, which was never finished. He died on the day of Deepawali, vikram samvat 1963, accordingly the date was 27 October 1906. Actually speaking he did not die but took a jal samaadhi (en.water-drowning) in the pious river Ganga at Tehri. Not some but most of the people believe that he gave up his body to the mother river Ganga.A rare co-incidence was that he was born on Deepawali, took sanyas on Deepawali and left the world on Deepawali. A rare photo of Swami Ram Tirth just before his was published in an Indian Hindi Magazine Prabha in between 1920-30.

Literal Appreciation

Indian Revolutionary Pandit Ram Prasad Bismil had depicted the character of Swami Ram Tirth in a beatiful poem titled Yuva Sanyasi. This poem was published in his book Man Ki Lahar in the year 1920. Some of the heart touching lines are reproduced hereunder:

"Left old parents and, unmarried daughter left alone; Left sons uneducated, and spouce left alone.

Left lovable alma-mater, and left family away; Left all sobbing behind him, and went so far away.

Left charming better-half he, left river pious Ravi;

Left curled beautiful hair, and language Punjabi."#Young Monk (English Version of the above poem)

Legacy

Two of his closest disciples-S. Puran Singh and Narayan Swami, wrote the biographies of Ram Tirth. Puran Singh's The Story of Swami Rama: The Poet Monk of the Punjab appeared in 1924 and was published in English as well as in Hindi. Narayan Swami's untitled account was published in 1935 as a part of Ram Tirth's collected works. His sister's son H. W. L. Poonja, was a disciple of Ramana Maharishi who later became a noted Advaita teacher on his own. He was known as Papaji amongst his disciples and was based in Lucknow.

Paramahans Yoganand was a great admirer of Ram Tirth, translating many of Ram Tirth's poems from Bengali into English and putting some of them to music. One of Ram Tirth's poems, titled "Marching Light," appeared in Yoganand's book of Hindu chants, Cosmic Chants as "Swami Ram Tirth's Song."

Swami Ram Tirth Mission Ashram is located at Kotal Gaon Rajpura, near Dehradun in Uttarakhand state of India where his teachings are practiced regularly.

One of three campus of Hemvati Nandan Bahuguna Garhwal Central University situated at Badshahi Thaul, New Tehri by the name of Swamiji as the Swami Ram Tirth Parisar(SRTC). Hemant Goswami, the great grandson of Swami Ram Tirth is a social activist based in Chandigarh.

13

Ramana Maharshi

Sri Ramana Maharshi (December 30, 1879 – April 14, 1950), born Venkataraman Iyer, was a Hindu spiritual master ("Gyani"). He was born to a Tamil-speaking Brahmin family in Tiruchuzhi, Tamil Nadu. After experiencing at age 16 what he later described as liberation (moksha), he left home for Arunachala, a mountain considered sacred by Hindus. He lived at the mountain for the rest of his life. Although born a Brahmin, he declared himself an "Atiasrami," a Sastraic state of non-attachment to anything in life and beyond all caste restrictions. The ashram that grew around him, Sri Ramana Ashram, is situated at the foothill of Arunachala, to the west to the pilgrimage town of Tiruvannamalai.

Sri Ramana maintained that the purest form of his teachings was the powerful silence which radiated from his presence and quieted the minds of those attuned to it. He gave verbal teachings only for the benefit of those who could not understand his silence (or, perhaps, could not understand how to attain the silent state). His verbal teachings were said to flow from his direct experience of Atman as the only existing reality. When asked for advice, he recommended self-enquiry as the fastest path to moksha. Though his primary teaching is associated with Non-dualism, Advaita Vedanta, and Gyan yoga, he recommended Bhakti to those he saw were fit for it, and gave his approval to a variety of paths and practices.

Life

Family Background

Sri Ramana was born in a village called Tiruchuli (Tiruchuzhi) near Aruppukkottai, Madurai in Tamil Nadu, South India on Arudra Darshanam day, into an orthodox Hindu Tamil (Iyer) family, the second of four children of Sundaram Iyer (1845?-1892), from the lineage of Parashara, and Azhagammal (?-1922), and named Venkataraman at birth. His siblings were Nagaswamy (1877–1900), Nagasundaram (1886–1953) and sister Alamelu (1891/92-1953). Venkataraman's father was a respected pleader.

Childhood

Venkataraman seemed a normal child with no apparent signs of future greatness. He was popular, good at sports, very intelligent but lazy at school, indulged in an average amount of mischief, and showed little religious interest. He did have a few unusual traits. When he slept, he went into such a deep state of unconsciousness that his friends could physically assault his body without waking him up. He also had an extraordinary amount of luck. In team games, whichever side he played for, always won. This earned him the nickname 'Tangakai', which means 'golden hand'. When Venkataraman was about 11, his father sent him to live with his paternal uncle Subbaiyar in Dindigul because he wanted his sons to be educated in English so they would be eligible to enter government service, and only Tamil was taught at the village school in Tiruchuzhi. In 1891, when his uncle was transferred to Madurai, Venkataraman and his elder brother Nagaswami moved with him. In Dindigul, Venkataraman attended a British School.

The Awakening

In 1892, Venkataraman's father Sundaram Iyer suddenly fell seriously ill and unexpectedly died several days later at the age of 42. For some hours after his father's death he contemplated the matter of death, and how his father's body was still there, but the 'I' was gone from it.

After leaving Scott's Middle School, Venkataraman went to the American Mission High School. One November morning in 1895, he was on his way to school when he saw an elderly relative and enquired where the relative had come from. The answer was "From Arunachala." Krishna Bikshu describes Venkataraman's response: "The word 'Arunachala' was familiar to Venkataraman from his younger days, but he did not know where it was, what it looked like or what it meant. Yet that day that word meant to him something great, an inaccessible, authoritative, absolutely blissful entity. Could one visit such a place? His heart was full of joy. Arunachala meant some sacred land, every particle of which gave moksha. It was omnipotent and peaceful. Could one behold it? 'What? Arunachala? Where is it?' asked the lad. The relative was astonished, 'Don't you know even this?' and continued, 'Haven't you heard of Tiruvannamalai? That is Arunachala.' It was as if a balloon was pricked, the boy's heart sank."

A month later he came across a copy of Sekkizhar's Periyapuranam, a book that describes the lives of 63 Saivite saints, and was deeply moved and inspired by it. Filled with awe, and a desire for emulation, he began devotional visits to the nearby Meenakshi Temple in Madurai and, associated with this bhakti, later reported fever-like sensations. Soon after, on July 17, 1896, at age 16, Venkataraman had a life-changing experience. He spontaneously initiated a process of self-enquiry that culminated, within a few minutes, in his own permanent awakening. In one of his rare written comments on this process he wrote: 'Enquiring within Who is the seer? I saw the seer disappear leaving That alone which stands forever. No thought arose to say I saw. How then could the thought arise to say I did not see.' As Sri Ramana reportedly described it later:

"It was in 1896, about 6 weeks before I left Madurai for good (to go to Tiruvannamalai-Arunachala) that this great change in my life took place. I was sitting alone in a room on the first floor of my uncle's house. I seldom had any sickness and on that day there was nothing wrong with my health, but a sudden violent fear of death overtook me. There was nothing in my state of health to account for it nor was there any urge in me to find out whether there was any account for the fear. I just felt I was going to die and began thinking what to do about it. It did not occur to me to consult a doctor or any elders or friends. I felt I had to solve the problem myself then and there. The shock of the fear of death drove my mind inwards and I said to myself mentally, without actually framing the words: 'Now death has come; what does it mean? What is it that is dying? This body dies.' And at once I dramatised the occurrence of death. I lay with my limbs stretched out still as though rigor mortis has set in, and imitated a corpse so as to give greater reality to the enquiry. I held my breath and kept my lips tightly closed so that no sound could escape, and that neither the word 'I' nor any word could be uttered. 'Well then,' I said to myself, 'this body is dead. It will be carried stiff to the burning ground and there burn and reduced to ashes. But with the death of the body, am I dead? Is the body I? It is silent and inert, but I feel the full force of my personality and even the voice of I within me, apart from it. So I am the Spirit transcending the body. The body dies but the spirit transcending it cannot be touched by death. That means I am the deathless Spirit.' All this was not dull thought; it flashed through me vividly as living truths which I perceived directly almost without thought process. I was something real, the only real thing about my present state, and all the conscious activity connected with the body was centered on that I. From that moment onwards, the "I" or Self focused attention on itself by a powerful fascination. Fear of death vanished once and for all. The ego was lost in the flood of Self-awareness. Absorption in the Self continued unbroken from that time. Other thought might come and go like the various notes of music, but the I continued like the fundamental sruti note ["that which is heard" i.e. the Vedas and Upanishads] a note which underlies and blends with all other notes."

After this event, he lost interest in school-studies, friends, and relations. Avoiding company, he preferred to sit alone, absorbed in concentration on the Self, and went daily to the Meenakshi Temple, ecstatically devoted to the images of the Gods, tears flowing profusely from his eyes.

Venkataraman's elder brother, Nagaswamy, was aware of a great change in him and on several occasions rebuked him for his detachment from all that was going on around him. About six weeks after Venkataraman's absorption into the Self, on August 29, 1896, he was attempting to complete a homework assignment which had been given to him by his English teacher for indifference in his studies. Suddenly Venkataraman tossed aside the book and turned inward in meditation. His elder brother rebuked him again, asking, "What use is all this to one who is like this?" Venkataraman did not answer, but recognized the truth in his brother's words.

The Journey to Arunachala

He decided to leave his home and go to Arunachala. Knowing his family would not permit this, he slipped away, telling his brother he needed to attend a special class at school. Fortuitously, his brother asked him to take five rupees and pay his college fees on his way to school. Venkataraman took out an atlas, calculated the cost of his journey, took three rupees and left the remaining two with a note which read: "I have set out in quest of my Father in accordance with his command. This (meaning his person) has only embarked on a virtuous enterprise. Therefore, no one need grieve over this act. And no money need be spent in search of this. Your college fee has not been paid. Herewith rupees two."

At about noon, Venkataraman left his uncle's house and walked to the railway station. At about three o'clock the next morning, he arrived at Viluppuram and walked into the town at daybreak. Tired and hungry, he asked for food at a hotel and had to wait until noon for the food to be ready. He then went back to the station and spent his remaining money on a ticket to Mambalapattu, a stop on the way to Tiruvannamalai. From there, he set out, intending to walk the remaining distance of about 30 miles (48 km).

After walking about 11 miles (18 km), he reached the temple of Arayaninallur, outside of which he sat down to rest. When the priest opened the temple for puja, Venkataraman entered and sat in the pillared hall where he had a vision of brilliant light enveloping the entire place. He sat in deep meditation after the light disappeared until the temple priests who needed to lock up the temple roused him. He asked them for food and was refused, though they suggested he might get food at the temple in Kilur where they were headed for service. Venkataraman followed, and late in the evening when the puja ended at this temple, he asked for food and was refused again. The temple drummer who had been watching the rude behaviour of the priests implored them to hand over his share of the temple food to the strange youth. When he asked for water, he was directed to a Sastri's house. He set out but fainted and fell down, spilling the rice he had been given in the temple. When he regained consciousness, he began picking up the scattered rice, not wanting to waste even a single grain.

Muthukrishna Bhagavatar was amongst the crowd that gathered around Venkataraman when he collapsed. He was so struck by Venkataraman's extraordinary radiance and beauty and felt such compassion for him that he led the boy to his house, providing him with a bed and food. It was August 31, the Gokulastami day, the day of Sri Krishna's birth, and the Bhagavathar's wife was delighted that a young Brahmin boy with the appearance of a mendicant had visited their home that day, and was only too happy to feed him. Afterwards, Venkataraman asked Bhagavatar for a loan of four rupees on the pledge of his earrings so that he could complete his pilgrimage. Bhagavatar agreed and gave Venkataraman a receipt he could use to redeem his earrings. Venkataraman continued on his journey, tearing up the receipt immediately because he knew he would never have any need for the earrings.

On the morning of September 1, 1896, Venkataraman boarded the train and travelled the remaining distance. In Tiruvannamalai he went straight to the temple of Arunachaleswara. There, Venkataraman found not only the temple gates standing open, but the doors to the inner shrine as well, and not a single person, even a priest, was in the temple. He entered the sanctum sanctorum and addressed Arunachaleswara, saying: "I have come to Thee at Thy behest. Thy will be done." He embraced the linga in ecstasy. The burning sensation that had started back at Madurai (which he later described as "an inexpressible anguish which I suppressed at the time") merged in Arunachaleswara. Venkataraman was safely home.

Early Life at Arunachala

The first few weeks he spent in the thousand-pillared hall, but shifted to other spots in the temple and eventually to the Patala-lingam vault so that he might remain undisturbed. There, he would spend days absorbed in such deep samadhi that he was unaware of the bites of vermin and pests. Seshadri Swamigal, a local saint, discovered him in the underground vault and tried to protect him. After about six weeks in the Patala-lingam, he was carried out and cleaned up. For the next two months he stayed in the Subramanya Shrine, so unaware of his body and surroundings that food had to be placed in his mouth or he would have starved.

From there, he was invited to stay in a mango orchard next to Gurumurtam, a temple about a mile out of Tiruvannamalai, and shortly after his arrival, a sadhu named Palaniswami went to see him. Palaniswami's first darshan left him filled with peace and bliss, and from that time on his sole concern was serving Sri Ramana, joining him as his permanent attendant. From Gurumurtam to Virupaksha Cave (1899–1916) to Skandasramam Cave (1916–22), he was the instrument of divine protection for Sri Ramana, who would be without consciousness of the body and lost in inner bliss most of the time. Besides physical protection, Palaniswami would also beg for alms, cook and prepare meals for himself and Sri Ramana, and care for him as needed.

Gradually, despite Sri Ramana's silence, austerities, and desire for privacy, he attracted attention from visitors, and some became his disciples. Eventually, his family discovered his whereabouts. First his uncle Nelliappa Iyer came and pled with him to return home, promising that the family would not disturb his ascetic life. Sri Ramana sat motionless and eventually his uncle gave up. It was at the temple at Pavalakkunru, one of the eastern spurs of Arunachala, that his mother and brother Nagaswami found him in December 1898. Day after day his mother begged him to return, but no amount of weeping and pleading had any visible effect on him. She appealed to the devotees who had gathered around, trying to get them to intervene on her behalf until one requested that Sri Ramana writes out his response to his mother. He then wrote on a piece of paper, "In accordance with the prarabdha of each, the One whose function it is to ordain makes each to act. What will not happen will never happen, whatever effort one may put forth. And what will happen will not fail to happen, however much one may seek to prevent it. This is certain. The part of wisdom therefore is to stay quiet." At this point his mother returned to Madurai saddened.

Soon after this, in February 1899, Sri Ramana moved further up Arunachala where he stayed briefly in Satguru Cave and Guhu Namasivaya Cave before taking up residence at Virupaksha Cave for the next 17 years, using Mango Tree cave during the summers (except for a six month period at Pachaiamman Koil during the plague epidemic).

In 1902, a government official named Sivaprakasam Pillai, with writing slate in hand, visited the young Swami in the hope of obtaining answers to questions about "How to know one's true identity." The fourteen questions put to the young Swami and his answers were Sri Ramana's first teachings on Self-enquiry, the method for which he became widely known, and were eventually published as 'Nan Yar?', or in English, 'Who am I?'

Several visitors came to him and many became his disciples. Kavyakantha Sri Ganapati Sastri (literally, "One who has poetry in his throat"), a Vedic scholar of repute in his age with a deep knowledge of the Srutis, Sastras, Tantras, Yoga, and Agama systems, came to visit Sri Ramana in 1907. After receiving instructions from him, he proclaimed him as Bhagavan Sri Ramana Maharshi. Sri Ramana was known by this name from then on.

Discovery by Westerners

It was in 1911 that the first westerner, Frank Humphreys, then a policeman stationed in India, discovered Sri Ramana and wrote articles about him which were first published in The International Psychic Gazette in 1913. However, Sri Ramana only became relatively well known in and out of India after 1934 when Paul Brunton, having first visited Sri Ramana in January 1931, published the book A Search in Secret India, which became very popular. Resulting visitors included Paramahansa Yogananda, Somerset Maugham (whose 1944 novel The Razor's Edge models its spiritual guru after Sri Ramana), Mercedes de Acosta, Julian P. Johnson, and Arthur Osborne. Sri Ramana's relative fame spread throughout the 1940s. However, even as his fame spread, Sri Ramana was noted for his belief in the power of silence and his relatively sparse use of speech, as well as his lack of concern for fame or criticism. His lifestyle remained that of a renunciate.

Mother's Arrival

In 1912, while in the company of disciples, he was observed to undergo about a 15 minute period where he showed the outward symptoms of death, which reportedly resulted thereafter in an enhanced ability to engage in practical affairs while remaining in Sahaja Nirvikalpa Samadhi. In 1916 his mother Alagammal and younger brother Nagasundaram joined Sri Ramana at Tiruvannamalai and followed him when he moved to the larger Skandashram Cave, where Bhagavan lived until the end of 1922. His mother took up the life of a sannyasin, and Sri Ramana began to give her intense, personal instruction, while she took charge of the Ashram kitchen. Ramana's younger brother, Nagasundaram, then became a sannyasi, assuming the name Niranjanananda, becoming known as Chinnaswami (the younger Swami).

During this period, Sri Ramana composed The Five Hymns to Arunachala, his magnum opus in devotional lyric poetry. Of them the first is Akshara Mana Malai (the Marital Garland of Letters). It was composed in Tamil in response to the request of a devotee for a song to be sung while wandering in the town for alms. The Marital Garland tells in glowing symbolism of the love and union between the human soul and God, expressing the attitude of the soul that still aspires.

Mother's Death

Beginning in 1920, his mother's health deteriorated. On the day of her death, May 19, 1922, at about 8 a.m., Sri Ramana sat beside her. It is reported that throughout the day, he had his right hand on her heart, on the right side of the chest, and his left hand on her head, until her death around 8:00 p.m., when Sri Ramana pronounced her liberated, literally, 'Adangi Vittadu, Addakam' ('absorbed'). Later Sri Ramana said of this: "You see, birth experiences are mental. Thinking is also like that, depending on sanskaras (tendencies). Mother was made to undergo all her future births in a comparatively short time.." Her body was enshrined in a samadhi, on top of which a Siva lingam was installed and given the name Mathrubutheswara [Siva manifesting as mother]. To commemorate the anniversary of Ramana Maharshi's mother's death, a puja, known as her Aradhana or Mahapooja, is performed every year at the Mathrubutheswara.

After this, Sri Ramana often walked from Skandashram to her tomb. Then in December 1922, he came down from Skandashram permanently and settled at the base of the Hill, where Sri Ramanasramam is still located today. At first, there was only one hut at the samadhi, but in 1924 two huts, one opposite the samadhi and the other to the north were erected.

The Later Years

The Sri Ramanasramam grew to include a library, hospital, post-office and many other facilities. Sri Ramana displayed a natural talent for planning building projects. Annamalai Swami gave detailed accounts of this in his reminiscences. Until 1938, Annamalai Swami was entrusted with the task of supervising the projects and received his instructions from Ramana directly.

The 1940s saw many of Sri Ramana's most ardent devotees pass away. These included Echamma (1945), attendant Madhavaswami (1946), Ramanatha Brahmachari (1946), Mudaliar Granny and Lakshmi (1948). Sri Ramana was noted for his unusual love of animals and his assertion that liberation was possible not only for animals but also for plants: Ramana once spoke of a thorn bush gaining liberation by the Grace of a great saint. On the morning of June 18, 1948, he realized his favourite cow Lakshmi was near death. Just as he had with his own Mother, Sri Ramana placed his hands on her head and over her heart. The cow died peacefully at 11:30 a.m. and Sri Ramana later declared that the cow was liberated.

In 1939, at age 21, U.G. Krishnamurti met with Ramana Maharshi. U.G. related that he asked Ramana, "This thing called moksha, can you give it to me?"-to which Ramana Maharshi purportedly replied, "I can give it, but can you take it?" This answer completely altered U.G.'s perceptions of the "spiritual path" and its practitioners, and he never again sought the counsel of "those religious people." Later U.G. would say that Maharshi's answer-which he had originally perceived as "arrogant"-put him "back on track." "That Ramana was a real McCoy," said U.G Krishnamurti.

Sri Ramana was noted for his belief in the power of silence and relatively sparse use of speech. He led a modest and renunciate life, and depended on visitors and devotees for the barest necessities. However, a popular image of him as a person who spent most of his time doing nothing except silently sitting in samadhi is highly inaccurate, according to David Godman, who has written extensively about Sri Ramana. According to Godman, from the period when an Ashram began to rise around him after his mother arrived into his later years, Sri Ramana was actually quite active in Ashram activities until his health failed.

Final Years

In November 1948, a tiny cancerous lump was found on the Maharshi's arm and was removed in February 1949 by the ashram doctor. Soon, another growth appeared, and another operation was done by an eminent surgeon in March, 1949, with Radium applied. The doctor told Sri Ramana that a complete amputation of the arm to the shoulder was required to save his life, but he refused. A third and fourth operation were performed in August and December 1949, but only weakened him. Other systems of medicine were then tried; all proved fruitless and were stopped by the end of March when devotees gave up all hope. To devotees who begged him to cure himself for the sake of his followers, Sri Ramana is said to have replied, "Why are you so attached to this body? Let it go" and, "Where can I go? I am here."

By April 1950, Sri Ramana was too weak to go to the hall, and visiting hours were limited. Visitors would file past the small room where he spent his final days to get one final glimpse. Swami Satyananda, the attendant at the time, reports, "On the evening of 14 April 1950, we were massaging Sri Ramana's body. At about 5 o'clock, he asked us to help him to sit up. Precisely at that moment devotees started chanting 'Arunachala Siva, Arunachala Siva'. When Sri Ramana heard this, his face lit up with radiant joy. Tears began to flow from his eyes and continued to flow for a long time. I was wiping them from time to time. I was also giving him spoon full of water boiled with ginger. The doctor wanted to administer artificial respiration but Sri Ramana waved it away. Sri Ramana's breathing became gradually slower and slower and at 8:47 p.m. it subsided quietly." Henri Cartier-Bresson, the French photographer, who had been staying at the ashram for a fortnight prior to Sri Ramana's death, recounted the event:

"It is a most astonishing experience. I was in the open space in front of my house, when my friends drew my attention to the sky, where I saw a vividly-luminous shooting star with a luminous tail, unlike any shooting star I had before seen, coming from the South, moving slowly across the sky and, reaching the top of Arunachala, disappeared behind it. Because of its singularity, we all guessed its import and immediately looked at our watches – it was 8:47 – and then raced to the Ashram only to find that our premonition had been only too sadly true: the Master had passed into parinirvana at that very minute."

Cartier-Bresson took some of the last photographs of Sri Ramana on April 4, 1950 and went on to take pictures of the mahasamadhi preparations. The New York Times concluded: "Here in India, where thousands of so-called holy men claim close tune with the infinite, it is said that the most remarkable thing about Ramana Maharshi was that he never claimed anything remarkable for himself, yet became one of the most loved and respected of all.."

Teachings

Sri Ramana's teachings about self-enquiry, the practice he is most widely associated with, have been classified as the Path of Knowledge (Gyan marga) among the Indian schools of thought. Though his teaching is consistent with and generally associated with Hinduism, the Upanishads and Advaita Vedanta, there are some differences with the traditional Advaitic school, and Sri Ramana gave his approval to a variety of paths and practices from various religions.

His earliest teachings are documented in the book Nan Yar?(Who am I?), first written in Tamil. The original book was published by Sri Pillai, although the essay version of the book (Sri Ramana Nutrirattu) prepared by Sri Ramana is considered definitive as unlike the original it had the benefit of his revision and review. A careful translation with notes is available in English as 'The Path of Sri Ramana, Part One' by Sri Sadhu Om, one of the direct disciples of Sri Ramana. Selections from this definitive version follow:

- As all living beings desire to be happy always, without misery, as in the case of everyone there, is observed supreme love for one's self, and as happiness alone is the cause for love, in order to gain that happiness which is one's nature and which is experienced in the state of deep sleep where there is no mind, one should know one's self. For that, the path of knowledge, the inquiry of the form "Who am I?," is the principal means.
- Knowledge itself is 'I.' The nature of (this) knowledge is existence-consciousness-bliss.
- What is called mind is a wondrous power existing in Self. It projects all thoughts. If we set aside all thoughts and see, there will be no such thing as mind remaining separate; therefore, thought itself is the form of the mind. Other than thoughts, there is no such thing as the world.
- Of all the thoughts that rise in the mind, the thought 'I' is the first thought.
- That which rises in this body as 'I' is the mind. If one enquires 'In which place in the body does the thought

'I' rise first?', it will be known to be in the heart [spiritual heart is 'two digits to the right from the centre of the chest']. Even if one incessantly thinks 'I,' 'I,' it will lead to that place (Self)'

- The mind will subside only by means of the enquiry 'Who am I?'. The thought 'Who am I?', destroying all other thoughts, will itself finally be destroyed like the stick used for stirring the funeral pyre.
- If other thoughts rise, one should, without attempting to complete them, enquire, 'To whom did they arise?', it will be known 'To me.' If one then enquires 'Who am I?', the mind (power of attention) will turn back to its source. By repeatedly practising thus, the power of the mind to abide in its source increases.
- The place where even the slightest trace of the 'I' does not exist, alone is Self.

Self itself is God

Sri Ramana warned against considering self-enquiry as an intellectual exercise. Properly done, it involves fixing the attention firmly and intensely on the feeling of 'I', without thinking. It is perhaps more helpful to see it as 'Self-attention' or 'Self-abiding' (cf. Sri Sadhu Om-The Path of Sri Ramana Part I). The clue to this is in Sri Ramana's own death experience when he was 16. After raising the question 'Who am I?' he "turned his attention very keenly towards himself" (cf. description above). Attention must be fixed on the 'I' until the feeling of duality disappears.

Although he advocated self-enquiry as the fastest means to realization, he also recommended the path of bhakti and self-surrender (to one's Deity or Guru) either concurrently or as an adequate alternative, which would ultimately converge with the path of self-enquiry.

Sri Ramana's teachings and Advaita

Sri Ramana's teachings and the traditional Advaitic school of thought pioneered by Sri Adi Shankara have many things in common. Sri Ramana often mentioned and is known to have encouraged study of the following classical works: Ashtavakra Gita, Ribhu Gita and Essence of Ribhu Gita, Yoga Vasista Sara, Tripura Rahasya[ ], Kaivalya Navaneetam, Advaita Bodha Deepika, and Ellam Ondre. However, there are some practical differences with the traditional Advaitic school, which recommends a negationist neti, neti (Sanskrit, "not this," "not this") path, or mental affirmations that the Self was the only reality, such as "I am Brahman" or "I am He," while Sri Ramana advocates the enquiry "Nan Yar" (Tamil, "Who am I"). Furthermore, unlike the traditional Advaitic school, Sri Ramana strongly discouraged most who came to him from adopting a renunciate lifestyle.

To elaborate:

- The traditional Advaitic (non-dualistic) school advocates "elimination of all that is non-self (the five sheaths) until only the Self remains." The five kosas, or sheaths, that hide the true Self are: Material, Vital, Mental, Knowledge, and Blissful.
- Sri Ramana says "enquiry in the form 'Who am I' alone is the principal means. To make the mind subside, there

is no adequate means other than self-enquiry. If controlled by other means, mind will remain as if subsided, but will rise again."

Teachers in his Tradition

He considered his own guru to be the Self, in the form of the sacred mountain Arunachala. Sri Ramana did not publicize himself as a guru, never claimed to have disciples, and never appointed any successors. While a few who came to see him are said to have become enlightened through association, and there are accounts of private acknowledgements, he did not publicly acknowledge any living person as liberated other than his mother at death. Sri Ramana declared himself an atiasrama (beyond all caste and religious restrictions, not attached to anything in life), and did not belong to or promote any lineage. Despite his non-affiliations, there are numerous contemporary teachers who publicly associate themselves with Sri Ramana, and some who assert being in his lineage.

His method of teaching was characterized by the following:

1. He urged people who came to him to practice self-enquiry;
2. He directed people to look inward rather than seeking outside themselves for Realization. ("The true Bhagavan resides in your Heart as your true Self. This is who I truly am.");
3. He viewed all who came to him as the Self rather than as lesser beings. ("The Gyani sees no one as an Agyani. All are only Gyanis in his sight.");

4. He charged no money, and was adamant that no one ever ask for money (or anything else) in his name;
5. He never promoted or called attention to himself. Instead, Sri Ramana remained in one place for 54 years, offering spiritual guidance to anyone of any background who came to him, and asking nothing in return;
6. He considered humility to be the highest quality;
7. He said the deep sense of peace one felt around a Gyani was the surest indicator of their spiritual state, that equality towards all was a true sign of liberation, and that what a true Gyani did was always for others, not themselves.

Notable Followers

Over the course of Sri Ramana's lifetime, people from a wide variety of backgrounds, religions, and countries were drawn to him. Some stayed for the rest of their lives (or his) and served him with great devotion, and others came for a single darshan and left, deeply affected by the peace he radiated.

Quite a number of followers wrote books conveying Sri Ramana's teachings. Sri Muruganar (1893–1973), one of Sri Ramana's foremost devotees who lived as Sri Ramana's shadow for 26 years, recorded the most comprehensive collection of Sri Ramana's sayings in a work called Guru Vachaka Kovai (The Garland of Guru's Sayings). Sri Ramana carefully reviewed this work with Sri Muruganar, modifying many verses to most accurately reflect his teaching, and adding in additional verses.

Sri Muruganar was also instrumental in Sri Ramana's writing of Upadesha Saram (The Essence of Instruction) and Ulladu Narpadu (Forty Verses on Reality). Sri Sadhu Om (1922–1985) spent five years with Sri Ramana and about 28 years with Sri Muruganar. His deep understanding of Sri Ramana's teachings on self-enquiry are explained in his book The Path of Sri Ramana – Part One. Suri Nagamma wrote a series of letters to her brother in Telugu, describing Sri Ramana's conversations with devotees over a five year period. Each letter was corrected by Sri Ramana before it was sent. Attendants of Sri Ramana included Palaniswami (from 1897), Kunju Swami (from 1920), Madhava Swami, Ramanatha Brahmachari, Krishnaswami, Rangaswamy, Sivananda, Krishna Bhikshu and Annamalai Swami (from 1928). The devoted ladies who cooked for Bhagavan and his devotees in the ashram kitchen includes, Shantamma, Sampurnamma, Subbalakshmi Ammal, Lokamma, Gowri Ammal and few others.

Paul Brunton's writings about Sri Ramana brought considerable attention to him in the West. Other Westerners who wrote about Sri Ramana include Arthur Osborne (the first editor of the ashram journal, The Mountain Path), Major Chadwick (who ran the Veda Patasala during Ramana's time), Ethel Merston, and S.S. Cohen. More recently, David Godman, a former librarian at the ashram, has written about Sri Ramana's teaching, as well as a series of books (The Power of the Presence) vividly portraying the lives of a number of lesser-known attendants and devotees of Sri Ramana. Swami Ramdas visited Ramana Maharshi while on pilgrimage in 1922, and after darshan, spent the next 21 days meditating in solitude in a cave on Arunachala. Thereafter, he attained the direct realization that "All was Rama, nothing but Rama."

Maurice Frydman (a.k.a. Swami Bharatananda), a Polish Jew who later translated Nisargadatta Maharaj's work "I Am That" from Marathi to English, was also deeply influenced by Sri Ramana's teachings.

William Somerset Maugham, the English author, wrote a chapter entitled "The Saint" in his last book "Points of View." This chapter is devoted to Ramana Maharshi, whom Maugham had at one time visited before Indian independence.

Indian National Congress politician and freedom-fighter, O. P. Ramaswamy Reddiyar, who served as the Premier of Madras from 1947 to 1949, was also a devoted follower of Ramana Maharshi. Ramaswami Pillai, Balarama Reddy, Ramani Ammal, Kanakammal, Meenakshi Ammal, Perumalswami and Rayar are some of the other long standing devotees who came into the Samadhi of Bhagavan during his life at Sri Ramanashramam.

Another famous follower of Sri Ramana Maharshi is Jinnuru Nannagaru (born Bhupathiraju Venkata Lakshmi Narasimha Raju),who has taken upon himself the task of taking people to a 'sorrowless', and 'tension-free' state.

Aksharamanamalai

Many of Ramana Maharshi's followers asked for a hymn to sing while on their rounds for alms. They felt this would help distinguish them from other hermits. After much persuasion, Sri Ramana Maharshi composed Sri Arunachala

Aksharamanamalai (The Marital Garland of Letters) in praise of Lord Shiva, manifest as the mountain Arunachala. The hymn consists of 108 stanzas composed in poetic Tamil, praising the formless Shiva as Arunachala and the different aspects of life and salvation that it symbolizes.

Biographies

- Self-Realization: The Life and Teachings of Bhagavan Sri Ramana Maharshi, by B.V. Narasimha Swami (ISBN 81-88225-74-6)
- Ramana Maharshi and the Path of Self Knowledge, by Arthur Osborne online text
- Sri Ramana Leela, by Krishna Bhikshu (Telegu Original) PDF version online
- Timeless in Time: Sri Ramana Maharshi, by A.R. Natarajan (ISBN 81-85378-82-7)
- Ramana Maharshi: His Life, by Gabriele Ebert (ISBN 978-1411673502)
- Sage of Arunachala-A great documentary

Reminiscences

- Ramana pictorial souvenir commemorating the Kumbhabhishekam on 18-6-1967. Tiruvannamalai, India: Board of Trustees Sri Ramanasramam. 1969. OCLC 140712. (Anonymously edited volume with many appreciations and reminiscences from others, plus many quotes from Ramana Maharshi)
- A Sadhu's Reminiscences of Ramana Maharshi, by Major A. W. Chadwick (ISBN 81-88018-37-6)

- Living By The Words of Bhagavan, by David Godman (no ISBN) about Annamalai Swami
- The Power of the Presence, Part One, by David Godman (ISBN 0-9711371-1-0), about several devotees
- The Power of the Presence, Part Two, by David Godman (ISBN 0-9711371-0-2), about several devotees
- The Power of the Presence, Part Three, by David Godman (ISBN 0-9711371-2-9), about several devotees
- Letters from Sri Ramanasramam, by Suri Nagamma (ISBN 81-88018-10-4), contains 273 letters from the period 1945 to 1950, each one corrected by Sri Ramana.
- A Practical Guide to Know Yourself: Conversations with Sri Ramana Maharshi (ISBN 81-85378-09-6)
- Talks With Sri Ramana Maharshi: On Realizing Abiding Peace and Happiness (ISBN 1-878019-00-7)
- Guru Ramana, by S.S. Cohen (ISBN 81-88225-22-3)
- Moments Remembered, Reminiscences of Bhagavan Ramana, by V. Ganesan (ISBN 978-8188018437)
- Living with the Master, Reminiscences by Kunjuswami (ISBN 81-88018-99-6)
- Sri Ramana Reminiscences, by G. V. Subbaramayya

For Children

- Sri Ramana, Friend of Animals: Hobbler and the Monkeys of Arunachala ISBN 81-8288-047-5

- Sri Ramana, Friend of Animals: The Life of Lakshmi the Cow
- Ramana Thatha (Grand Father Ramana), by Kumari Sarada ISBN 81-85378-03-7
- Ramana Maharshi (Amar Chitra Katha: The Glorious Heritage of India series) ISBN 81-7508-048-5

14

Samarth Ramdas

Ramdas (1606–1682) was a prominent Marathi saint and religious poet in the Hindu tradition in Maharashtra, India. Samarth Ramdas was a devotee of Lord Hanuman and Lord Rama. His birth name was Narayan Suryajipant Kulkarni Thosar.

Early Life

Ramdas Swami was born in a Deshastha Rugvedi kayastha family to Suryaji and Ranu-Bai Thosar in Jamb in Jalna District of Maharashtra on Ram Navami (the birth festival of Lord Ram), 1530 according to "Shaliwahan Shak" calendar. His given name was Narayan.

As a child, Ramdas showed an inclination toward metaphysical contemplation and religion. One recorded incident tells how he was walking in the dark and bumped into something under a tree. Fetching a light, he saw a local villager who had been arbitrarily hanged by the Mughals, foreign rulers of India. This incident fired in him a desire to be free in all aspects of the world: free from foreign rule and also free from Maya, the illusion that prevents individual souls from realizing their unity with the greater Self, Ultimate Spirit.

When Ramdas was eight, his father died; and when he was 18, his mother arranged his marriage. However, he wanted to pursue a monastic life. He ran away in the middle of the wedding ceremony, before the marriage vows were exchanged.

During the Hindu marriage ceremony, the last word which seals the marriage is "Saavdhan" meaning, 'be careful'. Swami Ramdas interpreted that word to mean that he had to be careful not to get entangled in the bonds of Maya, and must seek Self realization.

Residences

Ramdas moved around quite a lot, and in the process, used several Ghal, which are small caves used for meditation. The famous ones include:

- Ramghal, on Sajjangad
- Morghal, at Morbag village near Sajjangad
- Tondoshi Ghal, North of Chaphal
- Taak Li, near Nashik
- Chandragiri, opposite Vasantgad, near Karad
- Helwak, near Helwak village
- Shinganwadi, near Chandragiri
- Shivthar Ghal, near Mahad.

Spiritual Development

For the next twelve years, Ramdas devoted himself to studying Hindu religious books, to meditation, and to prayers in a place named Panchavati, near Nashik on the banks of the Godavari River. At age 24 he took the name "Ramdas," meaning "servant of Lord Ram," an incarnation of God.

Ramdas practised physical yoga exercises as well as meditation. The Surya Namaskara or Sun Salutation was his favourite as it involves every part of the body. It is said that he would do 1,200 Sun Salutations every day, believing that no spirituality could be attained if the physical body was not strong.

In addition to his veneration of Ram, Ramdas worshipped Ram's divinely strong servant Lord Hanuman. He established 11 temples of Hanuman in Maharashtra and promoted physical exercise to develop a healthy society.

Writings

Ramdas Swami was a gifted composer. He produced considerable literature in verse form in Marathi. Among his works, two compositions particularly stand out: A small book of meditations, Shri Manache Shlok, advises ethical behaviour and love for God, and a large volume, Dasbodh, provides advice on both spiritual and practical topics. Ramdas also wrote the Shri Maruti Stotra, a poem in praise of Hanuman, the Aatmaa Raam, 11-Laghu Kavita and Raamayan (Marathi-Teeka).

His most popular composition is the Marathi song/prayer to Lord Ganesh Sukhkarta Dukhharta Varta Vighnachi. He also composed several other prayers such as Satrane Uddane

Hunkaar Vadani to Lord Hanuman and Panchanan haivahan surabhushan lila to Lord Khandoba.

Disciples

Samarth Ramdas had many disciples. Kalyan Swami worked as a writer for Ramdas, recording his songs and prayers. Ramdas tested him in many ways before giving him this responsible position. Other noteworthy disciples included Udhaw Swami, Vena Swami, Akka Bai, Bhim Swami, Dayanand Prabhu, and Diwakar Swami.

Chhatrapati Shivaji considered Samarth Ramdas his spiritual Guru and sought his advice many times. Shivaji requested Ramdas swami to move his residence to a fort named Parali & establish his permanent monastery there. The fort was subsequently renamed Sajjangad-Fort of the sacred.

In the 20th century, Nana Dharmadhikari undertook to spread the philosophy of Samarth Ramdas.

15

Satguru Ghasidas

Satguru Ghasidas is a Hindu saint, successor of the Satnam sect of Chhattisgarh, migrated from Narnaul Hariyana. Satguru Ghasidas was born on Monday 18 December 1718. The date of death of Satguru Ghasidas is unknown. No kabra, no samadhi place present of Satguru Ghasidas. According to folk stories in the last time, he came from Bhandarpuri to Chhata hill in the forest of Giroudpuri. He entered a cave (Satlokhi\Satlok) in front of chhata hill. He is immortal and living in Satlokhi Cave. He was born in village Girodhpuri in Raipur district in a Harivamsa family. Satguru Ghasidas saw the socio-political milieu of misrule, loot and plunder in the society. The local kings and administrator failed to stop this. Satguru Ghasidas underwent the exploitative experiences specific to human communities, which helped him the hierarchical and exploitative nature of social dynamics in a caste-ridden society.

From an early age, he started rejecting social inequity and to understand the problems faced by human community and to find solutions, he travelled extensively in Chhattisgarh by foot and by yogik power. And has done a lot of impossible welfare work.

1. Order for pure and nectar water, safe ground at any place by yogik power
2. Social Salvation
3. Spread the knowledge of "Satnam" seed and to built Universe Victory Pillar\Shrishti Vijay Stambh.

Life Story of Satguru Ghasidas

Satguru Ghasidas was a farmer in Giroud, he also worked for somedays as a farm worker of plougman. a village formerly in Bilaspur, Chhattisgarh and now in Raipur, near the Sonakan forests. In search of the right path he decided to go to Jaganath Puri and on his way at Sarangarh attained true knowledge. It is said that he announced Satnam and returned to Girodh. On his return, he stopped working as a farm worker and became engrossed in Tapasya. After spending six months in Sonakhan forests doing tapasya Satguru Ghasidas returned and formulated path-breaking principles of a new egalitarian social order.

Satguru Ghasidas was lettered from childhood from school. He was Guru (Teacher) from childhood. He plays play of Guru Chela (Teacher and Disciple) from Childhood with his friends. He was a Baalak Yogi (Child Yogi). He lettered with knowledge of Atharvaved and other parallel books. He also lettered with knowledge of English through Bible and Missionary. He is

Successor of King of whole world Parikshit. God provides a king for whole human community for stability, well administration. God always protects his Lineage. He travels whole chhattisgarh by foot and by yogik power. he has done a lot of impossible welfare work. He put Atharvaved in his Bhandarpuri Moti Mahal to run properly the empire. He was never dead, never took samadhi. no muth\kabra samadhi place present of Satguru Ghasidas. He is immortal. He is living in chhata hill cave in present time. He deeply resented with bad treatment with any living being and any non true action.

Mr. Chisholm's Writing

With a few additions. Mr. Chisholm gave a graphic account of the retirement of Satguru Ghasidas to the Sonakan forests for a period of six months, and of his reappearance and proclamation of his revelation on a fixed date before a great multitude of Satnamis, who had gathered from all parts to hear him. An inquiry conducted locally by Mr. Hira Lal in 1903 indicates that this story is of doubtful authenticity, though it must be remembered that Mr. Chisholm wrote only forty years after the event, and forty more had elapsed at the time of Mr. Hira Lal's investigation. Of the Satnamis Reformer himself Mr. Chisholm writes: Satguru Ghasidas was a man of

1. unusually uncomparable
2. fair
3. complexion
4. imposing appearance, 7-foot (2.1 m) height, powerful, powerful long arm (Mahaa Baahuve)

5. sensitive
6. silent
7. given to seeing visions

He was well known to the whole community, having travelled much among them; had the reputation of being exceptionally sagacious and was universally respected."

Another Writing

On one occasion he and his brother started on a pilgrimage to the temple at Puri, but only got as far as Sarangarh, whence they returned chanting "Satnam Satnam." As Purush Pita Satnam order to return and to engross in Tapasya. From this time Satguru Ghasidas began to adopt the life of an ascetic, retiring all day to the forest to meditate on a rocky chhata hillock about a mile from Giroud with dhooni of chandan wood. The two immortal tree of Aanwala and Dhanvana under which on a holy stone up side from ground it is said that he was accustomed to sit. This is a favourite place of pilgrimage of the Satnamis, and two Satnami temples have been built near it, which contain White Satguru Gaddi and Charann Khadaau (Wooden Shoes) of Chandan wood. These temples are annually and whole year, day and night visited by the All Satnami. In the course of time Satguru Ghasidas became venerated as a saintly character, and on some miracles being attributed to him, his fame rapidly spread. The People began to travel from long distances to venerate him, and those who entertained desires, such as for

1. The birth of a desired child and surely fulfilled (Garbh Nyaas)

2. such as the curing of snake-bite and reviving dead (Mrit Sanjivani Vidya),
3. To measure the 1 KM road by the body holding pair coconut in the front of gate of big temple of Satnam in Giroudpuri to fulfill any wish (Bhoomi Naapana)

A Muslim who suffer from very dangerous disease come to this place and he cured from near about death. after that he dances extremely the panthi dance.

The pilgrims carry away with them the water of Seven Nectar Tank to drink and to get Satlok\Amarlok (Top Most Heaven) (Probably only one real heaven).

Seven Nectar Tanks:

1. Charann Kund (Feet Tank)
2. Amrit Kund (Nectar tank)
3. Panch Kund 1 (Five Tanks 1)
4. Panch Kund 2 (Five Tanks 2)
5. Panch Kund 3 (Five Tanks 3)
6. Panch Kund 4 (Five Tanks 4)
7. Panch Kund 5 (Five Tanks 5)

This Nectar tanks are miracle, many cured from many diseases. Start Life from new starting with true character and away from meat, liquor and tobacco.

The Main Teaching of Satguru Ghasidas.

The main teaching of Satguru Ghasidas is only one word "Satnam" seed. Rest of all the things in world is stem, branches and leaves. And a 7 metre long Standard Cylindrical White

Universe Victory Pillar (Shrishti Vijay Stambh) with a white rectangular flag of Satnam. He always presents at all Jai Stambh, empty Satguru gaddi, white Satnam flag in the visual picturized soul in spiritual form. In the form of white bright Circlular point, which later picturize as Live Running, Walking, Talking Satpurush SATNAM Satguru Ghasidas. It is true.

Seven Teachings of Satguru Ghasidas

The Seven Teachings of Satguru Ghasidas:

1. Satya-Truth \True Action
2. Dhairya-Patience
3. Lagan-Dedication
4. Karoonna, Dayaa, Kshamaa-Kindness, Pardon
5. Karm – Karm Yog-Labour
6. Saralataa-Simplicity
7. Vyavahaar-Vyavahaarikata-practicality – Practical Life

The seven precepts of Satguru Ghasidas to a Brahman Writer:

1. abstinence from liquor, meat
2. certain red vegetables, such as lentils chillies and tomatoes, because they have the colour of blood,
3. the abolition of idol worship,
4. the prohibition of the employment of cows for cultivation, and of ploughing after midday or taking food to the fields,
5. and the worship of the name of one solitary and supreme God.

6. The use of _taroi_ is said to have been forbidden on account of its fancied resemblance to the horn of the buffalo,
7. and of the brinjal due to its likeness to the scrotum of the same animal.

Satguru Ghasidas Never made precepts, forcefully law. He teaches only one word Satnam (Truename \Name "True"). And free people to do anything which he wishes, which is in category of true action.

Miracle of Satguru Ghasidas

Satguru Ghasidas is incarnation of "Sat" \"Truth" in the human form. He is only one Satguru. He is only one God. His Place (Tapobhoomi) Giroudpuri is full of Welfare Spiritual Proof. He makes appearance to many people in that holy hill and forest area. He has supernatural powers.

1. He can revive the dead, as he did with Satimata Safura.
2. He had divine yogic powers. He can do any impossible work in universe.
3. He is Lord of Satlok and Universe.
4. He Can Order for a very good Environment Like Satlok.

However the key point is that Satguru Ghasidas has been accepted as a visionary social reformer and the high number of Satnam followers is a testimony to this fact. According to the 1901 census, there were around 4,00,000 people adhering to the principles of Satnam Panth. The fighter from Chhattisgarh in the Indian war of Independence of 1857, Veer Narayan Singh, was also deeply influenced by the teachings of Satguru Ghasidas.

Guru Mahima

The Guru Mahima is infinte. It cannot be written on a paper.

Satlok

Satlok is the Top Most Heaven. Satlok is a true thing. Many Knowledge and text about Satnam and many hills and forest come from Satlok. Satguru, Satpurush, SATNAM Gosain shows many people Satlok. We can understand Satguru's "Tantravad" by the tradition "Satlok." Satlok is comparable with the Yugnaddha of Buddhist tantra. Basically Satlok Or Yugnaddha means 'Ekya ke param siddhant mein dwait ka sanshlesham'. This theory has been elaborated in the fifth chapter of 'yugnadhkram'.

Satguru is living example of God He enlightens his disciple and makes him attain God. In all the "Panthi Geet" several steps have been written in the honour of Satguru. Satguru is not considered as a common man. There is no difference between Satguru and God. Satguru has been placed at par with father, mother and God.

Satguru can save you from Lord Shiva's anger but no one can save you from Satguru's anger.

Spiritual Welfare Tourism For World People

Miraculous Herbs and Plants in Sonakhan Forest

There are a lot of miraculous plants and herbs, grown by the blessing of Satguru Ghasidas. It contains a kind of good smelling Grass widespread in that area, Sanjivani Booti, Chandan,

Aanwala, Dhanvana, and many undefined and unresearched plants and herbs in highest genetic (DNA) state[immortal state]. and crossing the species criteria limit are present. That Herbal Medicine should be taken in only on the place Giroudpuri. For cure from Coma, Brain Dead, Head Injury, Traumatic brain injury, Cancer, Heart Diseases, all diseases. These herbs are actually blessing of Satguru Ghasidas. The main thing is Blessing of Satguru Ghasidas. The patient who suffers from any disease should Stay here for somedays (1 to 40 days). and drink the Water of Charann Kund, Amrit Kund, Amar Kund & Panch Kund and take some kinds of Grass and Herbs with prescription of local Vaidya.

Holy Stone Between Immortal Tree of Auvara and Dhauvara

This is tapasya place and addressing place of Satguru Ghasidas.

Charann Kund

This is the tank created by Satpurush in which Satguru Ghasidas washes his feet after Success in Tapasya. Charan kund is located near the main temple of Satguru, few steps down to the temple.

Amrit Kund

This is the Source of Nectar Created by Satpurush for Satguru Ghasidas.

Cave of Lord Vishnu [Narsinh Naath]

The Cave of Lord Vishnu (Narsinh Naath) is located on the Hill Upside Amrit Kund. This is a cave in which Lord Visnu Live in the form of Lion (Narsinh Nath). This is the most Dangerous and Mysterious area.

Panch Kund

These are five Nectar tanks, always filled with water in all seasons.

Chhata Pahaad

This is the sitting place of Satguru Ghasidas. Satguru Ghasidas is immortal and used to sit in Meditation inside the Chhata Hill.

Satlokhi Cave

This is the way to Satguru Ghasidas while in Meditation.

Yog River

This is river flowing between Giroudpuri and Shabari Narayan (The place of Shabari of Ramayan age).

Haathi Chattan

There is a hathi chattan (elephant shaped stone). There is clearly an elephant shaped stone bounded with sankal (chain). That is the elephant of a local King who came to see Satguru in anger. The elephant converted into stone in the middle of Yog River while crossing it due to the curse of Satpurush. Then the King arrived at Satguru's feet walking with bare feet and totally dedicated himself, his family, and his state in Satguru's feet.

Holy Hill and Forest area of Sonakhan

The whole hill and forest area of Giroudpuri and Sonakhan is full of miracle and mystery.

Satnam Dham \Places

Satnam Dhams are present all over the world. All are same.

1. Satnam Dham USA
2. Satnam Dham Ganga River

3. Satnam Barabanki Dham
4. Satnam Jagannath Dham
5. Chakravaay Satnam Dham
6. Chatua Satnam Dham
7. Khadua Satnam Dham
8. Khapari Satnam Dham
9. Pachari Akaltara Satnam Dham
10. Dulha Pahaad Satnam Dham
11. Amarpuri Satnam Dham
12. Bodsara Satnam Dham
13. Baradera Satnam Dham
14. Agam Satnam Dham
15. Siliyari Satnam Dham
16. Rajsthan Satnam Dham
17. Delhi Satnam Dham (Palace)
18. Hariyanna Satnam Dham
19. Amritsar Satnam Dham
20. Risali Bhilai Satnam Dham
21. Rajendra Nagar Raipur Satnam Dham
22. Dantewada Satnam Dham
23. Jagadalpur Satnam Dham
24. Rajnandgaon Satnam Dham
25. Khairagarh Satnam Dham
26. Sarguja Satnam Dham

27. Kondagaon Satnam Dham
28. Kanker Satnam Dham
29. Giroudpuri Dham (Residential Place)
30. Bhandarpuri Dham (Residential Place)
31. Dalli Rajhara Satnam Bhawan Satnam Dham (Iron Ore City)

Satnam Festival and Fairs

1. Main Fair at Giroudpuri is organized at the time of Panchami, Shashti, and Saptami of Falgun Month (Baba Guru Ghasidas Darshan Mela) (Baba Guru Ghasidas makes appearance at Chhata Pahaad).
2. Vijay Parv is celebrated at Bhandaarpuri Dhaam.

The Satnam Dharm

According to Satguru Ghasidas, Satnam Dharm is Religion of Whole Human Community.

The Satnam Panth

The Satnam Dharm is related to Satyug. Satnam Dharm is in existence from Satyug. Around 1300–1400 the successor of Satnam Dharm was King Saint Satkhojan Das Goswami (The King of Narnaul Kurukshetra).

Ancient history of Satnami

Satnamis are the lineage of King Parikshit of Great Kuru Kingdom, Narnaul Haryana Dwaapar/Mahabharat age Kurukshetra Hastinapur. According to ancient Satnam Granths Satnamis are ancient Kuru. Satnamis are long heighted, fair, true charactered man. According to Shree Mad Bhagvat Geeta, The

King Parikshit is king of whole world. The Satnam people in Chhattishgarh who migrated from arnaul Haryana has Mahabharat age iron chair and other several thing present in their home in villages in Chhattisgarh. Satguru Ghasidas is immortal & successor of King Parikshit. Presently Satguru Ghasidas is king for whole world as well as for whole universe. He is responsible for Whole World. Satguru Ghasidas is incarnation of Supreme and last God Satpurush SATNAM Goswami. Presently successor of Satguru Ghasidas in Bhandarpuri Dhaam is of a very true character, highly spiritually and highly Knowledged man Satguru Aashkaran Das Gosain. Satguru Aashkarann Das Gosain could be considered as the King For Whole World.

The Word Satnaam ("True" Name)

The word Satnam is in existence since Satyug. Satnam is exactly understood as the name "true."

Raja Sant Satguru Balakdas Gosain

Raja Sant Satguru Baalak Das was incarnation of Lord Vishnu (Narsinh Naath). He was a Great Yogi. He is successful in spreading the message of Satnam, Satnam Culture, Panthi Songs, Dance in the whole chhattisgarh. When his mission is complete by yogik power goes into the cave of Lord Vishnu upside Amrit Kund. Formerly an annual fair was held at Giroudpuri on the date of success of Satguru Ghasidas in Satnam Sadhana Tapasya to which all people of all community used to go.

Colonel Agnue's (Administrator of Raipur) Writing

Once Agnue said, "The character of chhattisgarhi people seems to be better than the people of other areas of India. There are no crimes, specially murder and theft. On the whole, people of Chhattisgarh are honest. People are not used to big crimes. Criminals have a habit of confessing their crimes without hesitation. People of Chhattisgarh are more inclined towards truth than people of any other areas in India."

Perhaps because of this, Satguru Ghasidas got inspired with Satnam. Whenever everything went beyond people's control, they took help of ojhas, who misguided them to be superstitious. People of Chhattisgarh were quite innocent. Moreover Chhattisgarh was surrounded by hills and its natives didn't have much interaction with the rest of the world. For them every river had a soul. On the whole they didn't even know that many diseases were spread because of polluted water. Before Satguru Ghasidas, the area was an area of superstition and lawlessness and because of his efforts and those of his followers it became a 'Rice Bowl'. All these changes were because of Satguru Ghasidas.

Role of Satguru Ghasidas

Satguru Ghasidas remains a major hero in the tradition. The Satnam Panth is said by many Satnamis to be based on these principles formulated by Satguru Ghasidas.

Satguru Ghasidas through Satnami principles initiated a socio-religious order, which rejected the premier position of castes and completely demolished the exploitative and hierarchical caste system. This new order was a challenge to the caste system and it treated all human beings as socially equal. According to Satnam Panth, truth is God and there is only one God, which is Able and Anant (Infinite). Satguru Ghasidas believed that idol worship was not a good way to worship God and therefore Satnam rejects any form of idol worship. Interestingly, Satguru Ghasidas had a holistic vision and felt that systemic reforms to remove social injustice and inequality would remain inadequate and incomplete without reforming the individuals. This underlying principle led to prohibition of liquor and non-vegetarian food for the followers of Satnam Panth.

While the idol worship was against the panth, Satnamis performed bhakti on Rama and Hanuman. Many still workship Rama, Krishna, and Hanuman.

Satguru Ghasidas also formulated some principles, which clearly reflect his love for animals and his desire to put an end to cruelty towards animals. The Satnami tradition also lives on in the form of a vast collection of panthi songs, commonly sung by groups during street procession. Many panthi songs vividly described Satguru Ghasidas's life.

Mechanism of Satnaam

Satnam Panth emphasizes more on Satguru. Satguru Ghasidas is considered Adi Guru. Satguru Ghasidas established a hereditary system for Satguru. The entire Indian Philosophy and religion accepts guruism. All the branches of Indian Philosophy are very mysterious as according to them, truth is far away from intellectualism and logic. 'Satya' travels from Satguru to his disciples in the world. There is one way by which truth can be attained i.e., by having faith in Satguru because only Satguru can make you feel the Satnam (Supreme Being).

Having faith in the Satguru is necessary for the spiritual upgradation of a disciple. A true disciple becomes a toy in the hands of the Satguru. This why, Satguru has been given the supreme status in Satnam Panth. Quite often Satguru becomes synonymous with the god or god can be achieved through Satguru.

Satguru is living example of God. He enlightens his disciple and makes them attain God. In all the "Panthi Geets" several steps have been written in the honour of Satguru. Satguru is not considered as a common man. There is no difference between Satguru and God. Satguru has been placed at par with father, mother and God. Satguru can save you from Lord Shiva's anger but no one can save you from Satguru's Anger.

We can understand Satguru's "Tantravad" by the tradition "Satlok." Satlok is comparable with the Yugnaddha of Buddhist tantra. Basically Satlok Or Yugnaddha means 'Ekya ke param siddhant mein dwait ka sanshlesham.' This theory has been elaborated in the fifth chapter of 'yugnadhkram.' There are several moral responsibilities of a Satguru. Satguru's office takes all the decisions related to social boycott. Satguru defines penalty for the social outcaste, when the outcaste is re-entered in the Satnam Panth. During the nomenclature of a child, Satguru makes him wear a "Kanthi," which is the token of child's entry into "Satnam Panth." It is not necessary for the Satguru to be present in all the ceremonies. These 'Anushthans' can be done in the meetings of the panth.

Most of the Satnamis come for Satguru's darshan at least once in a year. On that occasion a gift from the disciples is mandatory. There is no public place for the prayer for the Satnamis. There is no written scripture for them. Also, there is no pattern for prayer. When people are devoted to god, they are only supposed to recite Satnam and ask for the grace of the God.

Chhattisgarh in Year 1820

Satnamis were the most important community of Chhattisgarh in circa 1820. With the "Dharm Sansthapana" of Satguru Ghasidas, they worked so hard that today they acquire (Prepare) 1/4 of the agricultural land of Chhattisgarh. Around 1820, Chhattisgarh went through a revolution started by Satguru Ghasidas and its people became aware of their rights. Before this they had tolerated immense pain and had become ultra-tolerant. Satguru Ghasidas discarded the theory of tolerance and organized people who were ultra–tolerant. The samantwadi system was broken into pieces and a new panth was discovered, which can be called 'Ekeshwarwad.' So far, the illusion minded people hypnotized Satnamis, that they are bad. Satguru Ghasidas broke this hypnotized Satnamis, and brought them upper from others. By his efforts Satnamis became very powerful among Gram Pramukhs and Samants, Satnamis Started learning everything, they became hardworking and aware of their rights.

The social customs of the Satnamis

The Satnam people were frendly with all people and nature even from all living beings, Nature, rains, winds, etc. There was also a rule of the Satnamis not to accept cooked food from open market because of its chance of impurity. Satnamis celebrate the festival Krishna Janmashtami for the following reasons

1. Krishna's birthday
2. Birth Day of Satguru Balak Das [the incarnation of Lord Vishnu]

3. As Satnami are Lineage of Lord Vishnu

when vessels of milk and curd are broken over the heads of the worshippers and caught and eaten by all castes indiscriminately as a token of amity. Several points in the above description point to the conclusion that the Satnami movement is in essence a social revolt for awakening of people. A large proportion of the Satnamis are owners or tenants of land. It may be noted in conclusion, Christianity was accepted as part of the Satnami movement.

World Christianity Missions-Satnami influence on Christianity

The Donald and Mary McGavran's greatest contribution to World Christinity Missions

In the late 18th century, Satguru Ghasidas came to the Satnam Panth of India, and his new message found immediate and widespread acceptance:

1. Throw out your idols. Worship only the true God.
2. Wait for the coming of a red-faced man with a big book.

Do what he tells you. So to this People, which called themselves the Satnamis, Donald and Mary McGavran went in the feet of Satguru Ghasidas. God (Satguru Ghasidas) used this experience to prepare Mc Gavran for his greatest contribution to world missions during his later years. The McGavrans believed, the gospel had to be presented in the light of Satguru Ghasidas' message, since all world accepted Satguru Ghasidas as their own Guru. So he tied the gospel message to the message of the Christianity. by blessing and order of Satguru Ghasidas. The

Donald and Mary McGavran's greatest contribution to world missions during his later years was a blessing and order of Satguru Ghasidas. They had learnt the Satnami's principle, and with other missionaries translated the four Gospels of Satguru Ghasidas and the book of Acts of Christianity. McGavran noted that where the church was growing, it grew almost explosively along family lines until most of the related people had become Christians worldwide. The McGavrans dedicated it to Satguru Ghasidas. Every Church after that is powered (Siddh) by Satguru Ghasidas. The principles and laws of Satguru Ghasidas were also taken in the British Empire's rules and act. So the British Empire was successful in the world. In one respect, the British empire is grown by Satguru Ghasidas. Rembember, British were very few in number. British were very weak and got many defeat in many wars. Satguru Ghasidas, Satpurush SATNAM Prepare and call the British for world mission. British means not British people. British means British Law (Truth and management). British \Angrej actually belong to Angira Rishi. Modern Science age is also given by Satpurush SATNAM who understood properly the wish and complexity of god and walked with God.

The Spreading of Satnam Teaching

The Satnam Panth and ancient Satnami People are originator of Vedanta, Sufi mysticism and bhakti.

Dadu Dayal (1544-1603)

Dadu dayal was a Saint, mainly follower of Satnam teaching.

Jivandas

Jivandas, a mendicant. a disciple of Dadu Dayal.

Jagjiwan Das

Jagjivandas (1669–1760) a Som Vanshiya Chhatriya of Barabanki District Uttarpradesh who fought for the right of the human beings. He was disciple of two who Satnam Sages who come from Narnaul Haryana, the Prophet of the Sadh Satnami (Sadhak of Satnam) Sect of Upper India.

Guru Ghasidas University

Guru Ghasidas Vishwavidyalaya, is a Central University of India, located in Bilaspur C.G. State, established under Central Universities Act 2009, No. 25 of 2009. Formerly called Guru Ghasidas University (GGU), established by an Act of the State Legislative Assembly, was formally inaugurated on June 16, 1983.

16

Swami Dayananda Saraswati

Maharishi Dayanand Saraswati (Born:12 February 1824 – Died:30 October 1883) was an important Hindu religious scholar, reformer, and founder of the Arya Samaj, a Hindu reform movement. He was the first to give the call for Swarajya – "India for Indians" – in 1876, later taken up by Lokmanya Tilak. Denouncing the idolatry and ritualistic worship prevalent in Hinduism at the time, he worked towards reviving Vedic ideologies. Subsequently the philosopher and President of India, S. Radhakrishnan, called him one of "makers of Modern India," as did Sri Aurobindo.

One of his notable disciples was Shyamji Krishna Varma, who founded India House in London and guided other revolutionaries. Others who were influenced by and followed him included Madam Cama, Pran Sukh Yadav, Vinayak Damodar Savarkar, Lala Hardayal, Madan Lal Dhingra, Ram

Prasad Bismil, Bhagat Singh, Swami Shraddhanand Sukhabodhananda, Mahatma Hansraj and Lala Lajpat Rai. One of his most influential works is the book Satyarth Prakash, which contributed to the Indian independence movement. He was a sanyasi (ascetic) from boyhood, and a scholar, who believed in the infallible authority of the Vedas.

Dayananda advocated the doctrine of karma and skepticism in dogma, and emphasized the ideals of brahmacharya (celibacy) and devotion to God. The Theosophical Society and the Arya Samaj were united from 1878 to 1882, becoming the Theosophical Society of the Arya Samaj. Among Maharishi Dayananda's contributions are his promoting of the equal rights of women, such as the right to education and reading of Indian scriptures and his translation of the Vedas from Sanskrit into Hindi so that the common person might be able to read them.

Early Life

Dayananda was born on February 12 in 1824, in the town of Tankara, near Morvi (Morbi) in the Kathiawar region (since India's independence in 1947 Rajkot district) of the princely state of Gujarat, into the affluent and devout Saryupareen Brahmins family of Karshanji Lalji Tiwari and his wife Yashodabai. Since he was born under Mul Nakshatra, he was named "Mulshankar," and led a comfortable early life, studying Sanskrit, the Vedas and other religious texts to prepare himself for a future as a Hindu priest.

A number of incidents in early childhood resulted in Dayananda's questioning the traditional beliefs of Hinduism and inquiring about God. While still a young child, when his family went to a temple for overnight worship on the night of Maha Shivratri, he stayed up waiting for Lord Shiva to appear to accept the offerings made to his idol. While his family slept, Dayananda saw a mouse eating the offerings. He was utterly surprised and wondered how a God who cannot protect even his own offerings would protect humanity. He argued with his father that they should not be worshipping such a helpless God.

The deaths of his younger sister and his uncle from cholera caused Dayananda to ponder the meaning of life and death and he started asking questions which worried his parents. He was to be married in his early teens, as was common in nineteenth-century India, but he decided, marriage was not for him and in 1846 ran away from home.

Dayananda was disillusioned with classical Hinduism and became a wandering monk. He learned Panini's grammar to read Sanskrit texts, and understood from them that God can be found. After wandering in search of God for over two decades, he found Swami Virajananda near Mathura, Uttar Pradesh who became his guru. Swami Virajananda told him to throw away all his books, as he wished Dayananda to start from a clean slate and learn directly from the Vedas, the oldest and most foundational scriptures of Hinduism. Dayananda stayed under Swami Virjananda's tutelage for two and a half years. After finishing his education, Virjananda asked him to spread the knowledge of the Vedas in society as his gurudakshina, or tuition-dues.

Dayanand's Mission

Dayananda mission was to tell the humankind for Universal Brotherhood through nobility as spelt out in Vedas and his first step was to take up the difficult task of reforming Hinduism with dedication despite multiple repeated attempts on his life. He travelled the country challenging religious scholars and priests to discussions and won repeatedly on the strength of his arguments based on his knowledge of sanskrit and Vedas. He believed that Hinduism had been corrupted by divergence from the founding principles of the Vedas and that Hindus had been misled by the priesthood for the priests' self-aggrandizement. Hindu priests discouraged the laity from reading Vedic scriptures and encouraged rituals, such as bathing in the Ganges River and feeding of priests on anniversaries, which Dayananda pronounced as superstitions or self-serving practices. By exhorting the nation to reject such superstitious notions, his aim was to educate the nation to go back to the Vedas. While he wanted the people to follow the Vedic life, he also exhorted the nation to accept social reforms like the abolition of untouchability, sati, and dowry, education of women, swadeshi and importance of cows for national prosperity as well as the adoption of Hindi as the national language. Through his teachings, preachings, sermons and writings, he inspired the nation to aspire to Swarajya (self governance), nationalism, and spiritualism. He advocated the equal rights and respects to women and advocated the full education of a girl child.

Swami Dayananda did critical, logical and scientific analysis of all faiths i.e., Islam and Christianity as well as of other Indian faiths like Jainism, Buddhism and Sikhism, in addition to denouncing idolatry in Hinduism, as may be seen in his book Satyartha Prakash. He was against what he considered to be the corruption of the pure faith in his own country. Unlike many other reform movements within Hinduism, the Arya Samaj's appeal was addressed not only to the educated few in India, but to the world as a whole as evidenced in the sixth principle of the Arya Samaj. In fact his teachings professed universalism for the all living beings and not for any particular sect, faith, community or nation.

Arya Samaj allows and encourages converts to Hinduism. Dayananda's concept of dharma is stated in the "Beliefs and Disbeliefs" section of Satyartha Prakash. He said:

"I accept as Dharma whatever is in full conformity with impartial justice, truthfulness and the like; that which is not opposed to the teachings of God as embodied in the Vedas. Whatever is not free from partiality and is unjust, partaking of untruth and the like, and opposed to the teachings of God as embodied in the Vedas—that I hold as adharma."

He also said:

"He, who after careful thinking, is ever ready to accept truth and reject falsehood; who counts the happiness of others as he does that of his own self, I call him just." — Satyarth Prakash

Dayananda's Vedic message was to emphasize respect and reverence for other human beings, supported by the Vedic notion of the divine nature of the individual–divine because the body was the temple where the human essence (soul or "atma") had the possibility to interface with the creator ("Paramatma"). In the ten principles of the Arya Samaj, he enshrined the idea that "All actions should be performed with the prime objective of benefiting mankind," as opposed to following dogmatic rituals or revering idols and symbols. In his own life, he interpreted moksha to be a lower calling (due to its benefit to one individual) than the calling to emancipate others.

Dayananda's "back to the Vedas" message influenced many thinkers and philosophers the world over. Taking the clue from him, Sri Aurobindo decided to look for hidden psychological meanings in the Vedas.

Arya Samaj

Swami Dayananda's creation, the Arya Samaj, unequivocally condemns idol worship, animal sacrifice, ancestor worship, pilgrimages, priest craft, offerings made in temples, the caste system, untouchability, child marriages and discrimination against women on the grounds that all these lacked Vedic sanction. The Arya Samaj discourages dogma and symbolism and encourages skepticism in beliefs that run contrary to common sense and logic. To many people, the Arya Samaj aims to be a "universal society" based on the authority of the Vedas.

Death

In 1883 Dayananda was invited by the Maharaja of Jodhpur to stay at his palace. The Maharaja was eager to become his disciple and learn his teachings. One day Dayananda went to the Maharaja's rest room and saw him with a dance girl named Nanhi Jan. Dayananda boldly asked the Maharaja to forsake the girl and all unethical acts and follow dharma like a true Aryan. Dayananda's suggestion offended the dance girl and she decided to take revenge. She bribed Dayananda's cook to poison him. At bedtime, the cook brought him a glass of milk containing poison and powdered glass. Dayananda drank the milk and went to sleep only to wake up later with a burning sensation. He immediately realized that he had been poisoned and attempted to purge his digestive system of the poisonous substance, but it was too late. The poison had already entered his bloodstream. Dayananda was bedridden and suffered excruciating pain. Many doctors came to treat him but all was in vain. His body was covered all over with large bleeding sores. On seeing Dayananda's suffering, the cook was overcome with unbearable guilt and remorse. He confessed his crime to Dayananda. On his deathbed, Dayananda forgave him and gave him a bag of money and told him to flee the kingdom lest he be found out and executed by the Maharaja's men.

"A man of spirit has passed away from India. Pandit Dayananda Saraswati is gone, the irrepressible, energetic reformer, whose mighty voice and passionate eloquence for the last few years raised thousands of people in India from, lethargic, indifference and stupor Into active patriotism is no more." – Col Henry Steel Olcott

"Swami Dayananda Saraswati is certainly one of the most powerful personalities who has shaped modem India and is responsible for its moral regeneration and religious revival." – Subhash Chandra Bose.

Works

Dayananda Saraswati wrote more than 60 works in all, including a 14 volume explanation of the six Vedangas, an incomplete commentary on the Ashtadhyayi (Panini's grammar), several small tracts on ethics and morality, Vedic rituals and sacraments and on criticism of rival doctrines (such as Advaita Vedanta, Islam and Christianity). Some of his major works are Satyarth Prakash, Sanskarvidhi, Rigvedadi Bhashya Bhumika, Rigved Bhashyam (upto 7/61/2)and Yajurved Bhashyam. The Paropakarini Sabha located in the Indian city of Ajmer was founded by the Swami himself to publish and preach his works and Vedic texts.

Following are the Complete list of his Works:-

1. Sandhya (Unavailable) (1863)
2. Bhagwat Khandnam OR Paakhand Khandan OR Vaishnavmat Khandan (1866
3. Advaitmat Khandan (Unavailable) (1870)
4. Panchmahayajya Vidhi (1874 & 1877)
5. Satyarth Prakash (1875 & 1884)
6. Vedanti Dhwant Nivaran (1875)
7. Vedviruddh mat Khandan OR Vallabhacharya mat Khandan (1875)
8. Shiksha Patri Dhwant Nivaran OR Swami Narayan mat Khandan (1875)
9. Ved Bhashyam Namune ka PRATHAM Ank (1875)
10. Ved Bhashyam Namune ka DWITIYA Ank (1876)
11. Aryabhivinaya (Incomplete) (1876)
12. Sanskarvidhi (1877 & 1884)
13. Aaryoddeshya Ratna Maala (1877)
14. Rigved Aadib Bhasya Bhumika (1878)
15. Rigved Bhashyam (7/61/1,2 only) (Incomplete) (1877 to 1899)

16. Yajurved Bhashyam (Complete) (1878 to 1889)
17. Asthadhyayi Bhashya (2 Parts) (Incomplete) (1878 to 1879)
18. Vedang Prakash (Set of 16 Books viz 01. Varnoccharan Shiksha (1879) 02. Sanskrit Vakyaprabodhini (1879) 03. Vyavahar Bhanu (1879) 04. Sandhi Vishay 05. Naamik 06. Kaarak 07. Saamaasik 08. Taddhit 09. Avyayaarth 10. Aakhyatik 11. Sauvar 12. PaariBhaasik 13. Dhatupath 14. Ganpaath 15. Unaadikosh 16. Nighantu)
19. Gautam Ahilya ki katha (Unavailable) (1879)
20. Bhrantinivaran (1880)
21. Bhrmocchedan (1880)
22. Anu Bhrmocchedan (1880)
23. Gokaruna Nidhi (1880)
24. Chaturved Vishay Suchi (1971)
25. Gadarbh Taapni Upnishad (As per Babu Devendranath Mukhopadhyay) (Unavailable)
26. Hugli Shastrarth tatha Pratima Pujan Vichar (1873)
27. Jaalandhar Shastrarth (1877)
28. Satyasatya Vivek (Bareily Shastrarth) (1879)
29. Satyadharm Vichar (Mela Chandapur) (1880)
30. Kashi Shastrarth (1880)

Note:-For other miscellaneous Shastrarth, please read 1.Dayanand Shastrarth Sangrah published by Arsh

Sahitya Prachar Trust, Delhi and 2. Rishi Dayanand ke Shastrarth evam Pravachan published by Ramlal Kapoor Trust Sonipat (Haryana).

31. Arya Samaj ke Niyam aur Upniyam (30-11-1874)
32. Updesh Manjari (Puna Pravachan) (04-07-1875)
33. Swami Dayanand dwara swakathit Janm Charitra (During Puna pravachan) (04-08-1875)
34. Swami Dayanand dwara swakathit Janm Charitra (For The Theosophist Society's monthly Journal: Nov. & Dec 1880)
35. Swikar Patra (27-02-1883)
36. Rishi Dayanand ke Patra aur Vigyapan

17

Sai Baba of Shirdi

Sai Baba of Shirdi (September 28, 1835 – October 15, 1918), also known as Shirdi Sai Baba, was an Indian guru, yogi, and fakir who is regarded by his Hindu and Muslim devotees as a saint. Many Hindu devotees including Hemadpant who wrote the famous Shri Sai Satcharitra consider him an incarnation of Lord Krishna while other devotees consider him as an incarnation of Lord Dattatreya. Many devotees believe that he was a Satguru, an enlightened Sufi Pir, or a Qutub. He is a well-known figure in many parts of the world, but especially in India, where he is much revered.

Sai Baba's real name is unknown. The name "Sai" was given to him upon his arrival at Shirdi, a town in the west-Indian state of Maharashtra, by Mahalsapati, a devotee of Kandoba Raya at the temple stairs where he first saw him. No information is available regarding his birth and place of birth. Sai baba never spoke about his past life, though he did mention to several devotees like Shyama that their relationship exists since 72 births.

Sai is of Sanskrit origin, meaning "Sakshat Eshwar" or the divine. The honorific "Baba" means "father; grandfather; old man; sir" in Indo-Aryan languages. Thus Sai Baba denotes "holy father" or "saintly father."

Sai Baba remains a very popular saint, and is worshiped by people around the world. He had no love for perishable things and his sole concern was self-realization. He taught a moral code of love, forgiveness, helping others, charity, contentment, inner peace, and devotion to God and guru. Sai Baba's teaching combined elements of Hinduism and Islam: he gave the Hindu name Dwarakamayi to the mosque he lived in, practiced Hindu and Muslim rituals, taught using words and figures that drew from both traditions, and was buried in Shirdi. One of his well known epigrams, "Sabka Malik Ek" ("One God governs all"), is associated with Islam and Sufism. He always uttered "Allah Malik" ("God is King").

Sai Baba is revered by several notable Hindu religious leaders. Some of his disciples became famous as spiritual figures and saints, such as Mhalsapati, a priest of Kandoba temple in Shirdi, Upasni Maharaj, Saint Bidkar Maharaj, Saint Gangagir, Saint Jankidas Maharaj, and Sati Godavari Mataji.

Early Years

Little has been officially documented on the early life of Shirdi Sai Baba. There is absolutely no record of his Family, Parents, Name, Date of birth, Religion of birth, Place of birth. He simply manifested as a 16 year old boy in Shirdi, in deep meditation under a neem tree with amazing yogic powers and with the ability to heal and thenceforth became extremely famous. This is what adds to Baba's greatness, mysticism and divinity!

Baba reportedly arrived at the village of Shirdi in the Ahmednagar district of Maharashtra, British India, when he was about 16 years old. It is generally accepted that Sai Baba stayed in Shirdi for three years, disappeared for a year, and returned permanently around 1858.

Return to Shirdi

In 1858 Sai Baba returned to Shirdi. Around this time he adopted his famous style of dress consisting of a knee-length one-piece robe (kafni) and a cloth cap. Ramgir Bua, a devotee, testified that Sai Baba was dressed like an athlete and sported 'long hair flowing down to the end of his spine' when he arrived in Shirdi, and that he never had his head shaved. It was only after Baba forfeited a wrestling match with one Mohdin Tamboli that he took up the kafni and cloth cap, articles of typical Sufi clothing. This attire contributed to Baba's identification as a Muslim fakir, and was a reason for initial indifference and hostility against him in a predominantly Hindu village. According to B.V. Narasimhaswami, a posthumous follower who was widely praised as Sai Baba's "apostle," this attitude was prevalent up to 1854 even among some of his devotees in Shirdi.

For four to five years, Baba lived under a neem tree, and often wandered for long periods in the jungle around Shirdi. His manner was said to be withdrawn and uncommunicative as he undertook long periods of meditation. The Shri Sai Satcharita recounts the reaction of the villagers:

The people of the village were wonder-struck to see such a young lad practicing hard penance, not minding heat or cold. By day he associated with no one, by night he was afraid of nobody.

He was eventually persuaded to take up residence in an old and dilapidated mosque and lived a solitary life there, surviving by begging for alms, and receiving itinerant Hindu or Muslim visitors. In the mosque he maintained a sacred fire which is referred to as a dhuni, from which he gave sacred ashes ('Udhi') to his guests before they left. The ash was believed to have healing and apotropaic powers. He performed the function of a local hakim, and treated the sick by application of ashes. Sai Baba also delivered spiritual teachings to his visitors, recommending the reading of sacred Hindu texts along with the Qur'an. He insisted on the indispensability of the unbroken remembrance of God's name (dhikr, japa), and often expressed himself in a cryptic manner with the use of parables, symbols and allegories.

Sai Baba participated in religious festivals and was also in the habit of preparing food for his visitors, which he distributed to them as prasad. Sai Baba's entertainment was dancing and singing religious songs.

After 1910 Sai Baba's fame began to spread in Mumbai. Numerous people started visiting him, because they regarded him as a saint with the power of performing miracles, or even as an Avatar. They built his first temple at Bhivpuri, Karjat.

Teachings and Practices

Sai Baba opposed all persecution based on religion or caste. He was an opponent of religious orthodoxy – Christian, Hindu and

Muslim. Although Sai Baba himself led the life of an ascetic, he advised his followers to lead an ordinary family life.

In his personal practice, Sai Baba observed worship procedures belonging to Hinduism and Islam; he shunned any kind of regular rituals but allowed the practice of namaz, chanting of Al-Fatiha, and Qur'an readings at Muslim festival times. Occasionally reciting the Al-Fatiha himself, Baba also enjoyed listening to moulu and qawwali accompanied with the tabla and sarangi twice daily.

Sai Baba encouraged his devotees to pray, chant God's name, and read holy scriptures. He told Muslims to study the Qur'an, and Hindus to study texts such as the Ramayana, Bhagavad Gita, and Yoga Vasistha. He advised his devotees and followers to lead a moral life, help others, love every living being without any discrimination, and develop two important features of character: faith (Shraddha) and patience (Sabr). He criticized atheism. In his teachings, Sai Baba emphasized the importance of performing one's duties without attachment to earthly matters, and of being content regardless of the situation.

Sai Baba interpreted the religious texts of both Islam and Hinduism. He explained the meaning of the Hindu scriptures in the spirit of Advaita Vedanta. His philosophy also had numerous elements of bhakti. The three main Hindu spiritual paths – Bhakti Yoga, Gyan Yoga, and Karma Yoga – influenced his teachings.

Sai Baba said that God penetrates every thing and every being. He emphasized the complete oneness of God which was very close to the Islamic tawhid and the Hindu doctrine of the

Upanishads. Sai Baba said that the world is transient, and that only God and his gifts are eternal. He emphasized the importance of devotion to God – bhakti – and surrender to his will. He also talked about the need of faith and devotion to one's spiritual guru. He said that everyone was the soul and not the body. He advised his followers to develop a virtuous character, and taught them that all fate was determined by karma.

Sai Baba left no written works. His teachings were typically short, pithy sayings rather than elaborate discourses. Sai Baba would ask his followers for money (dakshina), some of which he would give to the poor and other devotees the same day, and the rest was used to buy wood to maintain Dhuni. According to his followers, this was done to rid them of greed and material attachment.

Sai Baba encouraged charity, and stressed the importance of sharing. He said: "Unless there is some relationship or connection, nobody goes anywhere. If any men or creatures come to you, do not discourteously drive them away, but receive them well and treat them with due respect. Shri Hari (God) will certainly be pleased if you give water to the thirsty, bread to the hungry, clothes to the naked, and your verandah to strangers for sitting and resting. If anybody wants any money from you and you are not inclined to give, do not give, but do not bark at him like a dog." Other favourite sayings of his were: "Why do you fear when I am here," and "He has no beginning... He has no end."

Sai Baba made Eleven assurances to his devotees. This is also known as "Akra Wachan" or "Gyarah Wachan."

1. Whosoever puts their feet on Shirdi soil, their sufferings will come to an end.
2. Whosoever climbs the steps of my Samadhi (tomb), His sorrows will vanish.
3. I shall be ever active and vigorous even after leaving this earthly body.
4. My Samadhi (tomb) shall bless and speak to the needs of my devotees.
5. I shall be active and vigorous even from my tomb.
6. Those who surrender to me, Will evolve and progress.
7. Those who look at me with love, I look back at them with love.
8. I will forever carry your burden, This is my promise to you.
9. If you seek my advice and help, it shall be given to you at once.
10. Whoever becomes one with me forever, I will forever be indebted to him.
11. Whoever takes my name,will receive my grace.

Worship and Devotees

The Shirdi Sai Baba movement began in the 19th century, while he was living in Shirdi. A local Khandoba priest-Mhalsapati Nagre-is believed to have been his first devotee. In the 19th century Sai Baba's followers were only a small group of Shirdi inhabitants and a few people from other parts of India. The movement started developing in the 20th century, with Sai

Baba's message reaching the whole of India. During his life, Hindus worshiped him with Hindu rituals and Muslims considered him to be a saint. In the last years of Sai Baba's life, Christians and Zoroastrians started joining the Shirdi Sai Baba movement.

Shirdi is among the major Hindu places of pilgrimage. The first Sai Baba temple is situated at Bhivpuri, Karjat. The Sai Baba Mandir (Hindu temple) in Shirdi is visited by around twenty thousand pilgrims a day and during religious festivals this number can reach up to a hundred thousand. Shirdi Sai Baba is especially revered and worshiped in the states of Maharashtra, Andhra Pradesh, and Gujarat.

The Shirdi Sai movement has spread to the Caribbean and to countries such as the United States, Australia, Malaysia, and Singapore. The Shirdi Sai Baba movement is one of the main Hindu religious movements in English-speaking countries.

Sai Baba had many disciples and devotees:

1. Nana Saheb Chandorkar: Deputy Collector – legend has it that Sai Baba saved this man's daughter from labour complications.
2. Ganapath Rao: police officer who resigned to become an ascetic,and also known as DasGanu, He was an itinerant who spread Sai Baba's message.
3. Tatya Patil: had immense faith in Sai Baba and served him until Sai Baba took samadhi. Sai Baba used to treat Tatya Patil as His nephew.
4. Baija Mai kote patil: Sai Baba treated her as His elder sister and equivalent to mother.She was Tatya Patil's mother.

5. Haji Abdul baba: He served Sai Baba until Sai Baba died in 1918.
6. Madhav Rao Deshpande: Later known as Shama, one of the staunch devotees of Sai Baba.
7. Govindrao Raghunath Dabholkar (Hemadpant): Sai Baba allowed him to write the Shri Sai Satcharita.
8. Mahalsapati Chimanji Nagare: A priest of Khandoba Temple.
9. Radha Krishna Mai: A great devotee of Baba, cleaned the temple every day and looked after Baba's needs.
10. Shirdi Sai Baba Slogans (mantras) are sung by devotees in praise of him as worship.

Reported Miracles

Sai Baba's millions of disciples and devotees believe that he performed many miracles such as bilocation, levitation, mind reading, materialization, exorcisms, making the river Yamuna, entering a state of Samadhi at will, and lightning lamps with water, removing his limbs or intestines and sticking them back to his body (khandayoga), curing the incurably sick, appearing beaten when another was beaten, after death rising on third day like Jesus Christ, preventing a mosque from falling down on people, and helping his devotees in a miraculous way. He also gave Darshan (vision) to people in the form of Rama, Krishna, Vithoba and many other Gods depending on the faith of devotees.

According to his followers he appeared to them in dreams after his death, and gave them advice. His devotees have documented many stories.

Historical Sources

Biographers of Sai Baba (e.g. Govindrao Raghunath Dabholkar, Acharya Ekkirala Bharadwaja, Smriti Srinivas, Antonio Rigopolous) have based their writing on primary sources. One such source is the Shirdi Diary by Ganesh Shri krishna Khaparde, which describes every day of the author's stay at Shirdi.

Speculation about the unknown episodes of Sai Baba's life are primarily based on his own words.

The most important source about Sai's life is the Shri Sai Satcharita, written in Marathi in 1916 by Govindrao Raghunath Dabholkar, whom Sai Baba nicknamed Hemadpant. Consisting of 53 chapters, it describes Sai Baba's life, teachings, and miracles. The book compares Sai Baba's love to a mother's love: caring and loving, but reprimanding when needed. It describes Baba's lifestyle, his selfless attitude, and his love for his devotees. The book describes how one should surrender one's egoism at God's feet and trust one's guru. It explains how God is supreme and His devotees should trust Him and love Him. It teaches that God is omnipresent in all living things, so that everything on Earth must be treated with love and respect.

Sri Sai Baba and His Teachings by Acharya Ekkirala Bharadwaja is an in-depth study of Sai Baba's life routine and activities. B.V. Narasimhaswamiji has written important books such as Sri Sai Baba's Charters and Sayings and Devotee's Experiences of Sai Baba.

In Various Religions

Hinduism

During Sai Baba's life, the Hindu saint Anandanath of Yewala declared Sai Baba a spiritual "diamond." Another saint, Gangagir, called him a "jewel." Sri Beedkar Maharaj greatly revered Sai Baba, and in 1873, when he met him he bestowed the title Jagad guru upon him. Sai Baba was also greatly respected by Vasudevananda Saraswati (known as Tembye Swami). He was also revered by a group of Shaivic yogis, to which he belonged, known as the Nath-Panchayat.

Other Religions

In Islam, Sai Baba mainly appears in Sufism as a Pir. Meher Baba declared Baba to be a Qutub-e-Irshad-the highest of the five Qutubs, a "Master of the Universe" in the spiritual hierarchy. Sai Baba is also worshipped by prominent Zoroastrians such as Nanabhoy Palkhivala and Homi Bhabha, and has been cited as the Zoroastrians' most popular non-Zoroastrian religious figure.

Meher Baba met Sai Baba only once in his lifetime, during World War I, in December 1915. Meher Baba was still a youngster named Merwan Sheriar Irani when he met Sai Baba for a few minutes during one of Sai Baba's processions in Shirdi. This event is considered as the most significant in Meher Baba's life. Shri Sai Satcharita (Sai Baba's life story), makes no mention of Meher Baba. But in Lord Meher, the life story of Meher Baba, there are innumerable references to Sai Baba. Meher Baba credited his Avataric advent to Upasni, Sai Baba, and three other Perfect Masters – Hazrat Babajan, Hazrat Tajuddin Baba, and

Narayan Maharaj.

Notable Disciples

Sai Baba left behind no spiritual heirs and appointed no disciples, and did not even provide formal initiation (diksha), despite requests. Some disciples of Sai Baba achieved fame as spiritual figures, such as Upasni Maharaj of Sakori. After Sai Baba died, his devotees offered the daily Aarti to Upasni Maharaj when he paid a visit to Shirdi, two times within 10 years.

Sathya Sai Baba (1926–2011) claimed to be a reincarnation of Sai Baba; he had a considerable number of followers in the 20th and 21st century.

In Culture

Sacred Art and Architecture

In India, its a common sight to find a Sai Baba temple in any city or town, in every large city or town there is at least one temple dedicated to Sai Baba. There are even some in towns and cities outside India. In the mosque in Shirdi in which Sai Baba lived, there is a life-size portrait of him by Shama Rao Jaykar, an artist from Mumbai. Numerous monuments and statues depicting Sai Baba, which serve a religious function, have also been made. One of them, made of marble by a sculptor named Balaji Vasant Talim, is in the Samadhi Mandir in Shirdi where Sai Baba was buried. In Sai Baba temples, his devotees play various kinds of devotional religious music, such as aarti.

Stamp

Indian Postal Service released a Sai Baba commemorative stamp in May 2008.

On July 30, 2009, the New and Renewable Energy Minister Farooq Abdullah inaugurated what has been acclaimed as the largest solar steam system in the world, at the Shirdi shrine. The Shri Sai Baba Sansthan Trust paid an estimated Rs.1.33 crore for the system, Rs.58.4 lakh of which was paid as a subsidy by the renewable energy ministry. It is said the system can cook 20,000 meals per day for pilgrims visiting the temple.

18

Sarada Devi

Sarada Devi (22 December 1853 – 20 July 1920), born Saradamani Mukhopadhyaya, was the wife and spiritual counterpart of Ramakrishna Paramahamsa, a nineteenth century mystic of Bengal. Sarada Devi is also reverentially addressed as the Holy Mother by the followers of the Ramakrishna monastic order. Sarada Devi played an important role in the growth of the Ramakrishna Movement.

Sarada Devi was born in Jayrambati. At the age of five she was betrothed to Ramakrishna, whom she joined at Dakshineswar when she was in her late teens. According to her traditional biographers, both lived lives of unbroken continence, showing the ideals of a householder and of the monastic ways of life. After Ramakrishna's death, Sarada Devi stayed most of the time either at Jayrambati or at the Udbodhan office, Calcutta. The disciples of Ramakrishna regarded her as their own mother, and after their guru's passing looked to her for advice and encouragement. The followers of the Ramakrishna movement regard Sarada Devi as an incarnation of the Divine Mother.

Biography

Birth and Parentage

Saradamani Devi was born of Brahmin parents as the eldest daughter on December 22, 1853, in the quiet village of Jayrambati in present day West Bengal, India. Her parents, Ramchandra Mukhopadhyaya and Syamasundari Devi, were poor and pious. Her father Ramchandra earned his living as a farmer and through the performance of priestly duties. According to traditional accounts, Ramachandra and Syamasundari had visions and supernatural events foretelling the birth of a divine being as their daughter.

Sarada lived the simple life of an Indian village girl. As a child Sarada—then known as Saradamani—was fascinated by traditional Hindu folklore and narratives. As in the case of most girls of rural upbringing, she did not receive any formal education but learned to serve others as she helped her mother run a large household and looked after her younger brothers. During the terrible famine of 1864, Sarada worked ceaselessly as her family served food to hungry people. She was interested in the clay models of goddesses Kali and Lakshmi, which she worshiped regularly. She is said to have started meditating from her childhood and traditional accounts recount her mystic visions and experiences. According to Sarada Devi, she used to see a bevy of eight girls of her age coming from an unknown place and escorting her in her chores during her childhood.

Betrothal

Ramakrishna—then known as Gadadhar Chattopadhaya and a priest of the Dakshineswar Kali Temple since 1855—was practicing spiritual austerities. His mother and brother thought that a marriage would be a good steadying effect on him, by diverting his attention away from spiritual austerities and visions. It is reported that Ramakrishna himself indicated Saradamani as the bride. In May 1859, Sarada was betrothed to Ramakrishna. Sarada was 5 years old and Ramakrishna was 23; the age difference was typical for 19th century rural Bengal.

After the betrothal, Sarada was left to the care of her parents and Ramakrishna returned to Dakshineswar. Sarada next met Ramakrishna when she was fourteen years old, and she spent three months with him at Kamarpukur. There, Ramakrishna imparted Sarada instructions on meditation, spiritual life. Ramakrishna's frequent samadhi (ecstasy) and unorthodox ways of worship led some onlookers to doubt his mental stability, while others regarded him as a great saint. Sarada joined Ramakrishna at Dakshineswar in 1872 on her own accord when she was eighteen, after hearing these rumors about his mental health. She found Ramakrishna to be a kind and caring person.

At Dakshineswar Kali Temple

At Dakshineswar, Sarada Devi stayed in a tiny room in the nahabat (music tower). She stayed at Dakshineswar until 1885, except for short periods when she visited Jayrambati. By this time Ramakrishna had already embraced the monastic life of a sannyasi; as a result, the marriage was never consummated. As a priest, Ramakrishna performed the ritual ceremony—the

Shodashi Puja where Sarada Devi was made to sit in the seat of goddess Kali, and worshiped as the divine mother. According to Saradananda a direct disciple of Ramakrishna, Ramakrishna married to show the world an ideal of a sexless marriage. Ramakrishna regarded Sarada as the incarnation of Divine Mother, addressing her as Sree Maa (Holy Mother) and it was by this name that she was known to Ramakrishna's disciples.

Sarada Devi's days began at 3 am. After finishing her ablutions in the Ganges, she would practice japa and meditation until daybreak. Ramakrishna taught her the sacred mantras, and instructed her how to initiate people and guide them in spiritual life. Sarada Devi is regarded as Ramakrishna's first disciple. Except for her hours of meditation, most of her time was spent in cooking for Ramakrishna and the growing number of his devotees. While Sarada Devi remained completely in the background, her unassuming, warm personality attracted some female devotees to become her lifelong companions.

During Ramakrishna's last days, during which he suffered from throat cancer, Sarada Devi played an important role in nursing him and preparing suitable food for him and his disciples. It is reported that after Ramakrishna's death in August 1886, when Sarada Devi tried to remove her bracelets as the customs dictated for a widow, she had a vision of Ramakrishna in which he said, "I have not passed away, I have gone from one room to another." According to her, whenever she thought of dressing like a widow, she had a vision of Ramakrishna asking her not to do so. After Ramakrishna's death, Sarada Devi continued to play an important role in the nascent religious movement. She remained the spiritual guide of the movement for the next 34 years.

Pilgrimage

After Ramakrishna's death, Sarada Devi began her pilgrimage through North India, accompanied by a party of women disciples including Lakshmi Didi, Gopal Ma, and Ramakrishna's householder and monastic disciples. The party visited the Vishwanath Temple of god Shiva at Banaras and the city of Ayodhya, which is associated with life of god Rama. Later, she visited Vrindavan which is associated with god Krishna. According to traditional accounts, at Vrindavan, she experienced nirvikalpa samadhi and began her role as guru. She initiated several of the Ramakrishna's disciples including Mahendranath Gupta, Yogen with a mantra. According to her traditional biographers and disciples, to call her "Mother" was no mere expression of respect and all those who met her became aware of a maternal quality in her.

At Calcutta

After the pilgrimage, Sarada Devi stayed alone in Kamarpukur, Ramakrishna's native village also where he was born. There, she endured poverty, verging on starvation for a year. In 1888, when the news reached the lay and monastic disciples of Ramakrishna that she needed their care and attention, they invited her to Calcutta and arranged for her stay. Swami Saradananda built a permanent house for Sarada Devi in Calcutta. The house was named the Udbodhan House, after the Bengali monthly magazine conducted by the Ramakrishna Math. It is also called Mayerbati ("Holy Mother's House"), where she spent the longest period of her life outside Jayrambati.

Sarada Devi went to Calcutta because she had many hardships in Kamarpukur. She had no financial resources and about no one could take care of her. She tried to hide her situation, but it leaked out. When the devotees at Calcutta heard this, they persuaded Sarada Devi to come to Calcutta.

At Udbodhan House, Sarada Devi was accompanied by other women disciples of Ramakrishna, Golap Ma, Yogin Ma, Lakshmi Didi and Gauri Ma being the best known. An increasing number of people began to flock for guidance, instructions and spiritual initiation. Other Western women followers of Ramakrishna Order including Sister Nivedita and Sister Devamata formed close relationship with her. According to her biographers, her innate motherliness put visitors at ease. Swami Nikhilananda, her direct disciple writes, "Though she had no children of the flesh, she had many of the spirit." She regarded all her disciples as her own children.

Sarada Devi received the highest reverence from the Ramakrishna Order and its devotees. Ramakrishna had bade her continue his mission after his passing away and wanted his disciples not to make any distinction between himself and her. According to her devotees and traditional biographers, the hospitality of Sarada Devi was unique and was characterized by motherly care and solicitude. Traditional accounts recount the mystical experiences of her devotees. Some dreamt of her as a goddess in human form though they had never seen her picture before. Others reportedly received their initiation from her in their dream. One such example is of Girish Chandra Ghosh, the father of Bengali drama, who reportedly saw Sarada Devi in a dream when he was nineteen years old and received a mantra. When he met her many years later, to his astonishment she was the same person in the dream.

Last Days

Sarada Devi spent her final years moving back and forth between Jayrambati and Calcutta. In January 1919, Sarada Devi went to Jayrambati and stayed there for over a year. During the last three months of her stay, her health seriously declined. Her strength was greatly impaired and she was brought back to Calcutta on February 27, 1920. For the next five months she continued to suffer. Before her death, she gave the last advice to the grief-stricken devotees, "But I tell you one thing—if you want peace of mind, do not find fault with others. Rather see your own faults. Learn to make the whole world your own. No one is a stranger my child: this whole world is your own!" This is considered as her last message to the world. She died at 1.30 am on July 20, 1920. Her body was cremated at the Belur Math.

Teachings and Quotes

Sarada Devi did not write any books; her utterances and reminiscences have been recorded by her disciples including Swami Nikhilananda, Swami Tapasyananda. Though uneducated, Sarada Devi's spiritual insight and utterances are highly regarded by scholars like Gayatri Chakravorty Spivak, who writes, "We have bits and pieces of her exquisite remarks as testimony."

- Practise meditation, and by and by your mind will be so calm and fixed that you will find it hard to keep away from meditation.
- The mind is everything. It is in the mind alone that one feels pure and impure. A man, first of all, must make his own mind guilty and then alone can he see another man's guilt.

- "I tell you one thing. If you want peace of mind, do not find fault with others. Rather see your own faults. Learn to make the whole world your own. No one is a stranger, my child; the whole world is your own."
- One must have devotion towards one's own guru. Whatever may be the nature of the guru, the disciple gets salvation by dint of his unflinching devotion towards his guru.

Impact and Legacy

Sarada Devi played an important role as the advisory head of a nascent organization that became a monastic order devoted to social work—the Ramakrishna Mission. Gayatri Spivak writes that Sarada Devi "performed her role with tact and wisdom, always remaining in the background." She also initiated several prominent monks into the Ramakrishna Order. Swami Nikhilananda, who was a freedom fighter and a follower of Mahatma Gandhi, accepted Sarada Devi as his guru and joined the Ramakrishna Order. He eventually founded the Ramakrishna-Vivekananda Center in New York. Though uneducated herself, Sarada Devi advocated education for women. She entrusted Devamata with the implementation of her dream—a girl's school on the Ganges, where Eastern and Western pupils could study together. In 1954, Sri Sarada Math and Ramakrishna Sarada Mission, a monastic order for women was founded in the honor of Sarada Devi.

19

Swami Vivekananda

Swami Vivekananda(12 January 1863 – 4 July 1902), born Narendranath Dutta, was the chief disciple of the 19th century mystic Ramakrishna Paramahansa and the founder of the Ramakrishna Math and the Ramakrishna Mission. He is considered a key figure in the introduction of Hindu philosophies of Vedanta and Yoga to the "Western" World, mainly in America and Europe and is also credited with raising interfaith awareness, bringing Hinduism to the status of a major world religion during the end of the 19th century C.E. Vivekananda is considered to be a major force in the revival of Hinduism in modern India. He is perhaps best known for his inspiring speech beginning with "Sisters and Brothers of America," through which he introduced Hinduism at the Parliament of the World's Religions at Chicago in 1893.

Swami Vivekananda was born in an aristocratic Bengali kayastha family of Calcutta on January 12, 1863. Swami's parents influenced his thinking—the father by his rational mind and the mother by her religious temperament. From his childhood, he showed inclination towards spirituality and God realization. As a guru, Ramakrishna taught him Advaita Vedanta (non-dualism) and that all religions are true, and service to man was the most effective worship of God. After the death of his Guru, Vivekananda became a wandering monk, touring the Indian subcontinent and getting first-hand knowledge of India's condition. He later sailed to Chicago and represented India as a delegate in the 1893 Parliament of World Religions. He conducted hundreds of public and private lectures and classes, disseminating Vedanta and Yoga in America, England and a few other countries in Europe. He also established the Vedanta societies in America and England.

Early life (1863-1888)

Birth and childhood

Swami Vivekananda was born in 3, Shimla Pally, Calcutta (presently known as Kolkata) on 12 January 1863, Monday at 6:49 A.M., during the Makara Sankranti festival in a traditional Kayastha family, and was given the name Narendranath Dutta. His father Viswanath Dutta was an attorney of Calcutta High Court. He was considered generous, and had a liberal and progressive outlook in social and religious matters. His mother Bhuvaneshwari Devi was pious and had practiced austerities and prayed to Vireshwar Shiva of Varanasi to give her a son. She reportedly had a dream in which Shiva rose from his meditation and said that he would be born as her son. Narendranath's thinking and personality were influenced by his parents—the father by his rational mind and the mother by her religious temperament. From his mother he learnt the power of self-control. One of the sayings of his mother Narendranath quoted often in his later years was, "Remain pure all your life; guard your own honor and never transgress the honor of others. Be very tranquil, but when necessary, harden your heart." He was reportedly adept in meditation and could reportedly enter the state of samadhi. He reportedly would see a light while falling asleep and he reportedly had a vision of Buddha during his meditation. During his childhood, he had a great fascination for wandering ascetics and monks.

Narendranath had varied interests and a wide range of scholarship in philosophy, religion, history, the social sciences, arts, literature, and other subjects. He evinced much interest in the Hindu scriptures like the Vedas, the Upanishads, the Bhagavad Gita, the Ramayana, the Mahabharata and the Puranas. He was also well versed in classical music, both vocal and instrumental and is said to have undergone training under two Ustads, Beni Gupta and Ahamad Khan. Since boyhood, he took an active interest in physical exercise, sports, and other organizational activities. Even when he was young, he questioned the validity of superstitious customs and discrimination based on caste and refused to accept anything without rational proof and pragmatic test.

When his father moved to Raipur in 1877 for 2 years then Narendranath along with the whole family shifted there. At that time there were no good schools in Raipur so he spent his time with his father and had discussions on spiritual topics. Narendranath learned Hindi in Raipur and for the first time the

Question of existence of God came to his mind. It is believed that once he experienced an ecstasy during this period of life. The family returned to Calcutta in 1879 but it is believed that these 2 years were the turning point in his life. Raipur is sometimes termed as the "Spiritual Birthplace" of Swami Vivekananda.

College and Brahmo Samaj

Narendranath started his education at home, later he joined the Metropolitan Institution of Ishwar Chandra Vidyasagar in 1871 and in 1879 he passed the entrance examination for Presidency College, Calcutta, entering it for a brief period and subsequently shifting to General Assembly's Institution. During the course, he studied western logic, western philosophy and history of European nations. In 1881 he passed the Fine Arts examination and in 1884 he passed the Bachelor of Arts.

Narendranath is said to have studied the writings of David Hume, Immanuel Kant, Johann Gottlieb Fichte, Baruch Spinoza, Georg W. F. Hegel, Arthur Schopenhauer, Auguste Comte, Herbert Spencer, John Stuart Mill, and Charles Darwin. Narendra became fascinated with the Evolutionism of Herbert Spencer, and translated Spencer's book on Education into Bengali for Gurudas Chattopadhyaya, his publisher. Narendra also had correspondence with Herbert Spencer for some time. Alongside his study of Western philosophers, he was thoroughly acquainted with Indian Sanskrit scriptures and many Bengali works. According to his professors, student Narendranath was a prodigy. Dr. William Hastie, the principal of Scottish Church College, where he studied during 1881-84, wrote, "Narendra is really a genius. I have travelled far and wide but I have never come across a lad of his talents and possibilities, even in German universities, among philosophical students." He was regarded as a srutidhara—a man with prodigious memory. After a discussion with Narendranath, Dr. Mahendralal Sarkar reportedly said, "I could never have thought that such a young boy had read so much!"

Narendranath became the member of a Freemason's lodge and the breakaway faction from the Brahmo Samaj led by Keshab Chandra Sen. His initial beliefs were shaped by Brahmo concepts, which include belief in a formless God and deprecation of the worship of idols. Not satisfied with his knowledge of Philosophy, he wondered if God and religion could be made a part of one's growing experiences and deeply internalized. Narendra went about asking prominent residents of contemporary Calcutta whether they had come "face to face with God." but could not get answers which satisfied him.

His first introduction to Ramakrishna occurred in a literature class in General Assembly's Institution, when he heard Principal Reverend W. Hastie lecturing on William Wordsworth's poem The Excursion and the poet's nature-mysticism. In the course of explaining the word trance in the poem, Hastie told his students that if they wanted to know the real meaning of it, they should go to Ramakrishna of Dakshineswar. This prompted some of his students, including Narendranath to visit Ramakrishna.

With Ramakrishna

Narendranath's meeting with Ramakrishna in November 1881 proved to be a turning point in his life. About this meeting,

Narendranath said, "Ramakrishna looked just like an ordinary man, with nothing remarkable about him. He used the most simple language and I thought "Can this man be a great teacher?" I crept near to him and asked him the question which I had been asking others all my life: "Do you believe in God, Sir?" "Yes," he replied. "Can you prove it, Sir?" "Yes." "How?" "Because I see Him just as I see you here, only in a much intenser sense." That impressed me at once. I began to go to that man, day after day, and I actually saw that religion could be given. One touch, one glance, can change a whole life." Even though Narendra did not accept Ramakrishna as his guru initially and revolted against his ideas, he was attracted by his personality and visited him frequently. He initially looked upon Ramakrishna's ecstasies and visions as, "mere figments of imagination," "mere hallucinations." As a member of Brahmo samaj, he revolted against idol worship and polytheism, and Ramakrishna's worship of Kali. He even rejected the Advaitist Vedantism of identity with absolute as blasphemy and madness, and often made fun of the concept.

Though at first Narendra could not accept Ramakrishna and his visions, he could not neglect him either. It had always been in Narendra's nature to test something thoroughly before he would accept it. He tested Ramakrishna, who never asked Narendra to abandon reason, and faced all of Narendra's arguments and examinations with patience. "Try to see the truth from all angles" was his reply. During the course of five years of his training under Ramakrishna, Narendra was transformed from a restless, puzzled, impatient youth to a mature man who was ready to renounce everything for the sake of God-realization. In time, Narendra accepted Ramakrishna as guru, and when he accepted, his acceptance was whole-hearted and with complete surrendering as disciple.

In 1885 Ramakrishna suffered from throat cancer and he was shifted to Calcutta and later to Cossipore. Vivekananda and his brother disciples took care of Ramakrishna during his final days. Vivekananda's spiritual education under Ramakrishna continued there. At Cossipore, Vivekananda reportedly experienced Nirvikalpa Samadhi. During the last days of Ramakrishna, Vivekananda and some of the other disciples received the ochre monastic robes from Ramakrishna, which formed the first monastic order of Ramakrishna. Vivekananda was taught that service to men was the most effective worship of God. It is reported that when Vivekananda doubted Ramakrishna's claim of avatar, Ramakrishna reportedly said, "He who was Rama, He who was Krishna, He himself is now Ramakrishna in this body." During his final days, Ramakrishna asked Vivekananda to take care of other monastic disciples and in turn asked them to look upon Vivekananda as their leader. Ramakrishna's condition worsened gradually and he expired in the early morning hours of August 16, 1886 at the Cossipore garden house. According to his disciples, this was Mahasamadhi.

Founding of the Ramakrishna Math

After the death of their master, the monastic disciples led by Vivekananda formed a fellowship at a half-ruined house at Baranagar near the river Ganges, with the financial assistance of the householder disciples. This became the first building of the

Ramakrishna Math, or the monastery of the disciples who constituted the first monastic order of Sri Ramakrishna.

The dilapidated house at Baranagar was chosen because of its low rent and proximity to the Cossipore burning-ghat where Ramakrishna was cremated. Narendra and other members of the Math often spent their time in meditation, discussing about different philosophies and teachings of spiritual teachers including Ramakrishna, Adi Shankara, Ramanuja, and Jesus Christ. Narendra reminisced about the early days in the monastery as follows-

"We underwent a lot of religious practice at the Baranagar Math. We used to get up at 3:00 am and become absorbed in japa and meditation. What a strong spirit of detachment we had in those days! We had no thought even as to whether the world existed or not."

In the early part of 1887, Narendra and eight other disciples took formal monastic vows. Narendra took the name of Swami Bibidishananda. Later he was coronated with the name Vivekananda by Ajit Singh, the Maharaja of Khetri.

In January 1899 the Baranagar Math was shifted to a newly acquired plot of land at Belur in the district of Howrah, now famous as the Belur Math.

As a wandering monk in India (1888-1893)

Later, In 1888, Vivekananda left the monastery as a Parivrajaka—the Hindu religious life of a wandering monk, "without fixed abode, without ties, independent and strangers wherever they go." His sole possessions were a kamandalu (water pot), staff, and his two favorite books—Bhagavad Gita and The Imitation of Christ. Narendranath travelled the length and breadth of India for five years, visiting important centers of learning, acquainting himself with the diverse religious traditions and different patterns of social life. He developed a sympathy for the suffering and poverty of the masses and resolved to uplift the nation. Living mainly on Bhiksha or alms, Narendranath travelled mostly on foot and railway tickets bought by his admirers whom he met during the travels. During these travels, he gained acquaintance and stayed with scholars, Dewans, Rajas and people from all walks of life—Hindus, Muslims, Christians, Pariahs (low caste workers) and Government officials.

Northern India

In 1888, he started his journey from Varanasi. At Varanasi, he met pandit and Bengali writer, Bhudev Mukhopadhyay and Trailanga Swami, a famous saint who lived in a Shiva temple. Here, he also met Babu Pramadadas Mitra, the noted Sanskrit scholar, to whom the Swami wrote a number of letters asking his advice on the interpretation of the Hindu scriptures. After Varanasi, he visited Ayodhya, Lucknow, Agra, Vrindavan, Hathras and Rishikesh. At Hathras he met Sharat Chandra Gupta, the station master who later became one of his earliest disciples as Sadananda. Between 1888-1890, he visited Vaidyanath, Allahabad. From Allahabad, he visited Ghazipur where he met Pavhari Baba, a Advaita Vedanta ascetic who spent most of his time in meditation. Between 1888-1890, he returned to Baranagore Math for a few times, because of ill health and to arrange for the financial funds when Balaram Bose and Suresh Chandra Mitra, the disciples of Ramakrishna who supported the Math had expired.

The Himalayas

In July 1890, accompanied by his brother monk, Swami Akhandananda, he continued his journey as a wandering monk and returned to the Math only after his visit to the West. He visited, Nainital, Almora, Srinagar, Dehradun, Rishikesh, Haridwar and the Himalayas. During this travel, he reportedly had a vision of macrocosm and microcosm, which seems to be reflected in the Gyan Yoga lectures he gave later in the West, "The Cosmos, The Macrocosm and The Microcosm." During these travels, he met his brother monks —Swami Brahmananda, Saradananda, Turiyananda, Akhandananda and Advaitananda. They stayed at Meerut for a few days where they passed their time in meditation, prayer and study of scriptures. At the end of January 1891, the Swami left his brother monks and journeyed to Delhi alone.

At Delhi, after visiting historical places, he journeyed towards Alwar, in the historic land of Rajputana. Later he journeyed to Jaipur, where he studied Panini's Ashtadhyayi with a Sanskrit scholar. He next journeyed to Ajmer, where he visited the palace of Akbar and the famous Dargah and left for Mount Abu. At Mount Abu, he met the maharaja, Ajit Singh of Khetri, who became his ardent devotee and supporter. Swami Tathagatananda, a senior monk of the Ramakrishna Order, and the Head of Vedanta Society, New York wrote as follows :

At Khetri, he delivered discourses to the Raja, became acquainted with the pandit Ajjada Adibhatla Narayana Dasu, and studied Mahabhashya on sutras of Panini. After two and a half months there, towards the end of October (Mahabhashya) 1891, he proceeded towards Rajasthan and Maharastra.

Western India

Continuing his travels, he visited Ahmedabad, Wadhwan, Limbdi. At Ahmedabad he completed his studies of Muslim and Jain culture. At Limbdi, he met Thakore Sahed Jaswant Singh who had himself been to England and America. From the Thakore Saheb, the Swami first got the idea of going to the West to preach Vedanta. He later visited Junagadh, where he was the guest of Haridas Desai, the Dewan of the State, who was so charmed with his company that every evening he, with all the State officials, used to meet the Swami and converse with him until late at night. From there he also visited Girnar, Kutch, Porbander, Dwaraka, Palitana, Nadiad where he stayed at Diwan Haridas Desai's house Nadiad ni haveli and Baroda. At Porbander he stayed three quarters of a year, in spite of his vow as a wandering monk, to perfect his philosophical and Sanskrit studies with learned pandits; he worked with a court pandit who translated the Vedas.

He later travelled to Mahabaleshwar and then to Pune. From Pune he visited Khandwa and Indore around June 1892. At Kathiawar, he heard of the Parliament of the World's Religions and was urged by his followers there to attend it. He left Khandwa for Bombay and reached there on July 1892. In a Pune bound train he met Bal Gangadhar Tilak. After staying with Tilak for few days in Poona, the Swami travelled to Belgaum in October 1892. At Belgaum, he was the guest of Prof.

G.S. Bhate and Sub-divisional Forest officer, Haripada Mitra. From Belgaum, he visited Panjim and Margao in Goa. He spent three days in the Rachol Seminary, the oldest convent-college of theology of Goa where rare religious literature in manuscripts and printed works in Latin are preserved. He reportedly studied important Christian theological works here. From Margao the Swami went by train to Dharwar, and from there directly to Bangalore, in Mysore State.

Southern India

At Bangalore, the Swami became acquainted with Sir K. Seshadri Iyer, the Dewan of Mysore state, and later he stayed at the palace as guest of the Maharaja of Mysore, Chamaraja Wodeyar. Regarding the Swami's learning, Sir Seshadri reportedly remarked, "a magnetic personality and a divine force which were destined to leave their mark on the history of his country." The Maharaja provided the Swami a letter of introduction to the Dewan of Cochin and got him a railway ticket.

From Bangalore, he visited Trichur, Kodungalloor, Ernakulam. At Ernakulam, he met Chattampi Swamikal, contemporary of Narayana Guru in early December 1892. From Ernakulam, he journeyed to Trivandrum, Nagercoil and reached Kanyakumari on foot during the Christmas Eve of 1892. At Kanyakumari, the Swami reportedly meditated on the "last bit of Indian rock," famously known later as the Vivekananda Rock Memorial, for three days. At Kanyakumari, Vivekananda had the "Vision of one India," also commonly called "The Kanyakumari resolve of 1892." He wrote.

"At Cape Camorin sitting in Mother Kumari's temple, sitting on the last bit of Indian rock—I hit upon a plan: We are so many sanyasis wandering about, and teaching the people metaphysics—it is all madness. Did not our Gurudeva use to say, 'An empty stomach is no good for religion?' We as a nation have lost our individuality and that is the cause of all mischief in India. We have to raise the masses."

From Kanyakumari he visited Madurai, where he met the Raja of Ramnad, Bhaskara Setupati, to whom he had a letter of introduction. The Raja became the Swami's disciple and urged him to go to the Parliament of Religions at Chicago. From Madurai, he visited Rameshwaram, Pondicherry, he travelled to Madras and here he met some of his most devoted disciples, who played important roles in collecting funds for Swami's voyage to America and later in establishing the Ramakrishna Mission in Madras. With the aid of funds collected by his Madras disciples and Rajas of Mysore, Ramnad, Khetri, Dewans and other followers Vivekananda left for Chicago on 31 May 1893 from Bombay assuming the name Vivekananda—the name suggested by the Maharaja of Khetri.

Visit to Japan (1893)

On his way to Chicago, Vivekananda visited Japan in 1893. He first reached the port city of Nagasaki, and then boarded a steamer to Kobe. From here he took the land route to Yokohama, visiting along the way, the three big cities of Osaka, Kyoto and Tokyo. He called the Japanese "one of the cleanest people on earth," and was impressed not only by neatness of their streets and dwellings but also by their movements, attitudes and gestures, all of which he found to be "picturesque."

This was a period of rapid military build-up in Japan-a prelude to the Sino-Japanese War and the Russo-Japanese War. These preparations did not escape the attention of Vivekananda, who wrote-"The Japanese seem now to have fully awakened themselves to the necessity of the present times. They have now a thoroughly organized army equipped with guns which one of their own officers has invented and which is said to be second to none. Then, they are continually increasing their navy." About the industrial progress he observed, "The match factories are simply a sight to see, and they are bent upon making everything they want in their own country.."

Contrasting the rapid progress of Japan with the situation back in India, he urged his countrymen-the "offspring of centuries of superstition and tyranny"-to come out of their narrow holes and have a look abroad.

"Only I want that numbers of our young men should pay a visit to Japan and China every year. Especially to the Japanese, India is still the dreamland of everything high and good. And you, what are you?... talking twaddle all your lives, vain talkers, what are you? Come, see these people, and then go and hide your faces in shame. A race of dotards, you lose your caste if you come out! Sitting down these hundreds of years with an ever-increasing load of crystallized superstition on your heads, for hundreds of years spending all your energy upon discussing the touchableness or untouchableness of this food or that, with all humanity crushed out of you by the continuous social tyranny of ages. What are you? And what are you doing now?... promenading the sea-shores with books in your hands –

repeating undigested stray bits of European brainwork, and the whole soul bent upon getting a thirty rupee clerkship, or at best becoming a lawyer – the height of young India's ambition – and every student with a whole brood of hungry children cackling at his heels and asking for bread! Is there not water enough in the sea to drown you, books, gowns, university diplomas, and all?

First visit to the West (1893-1897)

His journey to America took him through China, Canada and he arrived at Chicago in July 1893. But to his disappointment he learnt that no one without credentials from a bona fide organization would be accepted as a delegate. He came in contact with Professor John Henry Wright of Harvard University. After inviting him to speak at Harvard and on learning from him not having credentials to speak at the Parliament, Wright is quoted as having said, "To ask for your credentials is like asking the sun to state its right to shine in the heavens." Wright then addressed a letter to the Chairman in charge of delegates writing, "Here is a man who is more learned than all of our learned professors put together." On the Professor, Vivekananda himself writes "He urged upon me the necessity of going to the Parliament of Religions, which he thought would give an introduction to the nation."

Parliament of World's Religions

The Parliament of Religions opened on 11 September 1893 at the Art Institute of Chicago. On this day, Vivekananda gave his first brief address. He represented India and Hinduism. Though initially nervous, he bowed to Saraswati, the goddess of learning and began his speech with, "Sisters and brothers of America!" To these words he got a standing ovation from a crowd of seven thousand, which lasted for two minutes. When silence was restored, he began his address. He greeted the youngest of the nations in the name of "the most ancient order of monks in the world, the Vedic order of sannyasis, a religion which has taught the world both, tolerance and universal acceptance." And he quoted two illustrative passages in this relation, from the Bhagavad Gita—"As the different streams having their sources in different places all mingle their water in the sea, so, O Lord, the different paths which men take, through different tendencies, various though they appear, crooked or straight, all lead to Thee!" and "Whosoever comes to Me, through whatsoever form, I reach him; all men are struggling through paths that in the end lead to Me." Despite being a short speech, it voiced the spirit of the Parliament and its sense of universality.

Dr. Barrows, the president of the Parliament said, "India, the Mother of religions was represented by Swami Vivekananda, the Orange-monk who exercised the most wonderful influence over his auditors." He attracted widespread attention in the press, which dubbed him as the "Cyclonic monk from India." The New York Critique wrote, "He is an orator by divine right, and his strong, intelligent face in its picturesque setting of yellow and orange was hardly less interesting than those earnest words, and the rich, rhythmical utterance he gave them." The New York Herald wrote, "Vivekananda is undoubtedly the greatest figure in the Parliament of Religions. After hearing him, we feel how foolish it is to send missionaries to this learned nation." The American newspapers reported Swami Vivekananda as "the greatest figure in the parliament of religions" and "the most popular and influential man in the parliament."

He spoke several more times at the Parliament on topics related to Hinduism and Buddhism. The parliament ended on 27 September 1893. All his speeches at the Parliament had one common theme—Universality—and stressed religious tolerance.

Lecturing tours in America and England

"I do not come," said Swamiji on one occasion in America, "to convert you to a new belief. I want you to keep your own belief; I want to make the Methodist a better Methodist; the Presbyterian a better Presbyterian; the Unitarian a better Unitarian. I want to teach you to live the truth, to reveal the light within your own soul."

After the Parliament of Religions, held in September 1893 at The Art Institute of Chicago, Vivekananda spent nearly two whole years lecturing in various parts of eastern and central United States, appearing chiefly in Chicago, Detroit, Boston, and New York. By the spring of 1895, he was weary and in poor health, because of his continuous exertion. After suspending his lecture tour, the Swami started giving free and private classes on Vedanta and Yoga. In June 1895, for two months he conducted private lectures to a dozen of his disciples at the Thousand Island Park. Vivekananda considered this to be the happiest part of his first visit to America. He later founded the "Vedanta Society of New York."

During his first visit to America, he travelled to England twice—in 1895 and 1896. His lectures were successful there. Here he met Miss Margaret Noble, an Irish lady, who later became Sister Nivedita. During his second visit in May 1896, while living at a house in Pimlico, the Swami met Max Müller a renowned Indologist at Oxford University who wrote Ramakrishna's first biography in the West. From England, he also visited other European countries. In Germany he met Paul Deussen, another famous Indologist.

He also received two academic offers, the chair of Eastern Philosophy at Harvard University and a similar position at Columbia University. He declined both, saying that, as a wandering monk, he could not settle down to work of this kind.

He attracted several sincere followers. Among his other followers were, Josephine MacLeod, Miss Müller, Miss Noble, E.T. Sturdy, Captain and Mrs. Sevier—who played an important role in the founding of Advaita Ashrama and J.J. Goodwin—who became his stenographer and recorded his teachings and lectures. The Hale family became one of his warmest hosts in America. His disciples—Madame Louise, a French woman, became Swami Abhayananda, and Mr. Leon Landsberg, became Swami Kripananda. He initiated several other followers into Brahmacharya.

Swami Vivekananda's ideas were admired by several scholars and famous thinkers—William James, Josiah Royce, C. C. Everett, Dean of the Harvard School of Divinity, Robert G. Ingersoll, Nikola Tesla, Lord Kelvin, and Professor Hermann Ludwig Ferdinand von Helmholtz. Other personalities who were attracted by his talks were Harriet Monroe and Ella Wheeler Wilcox—two famous American poets, Professor William James of Harvard University; Dr. Lewis G. Janes, president of Brooklyn Ethical Association; Sara C. Bull, wife of

Ole Bull, the Norwegian violinist; Sarah Bernhardt, the French actress and Madame Emma Calvé, the French opera singer.

From West, he also set his Indian work in motion. Vivekananda wrote a stream of letters to India, giving advice and sending money to his followers and brother monks. His letters from the West in these days laid down the motive of his campaign for social service. He constantly tried to inspire his close disciples in India to do something big. His letters to them contain some of his strongest words. In one such letter, he wrote to Swami Akhandananda, "Go from door to door amongst the poor and lower classes of the town of Khetri and teach them religion. Also, let them have oral lessons on geography and such other subjects. No good will come of sitting idle and having princely dishes, and saying "Ramakrishna, O Lord!"—unless you can do some good to the poor." Eventually in 1895, the periodical called Brahmavadin was started in Madras, with the money supplied by Vivekananda, for the purpose of teaching the Vedanta. Subsequenly, Vivekananda's translation of first six chapters of The Imitation of Christ was published in Brahmavadin (1889).

Vivekananda left for India on 16 December 1896 from England with his disciples, Captain and Mrs. Sevier, and J.J. Goodwin. On the way they visited France, Italy, seeing Leonardo da Vinci's The Last Supper, and set sail for India from the Port of Naples on December 30, 1896. Later, he was followed to India by Max Müller and Sister Nivedita. Sister Nivedita devoted the rest of her life to the education of Indian women and the cause of India's independence.

Back in India (1897-1899)

Colombo to Almora

Vivekananda arrived in Colombo on January 15, 1897 and received an ecstatic welcome. Here, he gave his first public speech in East, India, the Holy Land. From there on, his journey to Calcutta was a triumphal progress. He travelled from Colombo to Pamban, Rameshwaram, Ramnad, Madurai, Kumbakonam and Madras delivering lectures. People and Rajas gave him enthusiastic reception. In the procession at Pamban, the Raja of Ramnad personally drew the Swami's carriage. On way to Madras, at several places where the train would not stop, the people squatted on the rails and allowed the train to pass only after hearing the Swami. From Madras, he continued his journey to Calcutta and continued his lectures up to Almora.While in the West he talked of India's great spiritual heritage, on return to India, the refrain of his 'Lectures from Colombo to Almora' was uplift of the masses, eradication of the caste virus, promotion of the study of science, industrialization of the country, removal of poverty, the end of the colonial rule.These lectures have been published as Lectures from Colombo to Almora. These lectures are considered to be of nationalistic fervor and spiritual ideology. His speeches had tremendous influence on the Indian leaders, including Mahatma Gandhi, Bipin Chandra Pal and Balgangadhar Tilak.

Founding of the Ramakrishna Mission

Advaita Ashrama, Mayavati, a branch of the Ramakrishna Math, founded on March 19, 1899, later published many of Swami Vivekananda's work, now publishes Prabuddha Bharata journal

On 1 May 1897 at Calcutta, Vivekananda founded the Ramakrishna Mission—the organ for social service. The ideals of the Ramakrishna Mission are based on Karma Yoga. Its governing body consists of the trustees of the Ramakrishna Math-the organ to carry out religious works. Due to the close association between the two, both have their headquarters at Belur, near Calcutta. This was the beginning of an organized social and religious movement to help the masses through educational, cultural, medical and relief work.

Two other monasteries were founded by him-one at Mayavati on the Himalayas, near Almora called the Advaita Ashrama and another at Madras. Two journals were also started, Prabuddha Bharata in English and Udbhodan in Bengali. The same year, the famine relief work was started by Swami Akhandananda at Murshidabad district.

Vivekananda had inspired Sir Jamshedji Tata to set up a research and educational institution when they had travelled together from Yokohama to Chicago on the Swami's first visit to the West in 1893. About this time the Swami received a letter from Tata, requesting him to head the Research Institute of Science that Tata had set up. But Vivekananda declined the offer saying that it conflicted with his spiritual interests.

Visit to Punjab

He later visited western Punjab with the mission of establishing harmony between the Arya Samaj which stood for reinterpreted Hinduism and the Sanatanaists who stood for orthodox Hinduism. At Rawalpindi, he suggested methods for rooting out antagonism between Arya Samajists and Muslims. His visit to Lahore is memorable for his famous speeches and his inspiring association with Tirtha Ram Goswami, then a brilliant professor of Mathematics, who later graced monasticism as Swami Rama Tirtha and preached Vedanta in India and America. He also visited other places, including Delhi and Khetri and returned to Calcutta in January 1896. He spent the next few months consolidating the work of the Math and training the disciples. During this period he composed the famous arati song, Khandana Bhava Bandhana during the event of consecration of Ramakrishna's temple at a devotees' house.

Second visit to the West and last years (1899-1902)

Vivekananda once again left for the West in June 1899, amid his declining health. He was accompanied by Sister Nivedita and Swami Turiyananda. He spent a short time in England, and went on to America. During this visit, he founded the Vedanta societies at San Francisco and New York. He also founded "Shanti Ashrama" (peace retreat) at California, with the aid of a generous 160-acre (0.65 km2) gift from an American devotee. Later he attended the Congress of Religions, in Paris in 1900. The Paris addresses are memorable for the scholarly penetration evinced by Vivekananda related to worship of Linga and authenticity of the Gita. From Paris he paid short visits to Brittany, Vienna, Istanbul, Athens and Egypt. For the greater part of this period, he was the guest of Jules Bois, the famous thinker. He left Paris on October 24, 1900, and arrived at the Belur Math on December 9, 1900.

Vivekananda spent few of his days at Advaita Ashrama, Mayavati and later at the Belur Math. Henceforth till the end he stayed at Belur Math, guiding the work of Ramakrishna Mission and Math and the work in England and America. Thousands of visitors came to him during these years including The Maharaja of Gwalior and in December 1901, the stalwarts of Indian National Congress including Lokamanya Tilak. In December 1901, he was invited to Japan to participate in the Congress of Religions, however his failing health made it impossible. He undertook pilgrimages to Bodhgaya and Varanasi towards his final days.

Death

His tours, hectic lecturing engagements, private discussions and correspondence had taken their toll on his health. He was suffering from asthma, diabetes and other physical ailments. A few days prior to his demise, he was seen intently studying the almanac. Three days before his death he pointed out the spot for this cremation—the one at which a temple in his memory stands today. He had remarked to several persons that he would not live to be forty.

On the day of his death, he taught Shukla-Yajur-Veda to some pupils in the morning at Belur Math. He had a walk with Swami Premananda, a brother-disciple, and gave him instructions concerning the future of the Ramakrishna Math.

Vivekananda died at ten minutes past nine P.M. on July 4, 1902 while he was meditating. According to his disciples, this was Mahasamadhi. Afterward, his disciples recorded that they had noticed "a little blood" in the Swami's nostrils, about his mouth and in his eyes. The doctors remarked that it was due to the rupture of a blood-vessel in the brain, but they could not find the real cause of the death. According to his disciples, Brahmarandhra — the aperture in the crown of the head — must have been pierced when he attained Mahasamadhi. Vivekananda had fulfilled his own prophecy of not living to be forty years old.

Teachings and Philosophy

Swami Vivekananda believed that the essence of Hinduism was best expressed in the Vedanta philosophy, based on the interpretation of Adi Shankara. He summarized the Vedanta's teachings as follows,

- Each soul is potentially divine.
- The goal is to manifest this Divinity within by controlling nature, external and internal.
- Do this either by work, or worship, or mental discipline, or philosophy—by one, or more, or all of these—and be free.
- This is the whole of religion. Doctrines, or dogmas, or rituals, or books, or temples, or forms, are but secondary details.
- So long as even a single dog in my country is without food my whole religion is to feed it and serve it, anything excluding that is nonreligious.

According to Vivekananda, an important teaching he received from Ramakrishna was that "Jiva is Shiva" (each individual is divinity itself). This became his Mantra, and he coined the concept of daridra narayana seva-the service of God in and through (poor) human beings. "If there truly is the unity of Brahma underlying all phenomena, then on what basis do we regard ourselves as better or worse, or even as better-off or worse-off, than others?"-This was the question he posed to himself. Ultimately, he concluded that these distinctions fade into nothingness in the light of the oneness that the devotee experiences in Moksha. What arises then is compassion for those "individuals" who remain unaware of this oneness and a determination to help them.

Swami Vivekananda belonged to that branch of Vedanta that held that no one can be truly free until all of us are. Even the desire for personal salvation has to be given up, and only tireless work for the salvation of others is the true mark of the enlightened person. He founded the Ramakrishna Math and Mission on the principle of "Atmano Mokshartham Jagat-hitaya cha" (for one's own salvation and for the welfare of the World).

Vivekananda advised his followers to be holy, unselfish and have shraddha (faith). He encouraged the practice of Brahmacharya (Celibacy). In one of the conversations with his childhood friend Priya Nath Sinha, he attributes his physical and mental strengths, and eloquence to the practice of Brahmacharya.

Vivekananda did not advocate the emerging area of parapsychology and astrology (one instance can be found in his speech Man, the Maker of his Destiny, Complete-Works, Volume 8, Notes of Class Talks and Lectures) saying that this form of curiosity doesn't help in spiritual progress but actually hinders it.

Vivekananda and science

In his book Raja Yoga, Vivekananda explores traditional views on the supernatural and the belief that the practice of Raja Yoga can confer psychic powers such as 'reading another's thoughts,' 'controlling all the forces of nature,' become 'almost all-knowing,' 'live without breathing,' 'control the bodies of others' and levitation. He also explains traditional eastern spiritual concepts like kundalini and spiritual energy centres (chakras).

Vivekananda advocated to test thoroughly before making your decision of accepting or denying something:

"It is not the sign of a candid and scientific mind to throw overboard anything without proper investigation. Surface scientists, unable to explain various extraordinary mental phenomena, strive to ignore their very existence."

He further says in the introduction of the book that one should take up the practice and verify these things for oneself, and that there should not be blind belief.

"What little I know I will tell you. So far as I can reason it out I will do so, but as to what I do not know I will simply tell you what the books say. It is wrong to believe blindly. You must exercise your own reason and judgment; you must practise, and see whether these things happen or not. Just as you would take up any other science, exactly in the same manner you should take up this science for study."

In his paper read at the World Parliament of Religions, Chicago (1893), Vivekananda also hinted about the final goal of physics:

"Science is nothing but the finding of unity. As soon as

science would reach perfect unity, it would stop from further progress, because it would reach the goal. Thus Chemistry could not progress farther when it would discover one element out of which all other could be made. Physics would stop when it would be able to fulfill its services in discovering one energy of which all others are but manifestations.

All science is bound to come to this conclusion in the long run. Manifestation, and not creation, is the word of science today, and the Hindu is only glad that what he has been cherishing in his bosom for ages is going to be taught in more forcible language, and with further light from the latest conclusions of science."

The great electrical engineer, Nikola Tesla, after listening to Vivekananda's speech on Sankhya Philosophy, was much interested in its cosmogony and its rational theories of the Kalpas (cycles), Prana and Akasha. His notion based on the Vedanta led him to think that matter is a manifestation of energy. After attending a lecture on Vedanta by Vivekananda, Tesla also concluded that modern science can look for the solution of cosmological problems in Sankhya philosophy, and he could prove that mass can be reduced to potential energy mathematically.

Influence

Several leaders of 20th Century India and philosophers have acknowledged Vivekananda's influence. The first governor general of independent India, Chakravarti Rajagopalachari, said "Vivekananda saved Hinduism, saved India." According to Subhash Chandra Bose, Vivekananda is "the maker of modern

India" and for Mohandas Gandhi, Vivekananda's influence increased his "love for his country a thousandfold." National Youth Day in India is held on his birthday, January 12.

Swami Vivekananda is widely considered to have inspired India's freedom struggle movement. His writings inspired a whole generation of freedom fighters including Subhash Chandra Bose, Aurobindo Ghose and Bagha Jatin. Vivekananda was the brother of the revolutionary freedom fighter, Bhupendranath Dutta. Subhash Chandra Bose, one of the most prominent figures in Indian independence movement said.

"I cannot write about Vivekananda without going into raptures. Few indeed could comprehend or fathom him even among those who had the privilege of becoming intimate with him. His personality was rich, profound and complex... Reckless in his sacrifice, unceasing in his activity, boundless in his love, profound and versatile in his wisdom, exuberant in his emotions, merciless in his attacks but yet simple as a child, he was a rare personality in this world of ours."

Aurobindo Ghose considered Vivekananda as his spiritual mentor.

"Vivekananda was a soul of puissance if ever there was one, a very lion among men, but the definitive work he has left behind is quite incommensurate with our impression of his creative might and energy. We perceive his influence still working gigantically, we know not well how, we know not well where, in something that is not yet formed, something leonine, grand, intuitive, upheaving that has entered the soul of India and we say, "Behold, Vivekananda still lives in the soul of his Mother and in the souls of her children."

At the Belur Math, Mahatma Gandhi was heard to say that his whole life was an effort to bring into actions the ideas of Vivekananda.

Many years after Vivekananda's death, Rabindranath Tagore, a Nobel Poet Laureate told Romain Rolland,

"If you want to know India, study Vivekananda. In him everything is positive and nothing negative."

The French Nobel Laureate Romain Rolland writes.

"His words are great music, phrases in the style of Beethoven, stirring rhythms like the march of Händel choruses. I cannot touch these sayings of his, scattered as they are through the pages of books, at thirty years' distance, without receiving a thrill through my body like an electric shock. And what shocks, what transports, must have been produced when in burning words they issued from the lips of the hero!"

Vivekananda inspired Jamshedji Tata to set up Indian Institute of Science, one of India's finest Institutions. Abroad, he had some interactions with Max Müller. Scientist Nikola Tesla was one of those influenced by the Vedic philosophy teachings of the Swami Vivekananda. On November 11, 1995, a section of Michigan Avenue, one of the most prominent streets in Chicago, was formally renamed "Swami Vivekananda Way."

In many institutes, students have come together and formed organizations meant for promoting discussion of spiritual ideas and the practice of such high principles. Many of such organizations have adopted his name. One such group also exists at IIT Madras and is popularly known as Vivekananda

Study Circle. Another one exists at IIT Kanpur by the name Vivekananda Samiti. Additionally, Swami Vivekananda's ideas and teachings have carried on globally, being practiced in institutions all over the world.

In 2011, during the anti-corruption Lokpal bill movement, the prominent figure and Gandhian activist Anna Hazare repeatedly mentioned that he was greatly inspired by Swami Vivekananda's thoughts.

Works

Vivekananda left a body of philosophical works (see Vivekananda's complete works). Vivekananda observed that the billions of people on the earth could be classified into four basic types-those who were in constant activity, or the worker; those who were driven by their inner urge to achieve something in life, or the lover; those who tended to analyze the working of their minds, or the mystic and those who weighed everything with reason, or the philosopher. His books (compiled from lectures given around the world) on the four Yogas (Karma yoga for the worker, Bhakti yoga for the lover, Raja yoga for the mystic, and Gyan yoga for the philosopher) are very influential and still seen as fundamental texts for anyone interested in the Hindu practice of Yoga. His letters are of great literary and spiritual value. He was also considered a very good singer and a poet. By the time of his death, he had composed many songs including his favorite Kali, the Mother. He used humour for his teachings and was also an excellent cook. His language is very free flowing. His own

Bengali writings stand testimony to the fact that he believed that words-spoken or written-should be for making things easier to understand rather than show off the speaker or writer's knowledge.

20

Tulsidas

Tulsidas, (1497/1532 –1623) was a Hindu poet-saint, reformer and philosopher renowned for his devotion for the god Rama. A composer of several popular works, he is best known for being the author of the epic Ramcharitmanas, a retelling of the Sanskrit Ramayana in the vernacular Awadhi, which is a popular Hindu scripture often referred to as the Bible of North India. Tulsidas was acclaimed in his lifetime to be a reincarnation of Valmiki, the composer of the original Ramayana in Sanskrit. He is also considered to be the composer of the Hanuman Chalisa, a popular devotional hymn dedicated to Hanuman, the divine monkey helper and devotee of Rama. Tulsidas lived permanently and died in the city of Varanasi. The Tulsi Ghat in Varnasi is named after him. He founded the Sankatmochan Temple dedicated to Hanuman in Varanasi, believed to stand at the place where he had the sight of Hanuman. Tulsidas started the Ramlila plays, a folk-theatre adaption of the Ramayana. He has been acclaimed as one of the greatest poets in Hindi, Indian, and world literature. The impact of Tulsidas and his works on the art, culture and society in India is widespread and is seen to date in vernacular language, Ramlila plays, Hindustani classical music, popular music, and television series.

Transliteration and Etymology

The Sanskrit name of Tulsidas can be transliterated in two ways. Using the IAST transliteration scheme, the name is written as Tulasidasa, as pronounced in Sanskrit. Using the Hunterian transliteration scheme, it is written as Tulsidas, as pronounced in Hindi. The name is a compound of two Sanskrit words: Tulasi, which is an Indian variety of the basil plant considered auspicious by Vaishnavas (devotees of god Vishnu and his avatars like Rama), and Dasa, which means a slave or servant and by extension, a devotee. Tulsidas, thus means a servant of the plant Tulsi.

Life

Sources

Tulsidas himself has given only a few facts and hints about events of his life in various works. Till late nineteenth century, the two widely known ancient sources on Tulsidas' life were the Bhaktamal composed by Nabhadas between 1583 and 1639, and a commentary on Bhaktamal titled Bhaktirasbodhini composed by Priyadas in 1712. Nabhadas was a contemporary of Tulsidas and wrote a six-line stanza on Tulsidas describing him as an incarnation of Valmiki. Priyadas' work was composed around a hundred years after the death of Tulsidas and had eleven additional stanzas, describing seven miracles or spiritual experiences from the life of Tulsidas. During the 1920s, two more ancient biographies of Tulsidas were published based on old manuscripts – the Mula Gosain Charit composed by Veni Madhav Das in 1630 and the Gosain Charit composed by Dasanidas (also known as Bhavanidas) around 1770. Veni Madhav Das was a disciple and contemporary of Tulsidas and his work gave a new date for Tulsidas' birth. The work by Bhavanidas presented more narratives in greater detail as compared to the work by Priyadas. In the 1950s a fifth ancient account was published based on an old manuscript, the Gautam Chandrika composed by Krishnadatta Misra of Varanasi in 1624. Krishnadatta Misra's father was a close companion of Tulsidas. The accounts published later are not considered authentic by some modern scholars, whereas some other scholars have been unwilling to dismiss them. Together, these five works form a set of traditional biographies on which modern biographies of Tulsidas are based.

Incarnation of Valmiki

Tulsidas is believed to be a reincarnation of Valmiki. In the Hindu scripture Bhavishyottar Purana, the god Shiva tells his wife Parvati how Valmiki, who got a boon from Hanuman to sing the glory of Rama in vernacular language, will incarnate in future in the Kali Yuga (the present and last Yuga or epoch within a cycle of four Yugas).

"O Goddess [Parvati]! Valmiki will become Tulsidas in the Kali age, and will compose this narrative of Rama in the vernacular language. Bhavishyottar Purana, Pratisarga Parva, 4.20"

Nabhadas wrote in the Bhaktamal (literally, the Garland of Saints) that Tulsidas was the incarnation of Valmiki in the Kali Yuga. The Ramanandi sect believes that it was Valmiki himself who incarnated as Tulsidas in the Kali Yuga.

According to a traditional account, Hanuman went to Valmiki several times to hear him sing the Ramayana, but Valmiki turned down the request saying that Hanuman being a monkey was unworthy of hearing the epic. After the victory of Rama over Ravana, Hanuman went to the Himalayas to continue his worship of Rama. There he scripted a play version of the Ramayana called Mahanataka or Hanuman Nataka engraved on the Himalayan rocks using his nails. When Valmiki saw the play written by Hanuman, he anticipated that the beauty of the Maha Nataka would eclipse his own Ramayana. On Valmiki's request, Hanuman cast all the rocks into the ocean, some parts of which are available today as Hanuman Nataka. After this, Valmiki was instructed by Hanuman to take birth as Tulsidas and compose the Ramayana in the vernacular.

Early Life

Birth

Tulsidas was born on the seventh day of the bright half of the lunar Hindu month Shraavana (July–August). Although as many as seven places are mentioned as his birth-place, most scholars identify the place with Rajapur (Chitrakuta), a village on the banks of the Yamuna river in modern-day Uttar Pradesh. His parents were Hulsi and Atmaram Dubey. Most sources identify him as a Saryupareen Brahmin of the Parashar Gotra (lineage), although some sources claim he was a Kanyakubja or Sanadhya Brahmin.

There is difference of opinion among biographers regarding the year of birth of Tulsidas. Many sources rely on Veni Madhav Das' account in the Mula Gosain Charita, which gives the year of Tulsidas' birth as Vikrami Samvat 1554 (1497 CE). These sources include Shivlal Pathak, popular editions of Ramcharitmanas (Gita Press, Naval Kishore Press and Venkateshvar Press), Edwin Greaves, Hanuman Prasad Poddar, Ramanand Sarasvati, Ayodhyanath Sharma, Ramchandra Shukla, Narayandas, and Rambhadracharya. A second group of biographers led by Sant Tulsi Sahib of Hathras and Sir George Grierson give the year as Vikram 1589 (1532 CE). These biographers include Ramkrishna Gopal Bhandarkar, Ramghulam Dwivedi, James Lochtefeld, Swami Sivananda and others. A third small group of authors which includes H. H. Wilson, Garse De Tasse and Krishnadatta Mishra gives the year as Vikram 1600 (1543 CE).

The year 1497 appears in most current-day biographies and in popular culture. Biographers who disagree with this year argue that it makes the life span of Tulsidas equal 126 years, which in their opinion is unlikely if not impossible. In contrast, Ramchandra Shukla says that an age of 126 is not impossible for Mahatmas (great souls) like Tulsidas. The Government of India and provincial governments celebrated the 500th birth anniversary of Tulsidas in the year 1997 CE, according to the year of Tulsidas' birth in popular culture.

Childhood

Legend goes that Tulsidas was born after staying in the womb for 12 months, he had all 32 teeth in his mouth at birth, his health and looks were like that of a five-year old boy, and he did not cry at the time of his birth but uttered Rama instead. He was therefore named Rambola (literally, he who uttered Rama), as Tulsidas himself states in Vinayapatrika. As per the Mula Gosain Charita, he was born under the Abhuktamula constellation, which according to Jyotisha (Hindu astrology) causes immediate danger to the life of the father. Due to the inauspicious events at the time of his birth, he was abandoned by his parents on the fourth night, sent away with Chuniya (some sources call her Muniya), a female servant of Hulsi. In his works Kavitavali and Vinayapatrika, Tulsidas attests to his parents abandoning him after birth due to an inauspicious astrological configuration.

Chuniya took the child to her village of Haripur and looked after him for five and a half years after which she passed away. Rambola was left to fend for himself as an impoverished orphan, and wandered from door to door begging for alms. It is believed that the goddess Parvati assumed the form of a Brahmin woman and fed Rambola every day.

Initiation from Guru and Learning

At the age of five years, Rambola was adopted by Narharidas, a Vaishnava ascetic of Ramananda's monastic order who is believed to be the fourth disciple of Ramananda, or alternately, the disciple of Anantacharya. Rambola was given the Virakta Diksha (Vairagi initiation) with the new name of Tulsidas. Tulsidas narrates the dialogue that took place during the first meeting with his guru in a passage in the Vinayapatrika. When he was seven years old, his Upanayana ("sacred thread ceremony") was performed by Narharidas on the fifth day of the bright half of the month of Magha (January–February) at Ayodhya, a pilgrimage-site related to Rama. Tulsidas started his learning at Ayodhya. After some time, Narharidas took him to a particular Varaha Kshetra (a holy place with temple dedicated to Varaha-the boar avatar of Vishnu), where he first narrated the Ramayana to Tulsidas. Tulsidas mentions this in the Ramcharitmanas.

"And then, I heard the same narrative from my Guru in a Sukarkhet (Varaha Kshetra). I did not understand it then, since I was totally without cognition in childhood. Ramcharitmanas 1.30 (ka)."

Most authors identify the Varaha Kshetra referred to by Tulsidas with the Varaha temple on the second entrance of the pilgrimage of Kamadgiri in Chitrakuta. Some biographers believe this Sukarkshetra is the Soron Varaha Kshetra in modern-day Kanshi Ram Nagar, while some others believe it to be Paska-Rajapur Varaha Kshetra in current-day Gonda. Tulsidas further mentions in the Ramcharitmanas that his guru repeatedly narrated the Ramayana to him, which led him to understand it somewhat.

Tulsidas later came to the sacred city of Varanasi and studied Sanskrit grammar, four Vedas, six Vedangas, Jyotisha and the six schools of Hindu philosophy over a period of 15–16 years from guru Shesha Sanatana who was based at the Pancaganga Ghat in Varanasi. Shesha Sanatana was a friend of Narharidas and a renowned scholar on literature and philosophy. After completing his studies, Tulsidas came back to his birthplace

Rajapur with the permission of Shesha Sanatana. Here he found that his family was no more, with his parents dead. Tulsidas performed the Shraddha ceremony (which deals with giving offerings to the ancestors) of his parents. He started living in his ancestral home and narrating the Katha ("story") of Ramayana in Chitrakuta.

Marriage and Renunciation

According to the Mula Gosain Charita and some other works, Tulsidas was married to Ratnavali on the thirteenth day of the bright half of the Jyeshta month (May–June) in Vikram 1583 (1526 CE). Ratnavali was the daughter of Dinbandhu Pathak, a Brahmin of the Bharadwaja Gotra, who belonged to Mahewa village of Kaushambi district. They had a son named Tarak who died as a toddler. Once when Tulsidas had gone to a Hanuman temple, Ratnavali went to her father's home with her brother. When Tulsidas came to know this, he swam across the Yamuna river in the night to meet his wife. Ratnavali chided Tulsidas for this, and remarked that if Tulsidas was even half as devoted to God as he was to her body of flesh and blood, he would have been redeemed. Tulsidas left her instantly and left for the holy city of Prayag. Here, he renounced the Grihastha (householder's life) stage and became a Sadhu (Hindu ascetic).

Some authors consider the marriage episode of Tulsidas to be a later interpolation and maintain that he was a bachelor. They include Rambhadracharya, who interprets two verses in the Vinayapatrika and Hanuman Bahuka to mean that Tulsidas never married and was a Sadhu from childhood.

Later Life

Travels

After renunciation, Tulsidas spent most of his time at Varanasi, Prayag, Ayodhya, and Chitrakuta but visited many other nearby and far-off places. He travelled across India to many places, studying different people, meeting saints and Sadhus and meditating. The Mula Gosain Charita gives an account of his travels to the four pilgrimages of Hindus (Badrinath, Dwarka, Puri and Rameshwaram) and the Himalayas. He visited the Manasarovar lake in current-day Tibet, where tradition holds that he had Darshan (sight) of Kakabhushundi, the crow who is one of the four narrators in the Ramcharitmanas.

Darshan of Hanuman

Tulsidas hints at several places in his works, that he had met face to face with Hanuman and Rama. The detailed account of his meetings with Hanuman and Rama are given in the Bhaktirasbodhini of Priyadas. According to Priyadas' account, Tulsidas used to visit the woods outside Varanasi for his morning ablutions with a water pot. On his return to the city, he used to offer the remaining water to a certain tree. This quenched the thirst of a Preta (a type of ghost believed to be ever thirsty for water), who appeared to Tulsidas and offered him a boon. Tulsidas said he wished to see Rama with his eyes, to which the Preta responded that it was beyond him. However, the Preta said that he could guide Tulsidas to Hanuman, who could grant the boon Tulsidas asked for. The Preta told Tulsidas that Hanuman comes everyday disguised in the mean attire of a leper to listen to his Katha, he is the first to arrive and last to leave.

That evening Tulsidas noted that the first listener to arrive at his discourse was an old leper, who sat at the end of the gathering. After the Katha was over, Tulsidas quietly followed the leper to the woods. In the woods, at the spot where the Sankat Mochan Temple stands today, Tulsidas firmly fell at the leper's feet, shouting "I know who you are" and "You cannot escape me." At first the leper feigned ignorance but Tulsidas did not relent. Then the leper revealed his original form of Hanuman and blessed Tulsidas. When granted a boon, Tulsidas told Hanuman that he wanted to see Rama face to face. Hanuman told him to go to Chitrakuta where he would see Rama with his own eyes.

At the beginning of the Ramcharitmanas, Tulsidas bows down to a particular Preta and asks for his grace (Ramcharitmanas, Doha 1.7). According to Rambhadracharya, this is the same Preta which led Tulsidas to Hanuman.

Darshan of Rama

As per Priyadas' account, Tulsidas followed the instruction of Hanuman and started living in an Ashram at Ramghat in Chitrakuta. One day Tulsidas went to perform the Parikrama (circumambulation) of the Kamadgiri mountain. He saw two princes, one dark and the other fair, dressed in green robes pass by mounted on horsebacks. Tulsidas was enraptured at the sight, however he could not recognize them and took his eyes off them. Later Hanuman asked Tulsidas if he saw Rama and his brother Lakshmana on horses. Tulsidas was disappointed and repentful. Hanuman assured Tulsidas that he would have the sight of Rama once again the next morning. Tulsidas recalls this incident in a song of the Gitavali and laments how "his eyes turned his own enemies" by staying fixed to the ground and how everything happened in a trice.

On the next morning, Wednesday, the new-moon day of Magha, Vikram 1607 (1551 CE) or 1620 (1564 CE) as per some sources, Rama again appeared to Tulsidas, this time as a child. Tulsidas was making sandalwood paste when a child came and asked for a sandalwood Tilaka (a religious mark on the forehead). This time Hanuman gave a hint to Tulsidas and he had a full view of Rama. Tulsidas was so charmed that he forgot about the sandalwood. Rama took the sandalwood paste and put a Tilaka himself on his forehead and Tulsidas' forehead before disappearing.

In a verse in the Vinayapatrika, Tulsidas alludes to a certain "miracle at Chitrakuta," and thanks Rama for what he did for him at Chitrakuta. Some biographers conclude that the deed of Rama at Chitrakuta referred to by Tulsidas is the Darshan of Rama.

Darshan of Yajgavalkya and Bharadwaja

In Vikram 1628 (1572 CE), Tulsidas left Chitrakuta for Ayodhya where he stayed during the Magha Mela (the annual fair in January). Six days after the Mela ended, he had the Darshan of the sages Yajgavalkya and Bharadwaja under a banyan tree. In one of the four dialogues in the Ramcharitmanas, Yajgavalkya is the speaker and Bharadwaja the listener. Tulsidas describes the meeting between Yajgnavalkya and Bharadvaja after a Magha Mela festival in the Ramcharitmanas, it is this meeting where Yajnavalkya narrates the Ramcharitmanas to Bharadwaja.

Attributed Miracles

In Priyadas' biography, Tulsidas is attributed with the power of working miracles. In one such miracle, he is believed to have brought back a dead Brahmin to life. While the Brahmin was being taken for cremation, his widow bowed down to Tulsidas on the way who addressed her as Saubhagyavati (a woman whose husband is alive). The widow told Tulsidas her husband had just passed away, so his words could not be true. Tulsidas said that the word has passed his lips and so he would restore the dead man to life. He asked everybody present to close their eyes and utter the name of Rama, on doing which the dead Brahmin was raised back to life.

In another miracle described by Priyadas, the emperor of Delhi summoned Tulsidas on hearing of his bringing back a dead man to life. Tulsidas was asked to perform a miracle, which Tulsidas declined by saying "It's a lie, all I know is Rama." The emperor imprisoned Tulsidas saying, "We will see this Rama." Tulsidas prayed to Hanuman and an army of monkeys wreaked havoc in all corners of Delhi, entering each home and the emperor's harem, scratching people and throwing bricks from ramparts. An old Hafiz told the emperor that this was the miracle of the imprisoned Fakir. The emperor fell at Tulsidas' feet, released him and apologized. Tulsidas stopped the menace of monkeys and asked the emperor to abandon the place. The emperor agreed and moved his fort to a new location.

"O Lord, how shall I describe today's splendour, for you appear auspicious. Tulsidas will bow down his head when you take the bow and the arrow in your hands."

When Tulsidas recited this couplet, the idol of Krishna holding the flute and stick in hands changed to the idol of Rama holding the bow and arrow in hands. Some authors have expressed doubts on the couplet being composed by Tulsidas.

Literary Life

Tulsidas started composing poetry in Sanskrit in Varanasi on the Prahlada Ghat. Tradition holds that all the verses that he composed during the day, would get lost in the night. This happened daily for eight days. On the eighth night, Shiva-whose famous Kashi Vishwanath Temple is located in Varanasi-is believed to have ordered Tulsidas in a dream to compose poetry in the vernacular instead of Sanskrit. Tulsidas woke up and saw both Shiva and Parvati who blessed him. Shiva ordered Tulsidas to go to Ayodhya and compose poetry in Awadhi. Shiva also predicted that Tulsidas' poetry would fructify like the Sama Veda. In the Ramcharitmanas, Tulsidas hints at having the Darshan of Shiva and Parvati in both dream and awakened state.

Composition of Ramcharitmanas

In the year Vikram 1631 (1575 CE), Tulsidas started composing the Ramcharitmanas in Ayodhya on Tuesday, Ramnavami day (ninth day of the bright half of the Chaitra month, which is the birthday of Rama). Tulsidas himself attests this date in the Ramcharitmanas. He composed the epic over two years, seven months and twenty-six days, and completed the work in Vikram 1633 (1577 CE) on the Vivaha Panchami day (fifth day of the bright half of the Margashirsha month, which commemorates the wedding of Rama and his wife Sita).

Tulsidas came to Varanasi and recited the Ramcharitmanas to Shiva (Vishwanath) and Parvati (Annapurna) at the Kashi Vishwanath Temple. A popular legend goes that the Brahmins of Varanasi, who were critical of Tulsidas for having rendered the Sanskrit Ramayana in the vernacular, decided to test the worth of the work. A manuscript of the Ramcharitmanas was kept at the bottom of pile of Sanskrit scriptures in the sanctum sanctorum of the Vishvanath temple in the night, and the doors of the sanctum sanctorum were locked. In the morning when the doors were opened, the Ramcharitmanas was found at the top of the pile. The words Satyam Shivam Sundaram were inscribed on the manuscript with the signature of Shiva. The words were also heard by the people present.

Per traditional accounts, some Brahmins of Varanasi were still not satisfied, and sent two thieves to steal the manuscript. The thieves tried to break into the Ashram of Tulsidas, but were confronted by two guards with bows and arrows, of dark and fair complexion. The thieves had a change of heart and came to Tulsidas in the morning to ask who the two guards were. Believing that the two guards could be none other than Rama and Lakshmana, Tulsidas was aggrieved to know that they were guarding his home at night. He sent the manuscript of Ramcahritmanas to his friend Rai Todar Mal, the finance minister of Akbar, and donated all his money. The thieves were reformed and became devotees of Rama.

Last Compositions

Around Vikram 1664 (1607 CE), Tulsidas was afflicted by acute pain all over his body, especially in his arms. He then composed the Hanuman Bahuk, where he describes his bodily pain and suffering in several stanzas. He was relieved of his pain after this composition. Later he was also afflicted by Bartod boils, which may have been the cause of his death.

The Vinaypatrika is considered as the last compositions of Tulsidas, believed to be written when Kali Yuga started troubling him. In this work of 279 stanzas, he beseeches Rama to give him Bhakti ("devotion"), and to accept his petition. Tulsidas attests in the last stanza of Vinaypatrika that Rama himself signed the manuscript of the work. The 45th stanza of the Vinaypatrika is sung as the evening Aarti by many Hindus.

Death

Tulsidas passed away at the Assi Ghat on the bank of the river Ganga in the Shraavan (July–August) month of the year Vikram 1680 (1623 CE). Like the year of his birth, traditional accounts and biographers do not agree on the exact date of his death. Different sources give the date as the third day of the bright half, seventh day of the bright half, or the third day of the dark half.

Works

Twelve works are widely considered by biographers to be written by Tulsidas, six major works and six minor works. Based on the language of the works, they have been classified into two groups as follows–

1. Awadhi works – Ramcharitmanas, Ramlala Nahachhu, Barvai Ramayan, Parvati Mangal, Janaki Mangal and Ramagya Prashna.
2. Braja works – Krishna Gitavali, Gitavali, Kavitavali, Dohavali, Vairagya Sandipani and Vinaya Patrika.

Besides these twelve works, four more works are popularly believed to be composed by Tulsidas which include Hanuman Chalisa, Hanuman Ashtak, Hanuman Bahuk and Tulsi Satsai.

Ramcharitmanas

Ramacharitamanas (1574–1576), literally The Holy Lake of Acts of Rama, is the Awadhi rendering of the Ramayana narrative. It is the longest and earliest work of Tulsidas, and draws from various sources including the Ramayana of Valmiki, the Adhyatma Ramayana, the Prasannaraghava and Hanuman Nataka. The work consists of around 12,800 lines divided into 1073 stanzas, which are groups of Chaupais separated by Dohas or Sorthas. It is divided into seven books (Kands) like the Ramayana of Valmiki, and is around one-third of the size of Valmiki's Ramayana. The work is composed in 18 metres which include ten Sanskrit metres (Anushtup, Shardulvikridit, Vasantatilaka, Vamshashta, Upajati, Pramanika, Malini, Sragdhara, Rathoddhata and Bhujangaprayata) and eight Prakrit metres (Soratha, Doha, Chaupai, Harigitika, Tribhangi, Chaupaiya, Trotaka and Tomara). It is popularly referred to as Tulsikrit Ramayana, literally The Ramayana composed by Tulsidas. The work has been acclaimed as "the living sum of Indian culture," "the tallest tree in the magic garden of medieval Indian poesy," "the greatest book of all devotional literature," "the Bible of Northern India," and "the best and most trustworthy guide to the popular living faith of its people."

Several manuscripts of the Ramcharitmanas are claimed to have been written down by Tulsidas himself. Grierson wrote in the late nineteenth century, two copies of the epic were said to have existed in the poet's own handwriting. One manuscript was kept at Rajapur, of which only the Ayodhyakand is left now, which bears marks of water. A legend goes that the manuscript was stolen and thrown into Yamuna river when the thief was being pursued, and only the second book of the epic could be rescued. Grierson wrote that the other copy was at Malihabad in Lucknow district, of which only one leaf was missing. Another manuscript of the Ayodhyakanda claimed to be in the poet's own hand exists at Soron in Etah district, one of the places claimed to be Tulsidas' birthplace. One manuscript of Balakanda, dated Samvat 1661, nineteen years before the poet's death, claimed to be corrected by Tulsidas, is at Ayodhya. Some other ancient manuscripts are found in Varanasi, including one in possession of the Maharaja of Benares that was written in Vikram 1704 (1647), twenty-four years after the death of Tulsidas.

Other major works

The five major works of Tulsidas apart from Ramcharitmanas include–

1. Dohavali, literally Collection of Dohas, is a work consisting of 573 miscellaneous Doha and Sortha verses mainly in Braja with some verses in Awadhi. The verses are aphorisms on topics related to tact, political wisdom, righteousness and the purpose of life. 85 Dohas from this work are also found in the Ramcharitmanas, 35 in Ramagya Prashna, two in Vairagya Sandipani and some in Rama Satsai, another work of 700 Dohas attributed to Tulsidas.

2. Kavitavali or Kavitta Ramayan (1608–1614), literally Collection of Kavittas, is a Braja rendering of the Ramayana, composed entirely in metres of the Kavitta family – Kavitta, Savaiya, Ghanakshari and Chhappaya. It consists of 325 verses including 183 verses in the Uttarkand. Like the Ramcharitmanas, it is divided into seven Kands or books and many episodes in this work are different from the Ramcharitmanas.

3. Gitavali, literally Collection of Songs, is a Braja rendering of the Ramayana in songs. All the verses are set to Ragas of classical music and suitable for singing. It consists of 328 songs divided into seven Kands or books. Many episodes of the Ramayana are elaborated while many others are abridged

4. Krishna Gitavali or Krishnavali, literally Collection of Songs to Krishna, is a collection of 61 songs in honor of Krishna in Braja. There are 32 songs devoted to the childhood sports (Balalila) and Rasa Lila of Krishna, 27 songs form the dialogue between Krishna and Uddhava, and two songs describe the episode of disrobing of Draupadi.

5. Vinaya Patrika, literally Petition of Humility, is a Braja work consisting of 279 stanzas or hymns. The stanzas form a petition in the court of Rama asking for Bhakti. It is considered to be the second best work of Tulsidas after the Ramcharitmanas, and is regarded as important from the viewpoints of philosophy, erudition, and eulogistic and poetic style of Tulsidas. The first 43 hymns are

addressed to various deities and Rama's courtiers and attendants, and remaining are addressed to Rama.

Minor works

Minor works of Tulsidas include–

1. Barvai Ramayana, literally The Ramayana in Barvai metre, is an abridged rendering of the Ramayana in Awadhi. The works consists of 69 verses composed in the Barvai metre, and is divided into seven Kands or books. The work is based on a psychological framework.
2. Parvati Mangal, literally The marriage of Parvati, is an Awadhi work of 164 verses describing the penance of Parvati and the marriage of Parvati and Shiva. It consists of 148 verses in the Sohar metre and 16 verses in the Harigitika metre.
3. Janaki Mangal, literally The marriage of Sita, is an Awadhi work of 216 verses describing the episode of marriage of Sita and Rama from the Ramayana. The work includes 192 verses in the Hamsagati metre and 24 verses in the Harigitika metres. The narrative differs from the Ramcharitmanas at several places.
4. Ramalala Nahachhu, literally The Nahachhu ceremony of the child Rama, is an Awadhi work of 20 verses composed in the Sohar metre. The Nahachhu ceremony involves cutting the nails of the feet before the Hindu Samskaras (rituals) of Chudakarana, Upanayana, Vedarambha, Samavartana or Vivaha. In the work, events take place in the city of Ayodhya, so it is considered to

describe the Nahachhu before Upanayana, Vedarambha and Samavartana.

5. Ramagya Prashna, literally Querying the Will of Rama, is an Awadhi work related to both Ramayana and Jyotisha (astrology). It consists of seven Kands or books, each of which is divided into seven Saptakas or Septets of seven Dohas each. Thus it contains 343 Dohas in all. The work narrates the Ramayana non-sequentially, and gives a method to look up the Shakuna (omen or portent) for astrological predictions.
6. Vairagya Sandipini, literally Kindling of Detachment, is a philosophical work of 60 verses in Braja which describe the state of Gyan (realization) and Vairagya (dispassion), the nature and greatness of saints, and moral conduct. It consists of 46 Dohas, 2 Sorathas and 12 Chaupai metres.

Popularly Attributed Works

The following four works are popularly attributed to Tulsidas–

1. Hanuman Chalisa, literally, Forty Verses to Hanuman, is an Awadhi work of 40 Chaupais and two Dohas and is a prayer to Hanuman. Although some authors do not consider it to be authored by Tulsidas, it is attributed to Tulsidas universally in popular belief and also contains the signature line of Tulsidas. It is one of the most read short religious texts in northern India, and is recited by millions of Hindus on Tuesdays and Saturdays. It is believed to have been uttered by Tulsidas in a state of Samadhi at the Kumbh Mela in Haridwar.

2. Sankatmochan Hanumanashtak, literally Eight verses for Hanuman, the Remover of Afflictions, is an Awadhi work of eight verses in the Mattagajendra metre, devoted to Hanuman. It is believed to have been composed by Tulsidas on the occasion of the founding of the Sankatmochan Temple in Varanasi. The work is usually published along with Hanuman Chalisa.
3. Hanuman Bahuka, literally The Arm of Hanuman, is a Braja work of 44 verses believed to have been composed by Tulsidas when he suffered acute pain in his arms at an advanced age. Tulsidas describes the pain in his arms and also prays to Hanuman for freedom from the suffering. The work has two, one, five and 36 verses respectively in the Chhappaya, Jhulna, Savaiya and Ghanakshari metre.
4. Tulsi Satsai, literally Seven Hundred Verses by Tulsidas, is a work in both Awadhi and Braja and contains 747 Dohas divided in seven Sargas or cantos. The verses are same as those in Dohavali and Ramagya Prashna but the order is different.

Doctrine

The philosophy and principles of Tulsidas are found across his works, and are especially outlined in the dialogue between Kakbhushundi and Garuda in the Uttar Kand of the Ramcharitmanas. Tulsidas' doctrine has been described as an assimilation and reconciliation of the diverse tenets and cultures of Hinduism. At the beginning of the Ramcharitmanas, Tulsidas says that his work is in accordance with various scriptures-the Puranas, Vedas, Upavedas, Tantra and Smriti.

Ram Chandra Shukla in his critical work Hindi Sahitya Ka Itihaas elaborates on Tulsidas' Lokmangal as the doctrine for social upliftment which made this great poet immortal and comparable to any other world littérateur.

Nirguna and Saguna Brahma

As per Tulsidas, the Nirguna Brahman (quality-less impersonal God) and Saguna Brahma (personal God with qualities) are one and the same. It is the devotion (Bhakti) of the devotee that forces the Nirguna Brahman which is quality-less, formless, invisible and unborn, to become Saguna Brahman with qualities. Tulsidas gives the example of water, snow and hail to explain this – the substance is the same in all three, but the same formless water solidifies to become hail or a mountain of snow – both of which have a form. Tulsidas also gives the simile of a lake – the Nirguna Brahman is like the lake with just water, while the Saguna Brahman is a lake resplendent with blooming lotuses. In the Uttar Kand of Ramcharitmanas, Tulsidas describes in detail a debate between Kakbhushundi and Lomasha about whether God is Nirguna (as argued by Lomasha adhering to monism) or Saguna (as argued by Kakbhushundi adhering to dualism). Kakbhushundi repeatedly refutes all the arguments of Lomasha, to the point when Lomasha becomes angry and curses Kakbhushundi to be a crow. Lomasha repents later when Kakbhushundi happily accepts the curse but refuses to give up the Bhakti of Rama, the Saguna Brahman. Though Tulsidas holds both aspects of God to be equal, he favours the qualified Saguna aspect and the devotees of the highest category in the Ramcharitmanas repeatedly ask for the qualified Saguna aspect of Rama to dwell in their mind. Tulsidas has at multiple places vigorously contradicted the denial of Avatar by Kabir. In several of his works, Kabir had said that the actual Rama is not the son of Dasharatha. In the Balkand of Ramcharitmanas, Shiva tells Parvati – those who say that the Rama whom the Vedas sing of and whom the sages contemplate on is different from the Rama of Raghu's race, are possessed by the devil of delusion and do not know the difference between truth and falsehood.

The name of Rama

At the beginning of the Ramcharitmanas, there is a section devoted to the veneration of the name of Rama. As per Tulsidas, repeating the name of Rama is the only means to attain God in the Kali age where the means suited for other ages like meditation, Karma, and Puja are ineffective. He says in Kavitavali that his own redemption is because of the power, glory and majesty of the name of Rama. In a couplet in the Gitavali, Tulsidas says that wishing for liberation without refuge in the name of Rama is like wishing to climb to the sky by holding on to the falling rain. In his view, the name of Rama is greater than both Nirguna and Saguna aspects of God – it controls both of them and is illuminates both like a bilingual interpreter. In a verse in the Dohavali, Tulsidas says that the Nirguna Brahma resides in his heart, the Saguna Brahman resides in his eyes and the name of Rama resides on his tongue, as if a radiant gemstone is kept between the lower and upper halves of a golden casket. He holds that Rama is superior to all other names of God, and argues that ra and ma being are the only two consonants that are written above all other consonants in the conjunct form in Sanskrit because they are the two sounds in the word Rama.

Rama as Brahma

At several places in Tulsidas' works, Rama is seen to be the higher than Vishnu and not as an avatar of Vishnu, which is the general portrayal of Rama. In the episode of the delusion of Sati in Ramcharitmanas, Sati sees many a Shiva, Brahma and Vishnu serving Rama and bowing at his feet. When Manu and Shatarupa perform penance, they crave to see that Supreme Lord "from a part of whose being emanate a number of Shivas, Brahmas and Vishnus." Brahma, Vishnu and Shiva come to them many times tempting them with a boon, but Manu and Shatarupa do not stop their penance. They are finally satisfied only by the appearance of Rama, on whose left side is Sita, from a part of whom are born "countless Lakshmis, Umas (Parvatis) and Brahmanis (Sarasvatis)." In the episode of marriage of Sita and Rama in Balkand, the trio of Brahma, Vishnu and Shiva are present-Brahma is astounded as he finds nowhere anything that is his own handiwork, while Vishnu is enchanted with Lakhmi on seeing Rama. In the Sundarkand, Hanuman tells Ravana that Brahma, Vishnu and Shiva can create, preserve and destroy by the might of Rama. In the Lanka and, Tulsidas presents the universe as the cosmic form of Rama, in which Shiva is the consciousness, Brahma is the reason and Vishnu is his intelligence. As per Tulsidas, Rama is not only an avatar, but also the source of avatars – Krishna is also an Avatar of Rama.

In the opinion of Urvashi Soorati, the Rama of Tulasidasa is an amalgamation of Vishnu who takes avatars, Vishnu in the abode of Ksheera Sagara, Brahma and the Para manifestation of the Pancharatra. Macfie concludes that Tulsidas makes a "double claim," i.e. Rama is an incarnation of both Vishnu and Brahma. In the words of Lutgendorf, Tulsidas' Rama is at once "Valmiki's exemplary prince, the cosmic Vishnu of Puranas, and the transcendent brahma of the Advaitins."

Vedanta, World and Maya

In the Sundarkand of Ramcharitmanas, Tulsidas says that Rama is knowable by Vedanta.

As per Tulsidas, Rama is the efficient and material cause (Nimitta and Upadana) of the world, which is real since Rama is real. In several verses of the Ramcharitmanas, Tulsidas says that the animate and inanimate world is a manifestation of Rama, and the universe is the cosmic form of Rama. Authors interpret these verses to mean that the world is real according to Tulsidas, in keeping with the Vishishtadvaita philosophy of Ramanuja. However, at some places in the Ramcharitmanas and Kavitavali, Tulsidas compares the world to a night or a dream and says it is Mithya (false or unreal). Some commentators interpret these verses to mean that in Tulsidas' opinion the world is unreal as per the Vivartavada doctrine of Adi Shankara, while some others interpret them to mean that the world is transient yet real as per the Satkhyativada doctrine of Ramananda. Uday Bhanu Singh concludes that in Tulsidas' view, the world is essentially the form of Rama and appears to be different from Rama due to Maya. Its visible form is transient, which is what Tulsidas means by Mithya. In the Vinayapatrika, Tulsidas says that the world in itself is neither true (Satya), nor false (Asatya), nor both true and false together (Satyasatya) – one who casts aside all these three illusions, knows oneself. This has been interpreted to mean that as per Tulsidas, the entire world is a Lila of Rama. At the beginning of the Ramcharitmanas, Tulsidas performs Samasti Vandana (obeisance to all beings) in which he bows down to the world also, saying it is "pervaded by" or "born out of" Sita and Rama. As per some verses in Ramcharitmanas and Vinaypatrika, when a Jiva (living being) knows the Self, Maya and Rama, it sees the world as being pervaded by Rama.

In the Balkand episode of the marriage of the princes of Ayodhya with the princesses of Mithila, Tulsidas presents a metaphor in which the four brides are compared with the four states of consciousness – the waking state (Jagrat), sleep with dreams (Swapna), dreamless sleep (Sushupti) and the fourth self-conscious state (Turiya). The four grooms are compared with the presiding divinity (Vibhu) of the four states – Vishva, Taijasa, Prajna and Brahma. Tulsidas says as the four states of consciousness with their presiding divinities reside in the mind of a Jiva, so the four brides with their grooms are resplendent in the same pavilion.

Tulsidas identifies Maya with Sita, the inseparable energy of Rama which takes avatar along with Rama. In his view, Maya is of two types – Vidya and Avidya. Vidya Maya is the cause of creation and the liberation of Jiva. Avidya Maya is the cause of illusion and bondage of the Jiva. The entire world is under the control of Maya. Maya is essentially the same but the two divisions are made for cognitive purposes, this view of Tulsidas is in accordance with Vaishnava teachers of Vedanta.

Views on other Hindu deities

As per Tulsidas, there is no incompatibility between devotion to Rama and attachment to Shiva. Tulsidas equates the Guru as an incarnation of Shiva, and a considerable part of the Balkand of Ramcharitmanas is devoted to the narrative of Shiva including the abandonment of Sati, the penance of Parvati, the burning of Kamadeva and the marriage of Parvati and Shiva. In addition, Tulsidas venerates the whole Hindu pantheon. The Ramcharitmanas begins with reverence of Ganesh, Sarasvati, Parvati, Shiva, the Guru, Valmiki and Hanuman. At the beginning of the Vinayapatrika, he bows to Ganesh, Surya, Shiva, Devi, Ganga, Yamuna, Varanasi and Chitrakoot, asking them for devotion towards Rama.

Bhakti

The Lord is to be approached by faith (bhakti) single minded devotion and surrender of self in perfect love, and all actions are to be purified of self-interest in contemplation of Him. Show love to all creatures, and thou wilt be happy; for when thou lovest all things, thou lovest the Lord, for He is all in all. The soul is from the Lord, and is submitted in this life to the bondage of works (karma); Mankind, in their obstinacy, keep binding themselves in the net of actions, and though they know and hear of the bliss of those who have faith in the Lord, they do not attempt the only means of release. The bliss to which the soul attains, by the extinction of desire, in the supreme home, is not absorption in the Lord, but union with Him in abiding individuality. This is emancipation (mukti) from the burden of birth and rebirth, and the highest happiness. But the practical end of all his writings is to inculcate bhakti addressed to Rama as the great means of salvation and emancipation from the chain of births and deaths, a salvation which is as free and open to men of the lowest caste as to Brahmins.

Critical Reception

From his time, Tulsidas has been acclaimed by Indian and Western scholars alike for his poetry and his impact on the Hindu society. Tulsidas mentions in his work Kavitavali that he was considered a great sage in the world. Madhusudana Sarasvati, one of the most acclaimed philosophers of the Advaita Vedanta tradition based in Varanasi and the composer of Advaitasiddhi, was a contemporary of Tulsidas. On reading the Ramcharitmanas, he was astonished and composed the following Sanskrit verse in praise of the epic and the composer.

Surdas, a devotee of Krishna and a contemporary of Tulsidas, called Tulsidas as Sant Shiromani (the highest jewel among holy men) in an eight-line verse extolling Ramcharitmanas and Tulsidas. Abdur Rahim Khankhana, famous Muslim poet who was one of the Navaratnas (nine-gems) in the court of the Mughal emperor Akbar, was a personal friend of Tulsidas. Rahim composed the following couplet describing the Ramcharitmanas of Tulsidas –

The historian Vincent Smith, the author of a biography of Tulsidas' contemporary Akbar, called Tulsidas as the greatest man of his age in India and greater than even Akbar himself. The Indologist and linguist Sir George Grierson called Tulsidas "the greatest leader of the people after the Buddha" and "the greatest of Indian authors of modern times;" and the epic

Ramcharitmanas "worthy of the greatest poet of any age." The work Ramcharitmanas has been called "the Bible of North India" by both nineteenth century Indologists including Ralph Griffith, who translated the four Vedas and Valmiki's Ramayana into English, and modern writers. Mahatma Gandhi held Tulsidas in high esteem and regarded the Ramcharitmanas as the "greatest book in all devotional literature." The Hindi poet Suryakant Tripathi 'Nirala' called Tulsidas "the most fragrant branch of flowers in the garden of the world's poetry, blossoming in the creeper of Hindi." Nirala considered Tulsidas to be a greater poet than Rabindranath Tagore, and in the same league as Kalidasa, Vyasa, Valmiki, Homer, Johann Wolfgang von Goethe and William Shakespeare. Edmour J. Babineau, author of the book Love and God and Social Duty in Ramacaritmanasa, says that if Tulsidas was born in Europe or the Americas, he would be considered a greater personality than William Shakespeare. In the words of the archaeologist F. R. Allchin, who translated Vinaypatrika and Kavitavali into English, "for people of a large part of North India Tulsidas claims reverence comparable to that accorded to Luther as translator of the Bible into the native German." Allchin also mentions that the work Ramcharitmanas has been compared to not only the Ramayana of Valmiki, but the Vedas themselves, the Bhagavad Gita, the Kuran and the Bible. Ernest Wood in his work An Englishman Defends Mother India considered the Ramcharitmanas to be "superior to the best books of the Latin and Greek languages." Tulsidas is also referred to as BhaktaœiromaGi, meaning the highest jewel among devotees.

Specifically about his poetry, Tulsidas has been called the "emperor of the metaphor" and one who excels in similes by several critics. The Hindi poet Ayodhyasingh Upadhyay 'Hariaudh' said of Tulsidas.

The Hindi poetess Mahadevi Verma said commenting on Tulsidas that in the turbulent Middle Ages, India got light from Tulsidas. She further went on to say that the Indian society as it exists today is an edifice built by Tulsidas, and the Rama as we know today is the Rama of Tulsidas.

21

Ved Vyasa

Vyasa is a central and revered figure in most Hindu traditions. He is also sometimes called Veda Vyasa, (the one who classified the Vedas into four parts) or Krishna Dvaipayana (referring to his complexion and birthplace). He is the author as well as a character in the Mahabharata and considered to be the scribe of both the Vedas, and the supplementary texts such as the Puranas. A number of Vaishnava traditions regard him as an Avatar of Vishnu. Vyasa is sometimes conflated by some Vaishnavas with Badarayana, the author of the Vedanta Sutras. Vyasa is also considered to be one of the seven Chiranjivins (long lived, or immortals), who are still in existence according to general Hindu belief.

The festival of Guru Purnima, is dedicated to him, and also known as Vyasa Purnima as it is the day, which is believed to be his birthday and also the day he divided the Vedas.

In the Mahabharata

Vyasa appears for the first time as the author of, and an important character in the Mahabharata. He was the son of Satyavati, daughter of a ferryman or fisherman, and the wandering sage Parashara. He was born on an island in the river Yamuna. The place is named after him as Vedvyas, possibly the modern-day town of Kalpi in the Jalaun district of Uttar Pradesh. He was dark-complexioned and hence may be called by the name Krishna (black), and also the name Dwaipayana, meaning 'island-born.'

Vyasa was grandfather to the Kauravas and Pandavas. Their fathers, Dhritarashtra and Pandu, adopted as the sons of Vichitravirya by the royal family, were fathered by him. He had a third son, Vidura, by a serving maid.

Veda Vyasa

Hindus traditionally hold that Vyasa categorised the primordial single Veda into four. Hence he was called Veda Vyasa, or "Splitter of the Vedas," the splitting being a feat that allowed people to understand the divine knowledge of the Veda. The word vyasa means split, differentiate, or describe.

It has been debated whether Vyasa was a single person or a class of scholars who did the splitting. The Vishnu Purana has a theory about Vyasa. The Hindu view of the universe is that of a cyclic phenomenon that comes into existence and dissolves repeatedly. Each cycle is presided over by a number of Manus, one for each Manvantara, that has four ages, Yugas of declining virtues. The Dvapara Yuga is the third Yuga. The Vishnu Purana says:

In every third world age (Dvapara), Vishnu, in the person of Vyasa, in order to promote the good of mankind, divides the Veda, which is properly but one, into many portions. Observing the limited perseverance, energy, and application of mortals, he makes the Veda fourfold, to adapt it to their capacities; and the bodily form which he assumes, in order to effect that classification, is known by the name of Veda-vyasa. Of the different Vyasas in the present Manvantara and the branches which they have taught, you shall have an account. Twenty-eight times have the Vedas been arranged by the great Rishis in the Vaivasvata Manvantara... and consequently eight and twenty Vyasas have passed away; by whom, in the respective periods, the Veda has been divided into four. The first... distribution was made by Svayambhu (Brahma) himself; in the second, the arranger of the Veda (Vyasa) was Prajapati... (and so on up to twenty-eight).

Author of the Mahabharata

Vyasa is traditionally known as author of this epic. But he also features as an important character in it. His mother later married the king of Hastinapura, and had two sons. Both sons died without issue and hence their mother asked Vyasa to go to the beds of the wives of her dead son Vichitravirya.

Vyasa fathers the princes Dhritarashtra and Pandu by Ambika and Ambalika. Vyasa told them that they should come alone near him. First did Ambika, but because of shyness and fear she closed her eyes. Vyasa told Satyavati that this child would be blind. Later this child was named Dhritarashtra. Thus Satyavati sent Ambalika and warned her that she should remain calm. But Ambalika's face became pale because of fear. Vyasa told her that child would suffer from anaemia, and he would not be fit enough to rule the kingdom. Later this child was known as Pandu. Then Vyasa told Satyavati to send one of them again so that a healthy child can be born. This time Ambika and Ambalika sent a maid in the place of themselves. The maid was quite calm and composed, and she got a healthy child later named as Vidura. While these are his sons, another son Shuka, born of his wife, sage Jabali's daughter Pinjala (Vatika), is considered his true spiritual heir. He makes occasional appearances in the story as a spiritual guide to the young princes.

In the first book of the Mahabharata, it is described that Vyasa asked Ganesha to aid him in writing the text, however Ganesha imposed a condition that he would do so only if Vyasa narrated the story without pause. To which Vyasa then made a counter-condition that Ganesha must understand the verse before he transcribed it.

Thus Lord VedVyas narrated the whole Mahabharata and all the Upanishads and the 18 Puranas, while Lord Ganesha wrote.

Vyasa is supposed to have meditated and authored the epic by the foothills of the river Beas (Vipasa) in the Punjab region.

There is an ashram of vedavyasa in Vedhagiri. It is believed that pandavas visited vyasa at vedhagiri and got advise during there vanavasa (exile period). The remnants of the ashram is still there on the top of Vedhagiri hill.

Vyasa's Jaya

Vyasa's Jaya, the core of Mahabharata is structured in the form of a dialogue between Dhritarashtra (the Kuru king and the father of the Kauravas, who opposed the Pandavas in the Kurukshetra War) and Sanjaya, his advisor and chariot driver. Sanjaya narrates each incident of the Kurukshetra War, fought in 18 days, as and when it happened. Dhritarashtra sometimes asks questions and doubts and sometimes laments, knowing about the destruction caused by the war, to his sons, friends and kinsmen.

In the beginning, Sanjaya gives a description of the various continents of the Earth, the other planets, and focuses on the Indian Subcontinent and gives an elaborate list of hundreds of kingdoms, tribes, provinces, cities, towns, villages, rivers, mountains, forests etc. of the (ancient) Indian Subcontinent (Bharata Varsha). He also explains about the 'military formations adopted by each side on each day, the death of each hero and the details of each war-racings. Some 18 chapters of Vyasa's Jaya constitutes the Bhagavad Gita, the sacred text of the Hindus. Thus, this work of Vyasa, called Jaya deals with diverse subjects like geography, history, warfare, religion and morality.

Ugrasrava Sauti's Mahabharata

The final version of Vyasa's work is today's Mahabharata, structured as a narration by Ugrasrava Sauti who was a professional story teller, to an assembly of (rishis) who had just attended the 12 years sacrifice of Saunaka also named as kulapati in the forest of Naimisha. Bharata is embedded inside it, and within it Jaya.

Reference to Writing

Within the Mahabharata, there is a tradition in which Vyasa wishes to write down or inscribe his work:

The Grandsire Brahma (creator of the universe) comes and tells Vyasa to get the help of Ganapati for his task. Ganapati writes down the stanzas recited by Vyasa from memory and thus the Mahabharata is inscribed or written. Ganapati could not cope with Vyasa's speed and he misses many words or even stanzas.

There is some evidence however that writing may have been known earlier based on archeological findings of styli in the Painted Grey Ware culture, dated between 1100 BC and 700 BC. and archeological evidence of the Brahmi script being used from at least 600 BC.

The difficulty faced by Ganapati (Ganesha) in writing down Mahabharata as described in the tradition, could be real, and was most probably faced by those people who first attempted to write it down as some reciter recited it continuously. This is because, the reciter will not be able to stop in the middle of recitation and then resume it, as the lines are committed to his memory as a continuous recording.

In the Puranas

Vyasa is also credited with the writing of the eighteen major, if not all, Puranas. His son Shuka is the narrator of the major Purana Bhagavat-Purana.

In Buddhism

Within Buddhism Vyasa appears as Kanha-dipayana (the Pali version of his name) in two Jataka tales: the Kanha-dipayana Jataka and Ghata Jataka. Whilst the former in which he appears as the Bodhisattva has no relation to his tales from the Hindu works, his role in the latter one has parallels in an important event in the Mahabharata.

In the 16th book of the epic, Mausala Parva, the end of the Vrishnis, clansmen of Vyasa's namesake and Krishna is narrated. The epic says: One day, the Vrishni heroes.. saw Vishvamitra, Kanwa and Narada arrived at Dwaraka. Afflicted by the rod of chastisement wielded by the deities, those heroes, causing Samba to be disguised like a woman, approached those ascetics and said, 'This one is the wife of Vabhru of immeasurable energy who is desirous of having a son. Ye Rishis, do you know for certain what this one will bring forth?Those ascetics, attempted to be thus deceived, said: 'This heir of Vasudeva, by name Samba, will bring forth a fierce iron bolt for the destruction of the Vrishnis and the Andhakas.

The important Bhagavata Purana (book 11) too narrates the incident in a similar manner and names the sages as Visvamitra, Asita, Kanva, Durvasa, Bhrigu, Angira, Kashyapa, Vamadeva, Atri, Vasishthha, along with Narada and others-it does not explicitly include Vyasa in the list.

The Ghata Jataka has a different version: The Vrishnis, wishing to test Kanha-dipayana's powers of clairvoyance, played a practical joke on him. They tied a pillow to the belly of a young lad, and dressing him up as a woman, took him to the ascetic and asked when the baby would be born. The ascetic replied that on the seventh day the person before him would give birth to a knot of acacia wood which would destroy the race of Vāásudeva. The youths thereupon fell on him and killed him, but his prophecy came true.

In the Arthashastra

The only non-religious book in which Vyasa has an interesting entry is the Arthashastra of Chanakya (Kautilya). In chapter 6 of the first Department, it says:

'Whosoever is of reverse character, whoever has not his organs of sense under his control, will soon perish, though possessed of the whole earth bounded by the four quarters. For example: Bhoja, known also by the name, Dándakya, making a lascivious attempt on a Bráhman maiden, perished along with his kingdom and relations; so also Karála, the Vaideha... Vátápi in his attempt under the influence of overjoy to attack Agastya, as well as the corporation of the Vrishnis in their attempt against Dwaipáyan.

This reference matches the Jataka version in including Vyasa as the sage attacked by the Vrishnis, though Vyasa does not die here.

Author of Brahma Sutra

The Brahma Sutra is attributed to Badarayana — which makes him the proponent of the crest-jewel school of Hindu philosophy, i.e., Vedanta. Vyasa is conflated with Badarayana by Vaishnavas with the reason that the island on which Vyasa was born is said to have been covered by Badara (Indian jujube/Ber/Ziziphus mauritiana) trees. Apart from Adi Shankara who refers to these two separately rather than as a single individual, many modern historians also think these were two different personalities.

Author of Yoga Bhashya

This text is a commentary on the Yoga Sutras of Patanjali. Vyasa is credited with this work also, though this is impossible, if Vyasa's immortality is not considered, as it is a later text.

22

Yukteswar Giri

Sri Yukteshwar Giri (also spelled Sriyukteshwar Giri and Sriyukteshvar Giri) (10 May 1855-9 March 1936) is the monastic name of Priyanath Karar, the guru of Swami Satyananda Giri and Paramhansa Yogananda. Sri Yukteshwar was an educator, astronomer, a Jyotisha (Vedic astrologer), a yogi, and a believer in the Bhagavad Gita and the Bible. He was a disciple of Lahiri Mahasaya of Varanasi and a member of the Giri branch of the swami order. Yogananda styled Sri Yukteswar Jnanavatar, or "Incarnation of Wisdom."

Biography

Sri Yukteswar was born Priyanath Karar in Serampore, India to Kshetranath Karar and Kadambini. Priyanath lost his father at a young age, and took on much of the responsibility for managing his family's land holdings. A bright student, he passed the entrance exams and enrolled in Srirampur Christian Missionary

College, where he developed an interest in the Bible. This interest would later express itself in his book, The Holy Science, which discusses the unity behind the scientific principles underlying Yoga and the Bible. He also attended Calcutta Medical College for almost two years.

After leaving college, Priyanath married and had a daughter. His wife died a few years after their marriage, and he eventually was formally intitiated into the monastic Swami order as "Sriyukteshvar Giri" (note: thus 'Sri' is not a separate honorific, but part of his given name).

In 1884, Priyanath met Lahiri Mahasaya, who became his Guru and initiated him into the path of Kriya Yoga. Sri Yukteswar spent a great deal of time in the next several years in the company of his guru, often visiting Lahiri Mahasaya in Benares. In 1894, while attending the Kumbha Mela in Allahabad, he met the Guru of Lahiri Mahasaya, Mahavatar Babaji, who asked Sri Yukteswar to write a book comparing Hindu scriptures and the Christian Bible. Mahavatar Babaji also bestowed on Sri Yukteswar the title of 'Swami' at that meeting. Sri Yukteswar completed the requested book in 1894, naming it Kaivalya Darsanam, or The Holy Science.

A Revolutionary Interlude

"Priyanath Karar" has been mentioned by James Campbell Ker in the Bihar and Orissa History Sheet (p. 498) of his Political Trouble in India, A Confidential Report, 1917, First Reprint 1973. Arun Chandra Guha writes that when Bankimchandra Chatterjee was a Deputy Magistrate at Chinsura, patriotic literary figures like Yogendra Vidyabhushan, Bhudev Mukherjee, Nabin Chandra Sen, Hemchandra Banerjee used to meet in his house. Under their inspiration and advice, Tincowri Chatterjee started physical culture centres at Chandernagore, Chinsura and Serampore. Professor Charu Chandra Roy organised them into revolutionary groups during the agitations against the Partition of Bengal in 1905. The famous Tantric saint Tarapada Banerjee, alias Tara Khepa, openly advocated rebellion against British rule while holding classes on the Gita and the Chandi. Preonath Karar was a member of those centres.

"A few months before the session of the Surat Congress, Suranath travelled in the guise of a Tantric priest all over Bengal preaching sedition went to Calcutta and stayed there for a month at the Sandhya office. He then formed a central committee, Mokshada, Shyamsundar Chakravarti, Arabinda Ghose, Tara Khepa, Annada Kaviraj and others as members." A few days before the publication of the Yugantar, at Benares, Preonath with Hrishikesh and Suranath "convened a public meeting as well as a meeting of the pundits wherein it was settled by quotations from the Hindu Astrology and Astronomy and announced firmly that the sinful Iron Age was now over..."

Spiritual Life

Sri Yukteswar converted his large two-story family home in Serampore into an ashram, named "Priyadham," where he resided with students and disciples. In 1903, he also established an ashram in the seaside town of Puri, naming it "Kararashram." From these two ashrams, Sri Yukteswar taught students, and began an organization named "Sadhu Sabha."

An interest in education resulted in Sri Yukteswar developing a syllabus for schools, on the subjects of physics, physiology, geography, astronomy, and astrology He also wrote a book for Bengalis on learning basic English and Hindi called "First Book," and wrote a basic book on astrology. Later, he became interested in the education of women, which was uncommon in Bengal at that time.

Sri Yukteswar was especially skilled in Jyotica (Indian astrology), and prescribed various astrological gemstones and bangles to his students. He also studied astronomy and science, as evidenced in the formulation of his Yuga theory in The Holy Science.

He had only a few long-term disciples, but in 1910, the young Mukunda Lal Ghosh would become Sri Yukteswar's most well known disciple, eventually spreading the teachings of Kriya Yoga throughout the world as Paramhansa Yogananda. Yogananda attributed Sri Yukteswar's small number of disciples to his strict training methods, which Yogananda said "cannot be described as other than drastic."

Regarding the role of the Guru, Sri Yukteswar said:

Look, there is no point in blindly believing that after I touch you, you will be saved, or that a chariot from heaven will be waiting for you. Because of the guru's attainment, the sanctifying touch becomes a helper in the blossoming of Knowledge, and being respectful towards having acquired this blessing, you must yourself become a sage, and proceed on the path to elevate your Soul by applying the techniques of sadhana given by the guru.

Author W.Y. Evans-Wentz described his impression of Sri Yukteswar in the preface to Yogananda's Autobiography of a Yogi:

"Sri Yukteswar was of gentle mien and voice, of pleasing presence, and worthy of the veneration, which his followers spontaneously accorded to him. Every person who knew him, whether of his own community or not, held him in the highest esteem. I vividly recall his tall, straight, ascetic figure, garbed in the saffron-colored garb of one who has renounced worldly quests, as he stood at the entrance of the hermitage to give me welcome. His hair was long and somewhat curly, and his face bearded. His body was muscularly firm, but slender and well-formed, and his step energetic."

Sri Yukteswar died at his Puri ashram on March 9, 1936.

The Holy Science

Sri Yukteswar wrote The Holy Science in 1894. In the introduction, he wrote:

"The purpose of this book is to show as clearly as possible that there is an essential unity in all religions; that there is no difference in the truths inculcated by the various faiths; that there is but one method by which the world, both external and internal, has evolved; and that there is but one Goal admitted by all scriptures."

The work introduced many ideas that were revolutionary for the time — for instance Sri Yukteswar broke from Hindu tradition in stating that the earth is not in the age of Kali Yuga, but has advanced to Dwapara Yuga. His proof was based on a new perspective of the precession of the equinoxes. He also introduced the idea that the sun takes a 'star for its dual,' and revolves around it in a period of 24,000 years, which accounts for the precession of the equinox. Research into this theory is being conducted by the Binary Research Institute, which produced a documentary on the topic titled The Great Year, narrated by James Earl Jones. A sign of the ubiquity of Sri Yukteswar's calculations in modern culture is that there is an iPhone Application for calculating them, just as there are calculators for currencies, lengths, areas and volumes.

The theory of the Sun's binary companion expounded by Sri Yukteswar in The Holy Science has attracted the attention of David Frawley, who has written about it in several of his books. According to Frawley, the theory offers a better estimate of the age of Rama and Krishna and other important historical Indian figures than other dating methods, which estimate some of these figures to have lived millions of years ago — belying accepted human history.

Chanakya : Unparalleled Diplomat

By P. K. Das & M. K. Singh

CHANAKYA

Price	:	₹ 149
Pages	:	224
Size	:	5.25 × 7.75 inches
Binding	:	Paperback
Language	:	English
Subject	:	Biography
ISBN	:	9788183520980

Nelson Mandela : The Herald of Freedon

By P. K. Das & M. K. Singh

Price	:	₹ 149
Pages	:	208
Size	:	5.25 × 7.75 inches
Binding	:	Paperback
Language	:	English
Subject	:	Biography
ISBN	:	9788183520997

NELSON MANDELA

Swami Vivekananda : A Journey to Absolute

By P. K. Das & M. K. Singh

SWAMI VIVEKANANDA

Price	:	₹ 149
Pages	:	248
Size	:	5.25 × 7.75 inches
Binding	:	Paperback
Language	:	English
Subject	:	Biography
ISBN	:	9788183520232

Tales from India

By Rudyard Kipling

Price : ₹ 175
Pages : 320
Size : 5.5 × 8.5 inches
Binding : Paperback
Language : English
Subject : Fiction/Classics
ISBN : 9788183520652

Kim

By Rudyard Kipling

Price : ₹ 149
Pages : 312
Size : 5.5 × 8.5 inches
Binding : Paperback
Language : English
Subject : Fiction/Classics
ISBN : 9788183520638

1984

By George Orwell

Price : ₹ 149
Pages : 328
Size : 4.75 × 7 inches
Binding : Paperback
Language : English
Subject : Fiction/Classics
ISBN : 9788183520706

Prophet

By Kahlil Gibran

Price : ₹ 75
Pages : 112
Size : 5.25 × 7.75 inches
Binding : Paperback
Language : English
Subject : Classics
ISBN : 9788183520560

A Tear and a Smile

By Kahlil Gibran

Price : ₹ 99
Pages : 174
Size : 5.25 × 7.75 inches
Binding : Paperback
Language : English
Subject : Classics
ISBN : 9788183520683

The Broken Wings

By Kahlil Gibran

Price : ₹ 60
Pages : 120
Size : 5.25 × 7.75 inches
Binding : Paperback
Language : English
Subject : Classics
ISBN : 9788183520621

Anna Hazare

By Sanjay Dutta

Price : ₹ 175
Pages : 208
Size : 5.5 × 8.5 inches
Binding : Paperback
Language : English
Subject : Biographies
ISBN : 9788183520867

Tiger in Woods

By Pradeep Thakur

Price : ₹ 199
Pages : 208
Size : 5.5 × 8.5 inches
Binding : Paperback
Language : English
Subject : Biographies/Sports
ISBN : 9788183520164

Angelina Jolie

By Pradeep Thakur

Price : ₹ 199
Pages : 192
Size : 5.75 × 7.75 inches
Binding : Paperback
Language : English
Subject : Biographies/Cinema
ISBN : 9788183520171

Spiritual Gurus Modern

By P. K. Das & M. K. Singh

Price	:	₹ 225
Pages	:	296
Size	:	5.25 × 7.75 inches
Binding	:	Paperback
Language	:	English
Subject	:	Spiritual
ISBN	:	9788183520348